liner notes

liner notes

on parents & children, exes & excess, death & decay, & a few of my other favorite things

LOUDON WAINWRIGHT III

BLUE RIDER PRESS | NEW YORK

blue
rider
press

An imprint of Penguin Random House LLC
375 Hudson Street
New York, New York 10014

Blue Rider Press is a registered trademark and its colophon
is a trademark of Penguin Random House LLC

Library of Congress Cataloging-in-Publication Data

Names: Wainwright, Loudon, III, date.
Title: Liner notes : on parents & children, exes & excess, death & decay,
& a few of my other favorite things / Loudon Wainwright III.
Description: New York, New York : Blue Rider Press, 2017.
Identifiers: LCCN 2017020391 (print) | LCCN 2017021211 (ebook) |
ISBN 9780698413085 (epub) | ISBN 9780399177026 (hardcover)
Subjects: LCSH: Wainwright, Loudon, III, date.|
Singers—United States—Biography.
Classification: LCC ML420.W124 (ebook) | LCC ML420.W124 A3 2017
(print) | DDC 782.42164092 [B]—dc23
LC record available at https://lccn.loc.gov/2017020391
p.   cm.

Printed in the United States of America
10   9   8   7   6   5   4   3   2   1

BOOK DESIGN BY MEIGHAN CAVANAUGH

For the family, and all we put us through

People will know when they see this show the kind of a guy I am
They'll understand just what I stand for and what I just can't stand
They'll perceive what I believe in and what I know is true
And they'll recognize I'm a one man guy, always was through and
through

I'm a one man guy in the morning, I'm the same in the afternoon
One man guy when the sun goes down, I whistle me a one man tune
One man guy, one man guy, only kind of guy to be
I'm a one man guy, a one man guy . . . and the one man is me

—"ONE MAN GUY," 1985

contents

1. my cool life   *1*

2. martha & loudon & loudie   *11*

3. the picture   *43*

4. swimming   *50*

5. the endless waves   *58*

6. shoot off the fence & liza   *61*

7. empire sand & stone   *67*

8. i remember sex   *72*

9. letter to ches baum   *78*

10. bright college days   *86*

11. the summer of love   *94*

12. watch hill back pages   *103*

13. milt   *107*

14. kate   *111*

15. scrambled eggs   *121*

16. disguising the man   *126*

17. bands   *131*

18. in your street   *136*

19. stinkin' to high heaven   *139*

20. nashville   *142*

21. suzzy   *147*

22. snafu   *152*

23. sir walter raleigh syndrome   *157*

24. the hollywood sign   *161*

25. a vulgar tribute to greatness   *166*

26. going for the laugh   *169*

27. the blues   *174*

28. another sort of love story   *180*

29. grammy chronicles   *184*

30. me & clive & david   *188*

31. sibs   *192*

32. oz   *196*

33. the sum of recollection just keeps growing   *199*

34. hospitals   *202*

35. nanny's ashes *206*

36. tracking the storm *209*

37. the home stretch *214*

38. day player blues *219*

39. paris *227*

40. over there, then back *230*

41. rite of passage *244*

42. montreal *247*

43. surviving twin *251*

44. me & my *mechuten* *258*

45. working the room *263*

46. my biggest fan *273*

47. graduation *279*

48. unplanned obsolescence *285*

49. memorial service *291*

50. the 75-90 *295*

acknowledgments *305*

1.
my cool life

Once upon a time there were songwriters and there were singers. The former wrote for the latter and the labor was usually divided rather than singular. Richard wrote the tune and Oscar wrote the lyrics. George did the music, brother Ira was in charge of the words. There were legendary musical tag teams: Gilbert and Sullivan, Comden and Green, Lerner and Loewe. Occasionally you'd get a genius who did it all—words *and* music—creative switch-hitters like Frank Loesser and Irving Berlin, but in Tin Pan Alley it was usually a two-person endeavor. And that continued right up into rock and roll. Goffin and King, Leiber and Stoller, Lennon and McCartney (or vice versa, as McCartney would now have it). Of course, Paul and John had themselves in mind as the singers and protagonists of their songs, in the same way that their hero Chuck Berry wrote and sang about his cool life. When John warbled, "I once had a girl / Or should I say she once had me," you felt sure that he was the actual guy being had. In traditional folk, blues, and country, few songwriters, if any, could read or write music. They made up songs about what was happening to and around them and then they had the audacity to sing and play the stuff themselves, using guitars, banjos, and harmonicas for self-accompaniment. These were the first singer-songwriters I heard on records, pioneers like Huddie Ledbetter, Robert Johnson, Woody Guthrie, Jimmie Rodgers, and Hank Williams. Guys with guitars telling it like it was. The "it" in question was the life they led. They spilled the beans and gave up the gory details. As a listener you felt you were getting something at its source, something simple, direct, and easy to identify with, because it turned out that their beans were not unlike your own. Everybody has pretty much the same gory details, which is why autobiography, and art, for that matter, work.

When I saw Bob Dylan at the Newport Folk Festival in 1963, there was a whole lotta identification going on. Here was a guy just a few years older than I was, writing and singing about what was happening in the world—his world *and* mine. These were the heady days of "Blowin' in the Wind" and "The Times They Are A-Changin'," when there were social issues to sing about and apostrophes in song titles. The not-so-nice Jewish boy from Hibbing, Minnesota, sounded like a sixty-year-old black bluesman who'd listened to a ton of Woody Guthrie, but Bob was young and just searching for himself. On his first recordings, Ray Charles all but impersonates his hero Nat King Cole. By the time Dylan went and, for that matter, became electric two years later at Newport, he'd become a fully formed original who'd left his contemporaries and his own influences in the dust. After 1965, Bob seemed to be pretty much focused on his cool, albeit rather cryptic, life. It had gone from "Hattie Carroll was a maid of the kitchen" to "You got a lotta nerve / To say you are my friend," which for my money is going from good to even better.

So what's the big rule/cliché when it comes to writing? Write about what you know? When I started writing songs in 1968 I didn't know about much. Raised in an affluent suburb of New York City, I'd gone to a boys' boarding school, dropped out of college, been busted for pot, and had survived a few disastrous puppy-love affairs. I'd mowed some lawns and had hitchhiked to New Canaan, Connecticut, but I hadn't harvested a single bale of cotton or ridden any rails. Still, I somehow managed to write two or three songs per week, drawn from my pathetic dearth of experience. Like most serious, young, egotistical artists, I thought my life, though yet to be cool, was nonetheless interesting. At least I was smart enough to know I had to make it *seem* interesting. So I put some work into presentation. To separate myself from the pack of bell-bottomed, ponytailed, guitar-toting song-slingers, I wore khakis and Brooks Brothers shirts and kept my hair unfashionably short. To cope with coffeehouse stage fright, while performing I physicalized my fear into strange, jerky body gyrations, replete with leg lifts, facial grimaces, and lots of tongue wagging. I was trying to make sure people noticed me and, within a year, Atlantic Records did. I made my first two albums for them. The records were positively retro, unadorned, without a trace of the drums, bass, and tasteful pedal-steel-guitar lickage that was going around at the time. My instincts paid off, at least for the critics, who were always looking for the next new thing and desperate to fill the Dylan vacuum (Bob was out of commission at that time, holed up in Woodstock, recovering from a motorcycle accident). I was, to shamelessly quote one hyperbolic journalist, "a blinding new talent." All my work on packaging had paid off. I'd been noticed. The songs I had written were also good. That helped. Once I began in earnest, I also decided to stop listening to the competition. I didn't want to check out this new guy David Bowie or hear what Dylan's latest was.

I put an embargo on any and all incoming influences, because I sensed it was important to be original, to not be like anyone else. If I was in a car and another singer-songwriter came on the radio, I'd turn it off or go looking for the jazz station. People always want to know what I listen to. My answer to that question has been and continues to be "Dead black piano players."

But nobody writes or works in a vacuum. There's a market out there, and unless you're writing, singing, shipbuilding, basket weaving, or whatever for the sheer pleasure of it, you have to deal with that market and all its vagaries. Since I've been in the music business I've earned a good enough living, mostly toiling away on the biz's outer peripheries. I've never written my songs for other people to sing and/or record, and, although I've had a few "covers"* as they call them in the biz (a term that brings to my mind Hudson's Bay blankets), there haven't been a lot of publishing royalty checks over the last forty-five years. I made fun of this rather sad fact in a song called, brace yourself, "A Song." The opening lines are:

> *Here's a song for someone else to sing*
> *With a universal and generic ring*
> *It's all about the same old stuff*
> *That you like and can't get enough of*
> *How's about a minor chord right here?*
> *Wasn't that rather pleasant in your ear?*

> —"A SONG," 1997

---

* Covers of note would include "The Man Who Couldn't Cry" by Johnny Cash, "I'm Alright" by Mose Allison, and "The Swimming Song" by Earl Scruggs. Also, it was a thrill to have my son, Rufus, record "One Man Guy."

In 1972, after releasing my two critically acclaimed but largely un-purchased LPs, Atlantic's crush on me was over and I was dropped. I was then picked up (yet another weird term, this one connotative of prostitution) by Columbia Records. On my third record, imagina-tively titled *Album III*, there were more songs of inexperience and autobiographical angst, but also a novelty tune I had made up in twelve minutes about a dead skunk I had run over while driving in northern Westchester County, New York. Dumb luck, great karma, plus some good old-fashioned payola all combined in a perfect storm, and the result was my only hit heretofore, number twelve on the *Bill-board* chart and number one in Little Rock, Arkansas, for six weeks. Suddenly, I did have a pretty cool life. I was the "Dead Skunk" guy.

Twenty-five years old and I pretty much had made it. The critics' darling was now a success. So what happened? Why is it that many people aren't quite sure who the hell I actually am? Where were the follow-up hits to "Dead Skunk," funny animal songs like "I Met Her at the Pet Store" and "Stay Away from My Aardvark"? I have bored a number of psychotherapists while coming up with answers to some of these questions and have chronicled quite a few of my resent-ments in song.

They spelled my name wrong again
With an E between the D and the N.
Some dope didn't know it should be an O.
They spelled my name wrong again.

—"T.S.M.N.W.A.," 1993

I continued to write about my life as it went all the way from cool to cheesy. By 1973, despite or possibly due to having had a hit song, I was miserable. Married and the father of two small children, I was never home, drunk a good deal of the time, and apparently felt it necessary to sleep with every waitress in North America and the United Kingdom. These beans have been spilt in song: "Mr. Guilty," "Drinking Song," and "The Waitress Song," to name three of dozens.

Now we've stumbled onto one of the big important questions: Is it necessary to feel like shit in order to be creative? I'd say the answer is, unless you're J. S. Bach, yes. Or to put it another way: It may not be *necessary* to feel like shit, but it couldn't hurt.

I know that those legit guys I mentioned earlier—Oscar, Richard, Irving, and Frank—had the blues from time to time, but when they wrote about it and got Ethel Merman or John Raitt to sing it, you felt sorry for Ethel and John, not for Oscar and Frank. I suppose that was the idea; the remove was placed there intentionally. Less messy, I guess. But I also know that when Hank Williams sings his very own "Hear that lonesome whippoorwill / He sounds too blue to fly," it's powerful and I doubt if Ethel, John, or even Sinatra could top his version. The very names of the legendary blues and R&B singer-songwriters tell it like they were: Howlin' Wolf, Muddy Waters, Lightnin' Hopkins, Screamin' Jay Hawkins, Mississippi John Hurt. These were performers and writers who were out to advertise their personas. They were musical memoirists. Autobiography was central to their ability to communicate not just their message but the emotion behind their message.

About twenty-five years ago, I wrote a song called "Hitting You." It was about hauling off and smacking one of my kids too hard. On the butt, I hasten to add. Nevertheless, she was five and I shouldn't have hit her. People were shocked when they heard the song, and some said I was very brave to sing it onstage. That's nice to hear, but I wasn't being brave. A stage—whether in a club, a concert hall, or a cow pasture—is usually a safe place for a performer. You appear to be exposed, but the reality is you're protected. There are lights, microphones, and often a fourth invisible wall separating you from the mob, a mob that hopefully happens to be partial to you. If you know what you're doing, you can get away with murder. And that, figuratively speaking, can be your intention. I've always held that provocation, unless totally gratuitous, is a good thing. Sometimes, like Barry Manilow, I write the songs that make the whole world cry, but often the response I'm going for is a shiver or a cringe. Making an audience uncomfortable for limited amounts of time ratchets up the dramatic tension. You then have the option to release that tension when and how you deem appropriate. Sounds like a bit of a cat-and-mouse game, doesn't it? I'm sure you've seen show biz movies where the performer states his desire and need to go out there and "kill 'em" or "knock 'em dead." Doing a show, or one's act as they used to call it, is a bit like cooking or sex. It's best not to hurry. Or so I've been told. Repeatedly.

Occasionally I get a reaction to a song that's not the one I expected. I assumed that people who heard "Hitting You" would be affected by their recollections of being whacked in the backseat by their own dads, and indeed some were, but many, if not most, identified not with the one being hit, but with the hitter. People came up after shows and talked to me about how they'd lost it and hit their kids and how awful and guilty they still felt about it. Now, that's entertainment!

Frequently I'm asked if writing and singing such personal songs is in any way therapeutic. It's true I have had people thank me for writing certain songs, usually ones about family, the passage of time, and death, just a few of my favorite topics (along with snowflakes on lashes and whiskers on kittens). I'm always happy to help someone, particularly a paying customer, make it through the night. As to whether what I do is therapeutic for myself, I doubt it. My career has provided me with a living and a half-assed identity, but having those things hasn't resolved any of my so-called stuff. I don't think songwriting is curative. In fact, it could be argued that, in the end, singing the blues just makes you bluer.

I never wanted to be a writer. It seemed like a hard, boring, and lonely life. Growing up, I saw my journalist father at work torturing himself while writing, trying to write, and, worst of all, not writing.

Being a writer looked to me like a stone drag and a must to avoid. By the time I was seven I knew that singing and performing would be part of my life equation. But I was surprised when wordplay entered the picture fifteen years later and I started writing my songs. Caressing a curvaceous guitar and singing my little ditties was nowhere near as lonely as trying to fill up blank pieces of paper. It was spare-time stuff, easy and fun. Unlike what my dad was doing, songwriting was quick. Who ever heard of a song (other than a Leonard Cohen song) taking six months or two years to write? In the end, I got to be like my old man, but in my own way, and for guys, that's hitting the Oedipal jackpot, like making out with your mom without having to actually do it.

But I don't want you to think I'm totally well-adjusted. Or ungrateful. My father loved writing and knew it was important, and I think I inherited some of that love and knowledge. The primary techniques I use in my work are description and detail. These are journalistic techniques, genetically passed on to me from my progenitor, and I use them in combination with sprinklings of humor, dollops of irony, and great lashings of unreliable narration.

When I first began writing, my songs were coming at a rate of two or three per week. Sadly, almost nothing comes at that rate anymore.

But when you're young, you're full of it and it pours out of you—piss and vinegar, fire and brimstone, and my personal favorites, Sturm und Drang. Later, the output slows down, and eventually you're left with just a trickle. If this is getting a little too urogenital for you, let's switch metaphors. Fishing. Writing songs is like fishing. You sit in the boat and you wait. It's true you have to know the best spot, time of day, what bait to use, the difference between a nibble and a strike, and most important, how to get the damn fish into the boat. Talent is essential, craft is crucial, but for me it's mostly down to waiting and luck. And in my line of work, luck is not random. It's definite and discerning. It's invisible, but it's there. It's mysterious and also obvious. I don't understand how inspiration works and I don't want to. Don't mess with grace and divinity. You can write songs with hard work, sharp pencils, and a rhyming dictionary, but without luck they won't swing. No luck means no fish.

I've been writing this book for the last few years, trying to fill up blank pieces of paper, but it hasn't been as lonely as I feared. That's because I've brought my family along for the ride. In my songs I've always written about the most important people in my life—my parents, my siblings, my children, and the women I fell for. These people, along with thoughts about my job, and my attending fears and doubts about myself, are what's in *Liner Notes*.

As to my choice of a title, let's say that a life is an LP, a sort of complicated, very-long-playing record. One of the things I enjoyed most when listening to LPs was reading their accompanying liner notes, and despite the fact that, like telephone answering machines, they're fast becoming vestigial, I've thought of these essays as just that—album liner notes; something extra, informative, and interesting (to me, anyway). The book is also peppered with a lot of my song lyrics. These (mostly) rhyming couplets were written primarily to be sung, but my hope is they also might be illustrative and revealing on the page.

About five years ago I reread all of my father's *Life* magazine columns and I realized that a lot of the themes and preoccupations we each wrote about overlapped. Selections of his elegant writing are included in these pages. I thought it would be cool to have my old man along for the aforementioned ride, in the shotgun seat.

2.
martha & loudon & loudie

My mother, Martha Taylor, grew up in south Georgia, in the two little towns of Tifton and Quitman. Wikipedia doesn't say much about Tifton except that "The Friendly City" is the county seat of Tift County and is also the home of the Georgia Firebirds of National Arena League football fame. About Quitman, on the other hand, there are a few interesting factual tidbits. It was the final home of James Pierpont, who, in addition to being the organist for the Presbyterian church in town, was the author of "Jingle Bells." There is also a city ordinance in Quitman prohibiting chickens from crossing the road.

My mom and her fraternal twin sister, Mary, were born on April 4, 1922, and with apologies to my cousins, Mary's kids, I'd have to say that Martha was the prettier of the two. They had an older sister, Peggy, and a younger one called Nan. Their father, Walter Taylor, was an itinerant tobacco farmer whom my mother always referred to as "a drunk," a pretty tough designation for one's own parent. My grandmother Rowena Long had a more elevated status because, as a young woman, she had attended the State Normal School, a teaching college located in Athens, Georgia. In 1929, a few years after my aunt Nan was born, Rowena went into the hospital to be treated for strep throat and wound up dying there. My mother, who was seven when this happened, was understandably traumatized by the event, so much so that throughout the rest of her life she insisted that she had been abandoned by her own mother. I and others would try to argue that Rowena's death from infection, though tragic, was a commonplace occurrence back then, and surely there was no maternal malice or intent involved. Still, Martha always insisted her mother had abandoned her.

Taylor family, about 1928—Walter, Rowena, and their four children: Peggy, Nan on Walter's lap, and the twins Martha (left) and Mary (right).

Suddenly, Walter Taylor had no wife to look after four little girls, all under the age of ten, so he did what a lot of widowed fathers did and still do: he hired a "housekeeper," in this case a middle-aged woman named Mrs. Morgan (pronounced "Mizz Maugan" by my mother and her sisters), who, in addition to cooking and keeping house, was also a live-in nanny. I hardly know anything about Mrs. Morgan or whether or not she brightened the sad little lives of the four motherless children, but because of my mom's lifelong abandonment issues I somehow doubt it.

Life's no picnic, that's a given
My mom's mom died when my mom was seven
My mom's father was a tragic guy
He was so distant, nobody knows why

—"A FATHER AND A SON," 1992

Walter wasn't around much—he was either traveling to work or just to look for it—but there is another clue as to why he was so distant. In 1918, while he was courting Rowena with a series of beautiful lovesick letters, Walter was being treated at a sanitarium in Florida for what he claimed was malaria. But a female cousin of Rowena's worked at the facility as a nurse and she had the lowdown on "Mr. Taylor." The disease my grandfather was being treated for was not malaria but instead venereal in nature, most likely syphilis or gonorrhea. Salvarsan, Dr. Ehrlich's magic bullet, had only recently been invented and was not easily available in those days, so there was no simple cure for Walter's shameful, dangerous malady, and there was certainly no way he could confess his awful secret to the woman he hoped to marry. The cousin wrote several letters to Rowena, urging her to forget about the older, previously married, devious, and most likely whorehouse-hopping Mr. Taylor. Nevertheless, my grandmother did marry him and bore him his four daughters. Whether or not Walter ever confessed to Rowena, or if she ever told him that she'd known all along, are Taylor family mysteries.

Rowena, my darling, please don't let me down
A few words from you can lift me off the ground
Your letters are treasures, you don't know their worth
Days I don't receive one I fall back to earth

Rowena, my darling, just a word or two
It means the world to me those few words from you
But when you don't send them, why can't you see?
It's as if the whole world had gone back on me

Tonight when I'm sleeping I will dream of you
Wishfully thinking. What else can I do?
Then in the morning it's always the same
When dreaming is done I call out your name

Tonight when I'm sleeping I will dream of you
Wishfully thinking. What else can I do?
Then in the morning I can only hope
For my heart's deliverance in an envelope

Rowena, my dear, yours to hand this a.m.
I'm holding your letter in heaven again
A few words from me now to make sure you know
As ever I'm yours, yes, and I love you so

—"ROWENA," 2009

My dad, Loudon Snowden Wainwright Jr., was born on December 16, 1924. He was an only child and he grew up in *Great Gatsby* country on the Gold Coast of Long Island. Both his parents came from money. The New York Wainwrights are genealogically connected to Peter Stuyvesant, my great-great-grandfather Howard Wainwright having married Margaret Livingston, who was a direct descendant of the renowned one-legged first governor of New Amsterdam. Our other famous relative, also a military man, was the four-star World

My dad with his parents in Watch Hill,
Rhode Island, early 1930s.

War II general Jonathan Mayhew "Skinny" Wainwright IV, who was
commander of Allied Forces in the Philippines at the time of their
surrender to the Japanese in 1942.

My father went to a private boys' boarding school, St. Andrew's,
in Middletown, Delaware, where he was pretty miserable. In his 1942
school yearbook, Dad was described thusly: "Literature is not Snow's
only accomplishment. His assets have been developing along the poetic, athletic, and dramatic lines as well." Among his classmates he
was voted "Wittiest." His favorite discussion topic was "Wine,
Women, and Camels." He came out on top in the categories of "Best
Dancer (Thinks He Is)" and "Done St. Andrew's for The Most." It
was predicted that he would be "First Married." Not a bad call, as it
turned out.

Both my parents enlisted in the Marine Corps, and that's where
they met. My mother and her twin, Mary, had joined up in 1943.
Mom became a training film projectionist, and somehow, at a mixer

My parents in uniform, 1943.

or a dance, I imagine, she met my father, who had joined at seventeen, right after graduating from St. Andrew's in 1942. As the saying goes, opposites attract, and the south Georgia country gal and the blue-blooded boy from Long Island got it on. Martha was three years older than Loudon and had a bit more "experience," having spent some time socializing on army bases before she joined the marines, whereas dating life for my father was mostly confined to fox-trotting and box-stepping at debutante balls in New York City and at the Watch Hill Yacht Club in Rhode Island. During his last few years at boarding school, Dad had a girlfriend from Hewlett named Pam who was very ambivalent about their romance and pretty much jerked him around. She was what they used to call a tease. When Loudon met sexy, southern Martha, I'll bet she didn't play those country-club ball-busting games, and though it's a terrible thing to say about your own mother, my guess is that Mom probably "put out." When my father's somewhat snobby mother, Eleanor Sloan, learned that her precious only son was contemplating marriage to a cracker chick from the Deep South, she was not at all pleased. My grandmother

("Nanny") would have much preferred Pam the ballbreaker, and she let Dad know it. Another of my theories is that Loudon married Martha to defy his mother, to go against her wishes. His father, Loudon I, had died in 1942, so he wasn't on the scene to weigh in, but I suspect he also would have opposed the match. As for Martha, she was surely smitten by the young, gangly, handsome "Loudie," with his smooth prep school manners and classy East Coast pedigree. And what a name! Loudon Snowden Wainwright Jr.—it almost has the ring of royalty to it. Here was my mom's ticket out of south Georgia.

My parents were near-total opposites—rich/poor, north/south, educated/uneducated. But my mother happened to be an excellent listener, which is what every unhappy guy craves, and maybe that's another reason why Dad fell for her. She grew up having to share her often absent father with her three sisters, and now, for the first time in her life, she had a man to herself. She was raring to listen. And this lonely only son had plenty to get off his chest. I imagine them lying in bed after sweaty summer sex—him smoking and talking, her taking

the occasional puff, naked under the sheet, punctuating his pauses with her south Georgia "Uh-uh"s, as if to say "Keep going, I understand, tell me more." After completion of the ultimate act of manhood, my dad reverts to being the hurt, lonely little boy. I sure did all that as a young married man: *Now that I've proved myself, let me tell you what I'm feeling. Now that I've been strong, let me tell you how*

My old man and me in 1946, both of us clueless.

weak I really am. The confession of weakness to a woman is so often a search for sweet absolution.

But the opposite-side-of-the-tracks thing turned out to be one of the fatal dynamics in my parents' marriage. After being discharged from the marines, the young couple married on September 13, 1945, and settled in Chapel Hill, North Carolina, where my dad studied journalism at UNC on the GI Bill. The southern, liberal college town was a good starting point, a compromise location. I was born there in 1946, and the following year my sister Martha (Teddy) arrived. The family moved up north two years later to settle near New York City so that Loudon could start his writing career, and things got more complicated. Now he was back on his home turf. After a few years in the affordable neutral zone of Fresh Meadows, Queens, and when my brother Andrew was born in 1950, we relocated forty miles farther north to the town of Katonah in Westchester County. When my dad joined the nearby Waccabuc Country Club, he started to reclaim his old identity. Now he was golfing, dancing, and drinking with young people from his own milieu, men and women of privilege who, like himself, had gone to boarding schools—St. What'shisname and Miss Whoseydingle. The uneducated white-trash girl from Georgia didn't fit in, and my grandmother Eleanor's dire predictions about my parents' unsuitability started to come true.

God knows my mother tried to fit in. She worked hard at tamping down her mellifluous southern drawl so she wouldn't sound so distinctly different from the lockjawed country clubbers around her. With some words, though, it was hopeless. Her pronunciation of the word "poetry" came out "poi-trie," and it made my father wince throughout their entire thirty-three-year marriage. To this day I still find myself using expressions like "I'll be dogged" or "I'm bone-tired." That's my mother talking. You can't take the red clay out of a

Georgia girl, and her accent would reassert itself without warning, particularly when she got angry with her kids. If my siblings and I got caught in an audacious lie or made the mistake of secretly scarfing down a last piece of pie she was saving for Dad, Mom could get "hopping mad" and she just might go and "cut a switch" in order to administer a little country discipline. She would break off a skinny branch from a bush that was handy, whittle it down with a paring knife, and then, while firmly grasping the wildly squirming, terrified offender's upper arm, administer a quick but fierce whipping to the backs of the youngster's naked legs. I have memories of this happening in the summer when we were conveniently wearing shorts or bathing suits. Although my father was a scary and imposing figure who possessed the power of the arched eyebrow, he never employed corporal punishment. But he could surely freeze you with a contemptuous look, or, if really pushed, a bellowed epithet. I still remember the terror my brother, Andy, and I experienced from our basement bedroom bunker whenever we heard the old man's footsteps and jingling pocket change overhead as he made his way across the floor to the top of the stairs to once and for all silence us with his raging *"Goddammit!"*

It should be said that some of my father's rage was alcohol-fueled or, perhaps more specifically, hangover-fueled. Booze has been a major component in our family dynamics for generations. My mother's dad, Walter, was a drunk. My grandfather Loudon I was a big-time drinker, and it's likely this was a contributing factor in his early death at the age of forty-three. My party-loving, jazz-age grandmother Eleanor loved her gin and tonics and thought there was something wrong, even perverse, about people who didn't drink. And by drink, I mean the hard stuff. Men who drank just beer, for instance, were considered by her to be "queer"—and by that she didn't mean unusual. Of course, in my grandparents' heyday people drank to excess; it was considered fashionable and charming, an almost lovable trait. William Powell would never had been able to solve all those murders in the Thin Man movies without his constant infusion of martinis, and Myrna Loy wouldn't have had it any other way. Not only did people drink to excess, they used to smoke constantly. There was a period of time in the 1960s when my father was smoking four packs of cigarettes a day. At his desk, when he was working, he would fire up another Tareyton and then realize he already had one going in the ashtray. In *The Great American Magazine*, his book about *Life*, where he worked for almost forty years, my father writes about all the drinking he and his colleagues did in and out of the office, referring cheerfully to "damp capers" and "gin blown strokes of genius." He almost boastfully recounts his arrest and overnight incarceration in 1954 after resisting arrest for drunkenly driving around Beverly Hills in the early-morning hours while tossing lit firecrackers out of the car windows.

'JULY FOURTH' DRIVER BOOKED

Loundon Wainwright apparently celebrated the end of the rainstorm a little too boisterously, because he was arrested at 2:30 this morning by officer R. E. Bennett who booked him at the Beverly Hills police station on a charge of drunk driving.

Bennett said Wainwright, who lives at 2578 Hutton Dr., Los Angeles, was driving his car erratically early this morning and tossing lighted firecrackers out of the window.

From the back pages of the *Los Angeles Times*, 1954. They spelled our name wrong again.

In January 1966, while I was in college at Carnegie Tech in Pittsburgh, our house in Bedford Village, New York, burned to the ground in under a half hour. The fire started in the middle of the night, when my parents and younger sisters, Teddy and Sloan, were fast asleep; it's a miracle everybody, with the exception of the family cat, got out alive. My dad devoted two of "The View from Here" columns that he wrote for *Life* to this terrifying event, but in print he's rather vague as to the actual cause of the fire, attributing it to "most likely faulty wiring." Our house was not particularly old and I think both he and my mother knew how the fire probably started. The old man was in the habit of staying up late at night, after everyone else had gone to bed, in order to read, smoke, and drink scotch. By the time he turned in he was often "in the bag" and, though there's no way of knowing for sure, a lit cigarette that dropped behind his big easy chair cushion is a far more likely cause for the blaze. Eventually, both my parents weaned themselves off the hard stuff, switching to large jugs of cheap white Almaden wine. Then, after he hit fifty, and with the help of AA, my father finally quit drinking.

The list of songs I've written that reference drinking is a long one. "Central Square Song," "Drinking Song," "Wine with Dinner," "Primrose Hill," "April Fools Day Morn," and "White Winos" are just a few. I wouldn't characterize myself as a lush, but I drank plenty throughout my twenties and thirties, and I consciously projected the image of a boozing, poetic singer-songwriter. I thought drinking was sexy and cool. Growing up, I watched my parents and their friends get shit-faced at parties, and it sure looked like fun. And, of course, there were also all those literary alcoholic geniuses to emulate, guys like Jack Kerouac, F. Scott Fitzgerald, Charles Bukowski, and Malcolm Lowry. The Kettle of Fish on MacDougal Street in Greenwich Village, an old haunt of Kerouac's, was where I perfected my barfly shtick when I was in my early twenties. In the company of harder-drinking folkie elders like Dave Van Ronk, Rosalie Sorrels, and Patrick Sky, I would belly up to the Kettle bar and order a shot of Jack Daniel's with a Heineken back. After a showy sip or two of the bourbon, and when no one was looking, I would surreptitiously pour most of the contents of the shot glass onto the sawdusted floor. Then I would order another round and, looking as cool as ever, get back to satisfying my real compulsion, my raison d'être for being in the saloon. That would be to pick up women. There are a few songs about that, too.

In this town, television shuts off at two
What can a lonely rock 'n' roller do?
The bed's so big, the sheets are clean
Your girlfriend said you were nineteen
The Styrofoam ice bucket is full of ice
Come up to my motel room, treat me nice

I don't wanna make no late-night New York calls
I don't wanna stare at those ugly grass-mat walls
Chronologically I know you're young
But when you kissed me in the club you bit my tongue
I'll write a song for you, I'll put it on my new LP
Come up to my motel room, sleep with me

There's a Bible in the drawer, don't be afraid
I'll put up a sign to warn the cleanup maid
There's lots of soap and lots of towels
Never mind those desk clerk scowls
I'll buy you breakfast, they'll think you're my wife
Come up to my motel room, save my life

—"MOTEL BLUES," 1971

My dad's ambition was to write literary fiction, and in the late forties he had three short stories published in *The New Yorker*, which, for a young writer, is about as auspicious a beginning as there can be.

My favorite of the three is called "Clean Jersey." In it, Harry, an insecure and overbearing husband and father, and his long-suffering wife, Fran, have traveled to their son Bill's boarding school to watch him play in a football game. Bill, much to his father's annoyance, spends most of the game warming the bench until he's substituted in the closing minutes due to a teammate's injury. He makes a key tackle and then manages to recover an even more important fumble. Harry is elated at his son's unexpected success until, on the last play of the game, Bill is thrown a Hail Mary pass that hits him in the back of the neck and knocks him to the ground. The home team loses, and after the game Harry cannot contain his disappointment. He insults his already humiliated son: "Bill looked at Harry and then slowly began rubbing the back of his neck. 'What's the matter, kid? Does it sting?' Harry said quietly. 'You might have done better if you'd used your hands.'" Rough stuff, and I suspect it was gleaned from my dad's real-life experience with his own father, who by all accounts was an impatient and judgmental man. Whenever my dad would verbally kick my ass or tell me I was full of shit, my mother would apologize for him by saying, "Well, Loudie, you know your daddy was treated very badly by his father," almost as if there had been some kind of emotional abuse involved. I suppose there might have been, though I never asked. Asking was not a big thing in our family.

In the early fifties, a Marine Corps buddy of my father's came, with his wife and small children, to visit our family. This man's kids called him "sir," and for some reason my dad was impressed by this. After the visitors left, Teddy, Andy, and I were told that from now on we were to call our father "sir" as opposed to "Daddy." We went along with it for a few days, until I meekly asked my old man one morning if he would agree to a compromise and allow us to just call him "Dad." That seemed to wake him up, and he suddenly saw the silliness of it all. The "sir" decree was lifted. Alas, the beat goes on. Whenever I took the hard line with my own kids when they were growing up, à la "Eat your fish," "Don't do it that way," or "That's all wrong," it would always backfire. All the hard line really did was widen the rifts between us.

Despite the glory of having three short stories published in *The New Yorker*, my father had to face the reality of supporting a wife and three kids, so he took a job at *Life*. That was an exciting and glamorous gig, and as a senior editor and widely read columnist he eventually enjoyed great success, but he always tortured himself about working for the magazine, feeling that he had somehow sold out. He admired and was envious of contemporaries like John Updike and John Cheever, because they had found a way and the will to stick with writing and publishing their own fiction. My father always felt that he postponed his original dream for so long that the dream got lost. There just wasn't enough time for him to be a real writer. He had to wake up every morning, take the train into town, and work his butt off five days a week. The grind of getting out a weekly magazine, coming up with ideas on the fly, the necessity of collaborating and, as a result, compromising, the travel, the constant pressure of deadlines, "putting the magazine to bed"—all of this was the antithesis of fiction writing, of sitting down in front of a typewriter for *x* hours every day to imagine and then create a story. Throughout the sixties and seventies, long after he had given up any hope of writing fiction again, my father signed book deals and took sabbaticals to write nonfiction books. There was the book about the judge, the book about the minister, and the book about the cop. There was plenty of talk and planning about getting this work done; offices were rented with the express purpose of providing a conducive and nondistracting writing environment. The words "the book," spoken around our house at first with unbridled enthusiasm and pride, were later delivered in a more subdued tone, and then with regret and resignation. The books were never written, and in some cases the advances had to be returned, the ultimate humiliation. However, after years of struggle, he completed *The Great American Magazine*, and it was published in 1986. The irony is that it was about *Life*, the beautiful behemoth that almost forty years earlier had lured my father away from his original dream.

In 1952 my dad was made *Life*'s West Coast bureau chief and our family moved to Los Angeles, where we lived until 1956. *Life* had by that time become America's premier photo magazine, nudging out its closest competitor, *Look*. The domination of television was still a ways off, and picture magazines were what everybody looked at for entertainment and as a connection to other places and cultures. The world's greatest photographers worked for *Life*: Margaret Bourke-White, Philippe Halsman, Robert Capa, and Gjon Mili. The up-and-comers were my dad's contemporaries and his drinking buddies—Ralph Crane, Gordon Parks, George Silk, and Robert Frank among them. Another of my father's L.A. friends was the folksinger Terry Gilkyson. His group, the Easy Riders, had a major hit in the fifties, "Marianne," and they wrote and were the vocal backup trio on the Dean Martin classic "Memories Are Made of This." My father had written a few songs himself on piano, including a great one called "Hand Full of Dust," which I adapted and recorded for my 1992 album *History*. At Terry's urging, Dad recorded "Hand Full of Dust" in 1952 at a demo studio, and I remember him bringing home the strange-looking acetate disc and playing it for us. My father wasn't much of a singer, but to me it seemed like an amazing thing to have done. As a gift, Terry also gave my father a lovely little Mexican nylon-string guitar, but after a few weeks of trying to play C, F, and G7, Dad gave up, unable to push past the fingertip-callous stage, and the guitar wound up in hall closets on both coasts for several years. Then, in the late fifties, the Kingston Trio were on TV and radio, and folk music suddenly became cool. Since I was the eldest and dominant sibling, I elbowed my younger brother and sister out of the way and laid claim to Dad's closeted six-string. It was my first ax, and after a few lessons at the Mt. Kisco School of Music, I progressed from hesitantly pluck-ing out the melody of "The Third Man Theme" to forcefully strum-ming "On Top of Old Smokey." Getting that guitar was a seminal event in my life, and learning to play it was a dreamed-of rite of pas-sage. At the age of thirteen, I had bested my father at something. Per-haps it would be possible to become my own man, instead of the son of the son of Loudon Wainwright. A sad footnote: The little Mexican nylon-string guitar was incinerated in the 1966 family fire.

I have to thank my father for that guitar, and I also owe him a debt of gratitude for his record collection, which reflected his wide and fairly eclectic musical taste. He was partial to singers, and his favorites

Dad singing along, me strumming a G chord on the Terry
Gilkyson ax, Westport, Connecticut, 1959.
Photograph by George Silk.

Dear Louds,

It was great to hear from you by letter and phone the same day, and I look forward to calling you on your birthday. In the meantime, though, here is the lyric of "A Handful of Dust", probably written about 1950. When I wrote it, I had in mind that it should be sung by some terrific black woman, like Lena Horne, and the language, I'm ashamed to say, had some ungrammatical stuff I thought was "black." I've removed most of that from this version.

or Eartha Kitt

You got a car, a wife, a gal downtown.
You got a place to lay your body down.
You got money in your pocket,
You can eat around the crust.
But a man is just a handful of dust.

You take the best of everything I got,
And taking all, still want I don't know what.
But you're a star about to tumble,
A balloon about to bust,
Cause a man is just a handful of dust.

Lovin' livin' ain't enough,
You devil-driven graveyard stuff.
Highest flyin', play the clown.
Ain't no flyin' six feet down.

No place worth goin' ain't already been,
No sin worth sinnin' ain't already sinned.
You get thunder in your lovin',
You get lightning in your lust.
But a man is just a handful of dust.

That's it. I'm glad you persuaded me to write it down again after all this time. My friend Todd Brewster and I will try to come up with a comprehensible version of the tune, which isn't all that great. We'll put it on tape.

Much love,

Dad

Dad   September 1, 1988

A letter to me from my father, September 1, 1988.

included Fred Astaire (number one), Sinatra, Ella Fitzgerald, Mahalia Jackson, and Joan Baez. He also had recordings of more esoteric artists like Leadbelly, Kid Ory, and Louis Prima. I'm pretty sure he bought the first Tom Lehrer 10-inch disc, though for some strange reason he didn't dig Stan Freberg. My dad loved the Tin Pan Alley songwriters, such as Irving Berlin and Cole Porter, and the musical-theater greats—Rodgers and Hart and Hammerstein, Frank Loesser, and Lerner and Loewe. He appreciated the Beatles, I think, but in general was not a fan of rock and roll, and, as far as I can remember, was not the least interested in Bob Dylan. Dad and my first wife, Kate McGarrigle, could sit around and shoot the shit about Glenn Gould's recordings of the Brandenburg Concertos till the cows came home. Speaking of concertos, in my late teenage years, when no one was at home, I used to sneak a few snorts from my parents' liquor cabinet, don my father's gigantically clunky plastic Koss headphones, and drop the needle on the guitarist Julian Bream's version of Rodrigo's Concierto de Aranjuez. As the fabulously dramatic, angst-filled music ebbed and swelled, I would drunkenly conduct the unseen orchestra being piped into my head, loudly howling and moaning, a crazed postadolescent would-be Leonard Bernstein.

My mother couldn't carry a tune, which probably meant that some-one, at some point—maybe her daddy Walter, or Mrs. Morgan, or some cruel grade school teacher down in Tifton—told her she couldn't and shouldn't sing. I have a memory of her starting to join in on family renditions of "Happy Birthday" and then meekly trailing off into silence. But she loved hearing me sing. Once, at the age of seven, I sang the folk song "Rosin the Bow" a cappella for my mom and my aunt Mary in my aunt's kitchen in Santa Ana, California. They were en-thralled, and when I finished, both of them showered me with lavish praise and loving approval, beaming it down on me in a powerful Doublemint Twin sort of way. "Oh, Loudie, that was so *beautiful*! You are just the *cutest* thing!" This incident sealed my fate; there were no more fireman or cowboy fantasies for me. I knew then and there, standing on those linoleum tiles, that show business would be my life.

I was seven when I sang you "Rosin the Bow"
There in Aunt Mary's kitchen and I don't guess I know
It's why I've done this for all of this time
But now playing and singing seems a game and a crime

—"HOMELESS," 2001

My mother not only encouraged me to succeed but, more important, she had the ability to calm and relax me. As a prepubescent boy I would occasionally get severe cramps in my legs, particularly in my calf muscles, and my mom would minister to me with massages and the laying on of hot-water bottles. When I played Little League baseball, Mom would come to watch me, and amazing things could

Young Loudie and Mom, 1956.

happen as a result. I was at best a marginal player, but on a number of occasions, when I was aware of her presence in the stands, I would step up to the plate and hit a home run. If my father was watching me play, I would be much more likely to tense up and strike out, blowing it like the son does in Dad's short story "Clean Jersey."

In 1955 everything suddenly changed for our family when my father confessed to my mother that he was having an affair with a married woman named Gloria, whom he worked with at the L.A. *Life* bureau. This was not a fling or a casual office dalliance, but a torrid and serious romance. My poor mother decided the best course of action to protect the family was to put three thousand miles between her husband and the evil Jezebel home wrecker. It was decided that we would move back east. Mom, my sister Teddy, my brother Andy, and I took the Santa Fe Super Chief train back to New York. My father flew ahead of us to locate new digs, and he found a house to rent in Westchester County, in Bedford Village. My mother, desperate to hold on to her man and keep her family intact, became pregnant again, and in 1956 my sister Sloan was born. Then we moved to the house that would later burn down, on Tarleton Road, and there things seemed to stabilize for a while, until the old man started to figure out ways to get back to L.A. and to Gloria. Not long after Dad died, in 1988, I learned from Martha Fay, with whom he lived for the last twenty years of his life, that he had always thought he might have fathered a child with Gloria. During their affair, Gloria discovered she was pregnant, but was able to convince or trick her cuckolded husband into believing the baby, a boy, was his. In a final Gothic twist to the tale, a few years later, Gloria and her husband were both killed in a car crash. Mercifully the child was not in the car, and, after the tragedy, he was adopted and brought up by a family member. So I might have a half brother out there somewhere, although there's a lot of mythology surrounding these events.

It's possible that this baby was not my father's, that Gloria was either lying to him or wasn't sure herself who the father was. Whatever happened, I'm happy to let it all remain a mystery. I've got enough stuff to work out with the people who I know are in my family.

I certainly remember the name Gloria being contemptuously mentioned by my mother throughout my childhood, and this always felt strange to me, because there had been another Gloria in my life. Back in the early fifties, at the Warner Avenue grammar school in Westwood, there was a second grader named Gloria who was a favorite with the boys because she enjoyed showing them—how shall I put it?—what was underneath her underpants. I had a younger sister, so I was not completely in the dark about what was being offered on view, but whenever there was a display of Gloria's secrets during recess, I was sure to be there, gawking with the other guys in the corner of the playground. Once or twice I was the lucky one Gloria gave her ever-so-slightly stained panties to hold before she began her sexy anatomy lesson. I don't remember if my Gloria was particularly pretty or not, but the memory of her tawny, slightly greasy skin has stayed with me for more than sixty years. Another early supercharged erotic moment was seeing my mother's older sister, Peggy, emerge naked from a steamed-up shower cabinet when I was eight. I had walked into the bathroom by mistake, and suddenly there it was, a real-life version of what I would observe years later in Gustave Courbet's painting *The Origin of the World*. My aunt had an amused and slightly lascivious expression on her face as she stepped onto the bath mat, and no wonder. Her dripping dark brown pudendum was just about at my eye level, and she saw that my world had been rocked.

Speaking of being rocked: Back east, in 1956, I began to monitor the musical earthquake that was taking place by listening to 77 WABC radio. Fittingly, the first thing that got me was "Whole Lotta Shakin'

Goin' On" by Jerry Lee Lewis, and that led to the purchase of my first 45 single, Elvis's seismic "All Shook Up." The B-side was "That's When Your Heartaches Begin," a message as to what lies ahead for most mortals. Soon the longhair wars began. After seeing the King on *Ed Sullivan*, boys naturally wanted sideburns and DAs (ducks' asses), a sort of Pinocchio real-boy variation on the Davy Crockett coonskin cap craze from a few years earlier. But I didn't stand a chance, because that was about the time my father decided to send me to Harvey, a private boys' school in nearby Hawthorne, named after William Harvey (1578–1657), the Englishman who figured out how blood circulates. I would have to repeat the sixth grade because I hadn't studied Latin, and not only did I have to keep my hair neatly trimmed, I also had to learn how to knot a necktie. This felt a little like the Marine Corps "sir" kerfuffle all over again, but this time my father was not going to relent. He was determined that I get a good education, and I suppose I owe him another thank-you for that. Still, I remember the pain and embarrassment of tearfully asking for his help in understanding my Latin declension homework. Turns out Dad had forgotten most of that shit himself.

So little Loudie went off to a private boys' school at the age of twelve. Since I was a day student, it wasn't exactly *Tom Brown's School Days*, though; my nights and weekends were spent at home with Mom, brother, sisters, a cat, and a dog. It was a much lonelier existence for the boarding students. One boarder, the cartoonist Garry Trudeau, was in the class behind me. Recently, he and I met, and we wound up reminiscing a bit about our years at Harvey. Mostly we spoke of two sadistic teachers, "masters," whom we both hated. One taught Latin and was a short, nasty, trim dictator of a man who'd been terrorizing boys at the school for decades. I've blocked out what he was like in the classroom, but he couldn't have been very good, because I took three years of Latin at Harvey and the only thing I remember are the words for "boy" and "farmer" (*puer* and *agricola*). What stayed with me about this guy was the little bully's ability to inflict humiliation at the lunch table. The dining room tables at the school were big and round, with a master seated at each one to serve the food and keep order. Nobody wanted to sit at the Latin teacher's table; just being there felt like a kind of detention. My most traumatic experience with him had to do with stewed tomatoes. I was not a picky eater. I pretty much liked everything, with the exception of squash, which I eventually grew to enjoy, and stewed tomatoes, which to this day I cannot abide. One lunchtime, after everyone else had been excused, this Master of His Universe made me remain at the table to eat my fucking stewed tomatoes. After what seemed like an eternity, I finally ingested the viscous, smelly stuff, occasionally gagging but somehow managing to keep it down. But not before I'd been reduced to tears of shame, which undoubtedly was the master's intention.

The other faculty sadist at Harvey whom Garry and I spoke of was a football coach. Also short, this thug was a crew-cut, angry, jaw-clenching man whose distinguishing characteristic was a tendency to administer very painful noogies to keep lively boys in line. He didn't just rub the victim's skull, à la Moe from the Three Stooges; he struck it, his descending hand clenched in a fist with the knuckle of the middle digit slightly protruding so as to create a sharp point of impact. Neither Trudeau nor I, sensitive artist alumni types that we are, have ever returned to the Harvey School. Some grudges should be held.

In Bedford, my parents' marriage continued to erode. Obviously, as a kid, I didn't know or understand all the particulars, but it was clear they were both just getting unhappier. My father's infidelities continued; his propensity for that kind of behavior is something he and I share. For years, in and out of shrinks' offices, I've been trying to work out and understand this tendency of ours. There's the

Dad with his customary glass of scotch, 1960s.

"variety is the spice of life" concept, or the happy-go-lucky Woody Guthrie explanation of "More Pretty Girls Than One," but the danger aspect also comes into play, the thrill of doing something "bad" and being caught and punished for it. Maybe it goes back to childhood, first getting in trouble with authority figures—parents and teachers—then eventually it's cops, wives, and husbands. When you're in hot water, you experience the charge of really getting to someone who you perceive is controlling you, and that can feel good to a kid (as well as to an errant adult). I wouldn't rule out wanting to hurt the ones we love, either, because the ones we love are the ones who can piss us off the most.

> *Call me Mr. Guilty, Mr. Guilty that's my name*
> *Without a doubt it's all my fault, I am the one to blame*
> *You say that you're unhappy and I suppose it's true*
> *And I'm the one, the no good bum*
> *That did it all to you*

> —"MR. GUILTY," 1975

I'm not sure I understand love, anyway. I have no doubt my parents fell in love, but there are all kinds of ways to crawl out of or be ejected from that hole. And I don't think people fall as much as they jump.

They run into someone they think or hope can ring their various bells, and then they take the leap. After my folks finally split up, in 1976, after many bumpy, often bruising years, my dad used to say to me, "I love your mother." That pissed me off. What I thought he really meant was "I used to love your mother." It was regret and guilt he was feeling, not love. My mother clung to the marriage, always insisting that she still loved my father, but I think she was simply terrified of losing him and being alone. Where would she go? Certainly not back to Georgia. When he finally did leave, the little girl from Tifton was abandoned once again.

Whatever happened to you?
Whatever happened to us?
Hey, we missed the proverbial boat,
The plane and the train and the bus
Push led to shove and we fell outta love
And we tore each other apart
Love is grand but I can't understand
Why you broke my proverbial heart

We used to be in love
But now we are in hate
You used to say I came too early
But it was you who came too late
Boy meets girl and they give it a whirl
And the very next thing you know
He thinks she's nuts and she hates his guts
And the bad blood starts to flow

—"WHATEVER HAPPENED TO US," 1975

. . .

IN 1976, up in my hometown of Bedford Village, on a warm spring Easter Sunday afternoon, after the ham, the string beans, and the scalloped potatoes, my dad asked me if I would take a walk with him. He sounded serious, and there was a tinge of sadness in his eyes. It wasn't a long walk, just a few hundred yards down the dirt road our house was on. Faron, my sister Sloan's very social Siamese cat, tagged along on the stroll. My father then proceeded to tell me he was leaving my mother, his beloved Martha, his wife of thirty years and the mother of his four children. He was leaving her for a much younger woman—someone my age, in fact—whom he'd met and worked with in the city. I was not at all shocked. I knew my parents' marriage was a troubled one and that he'd had several affairs. So had I, for that matter. My five-year marriage to my wife Kate, the mother of Rufus and his sister, Martha, was shredding at that same time, largely due to my infidelities. I asked my father for a few details. Would Mom keep the house? For now, yes. Did my brother and sisters know? Yes. When was he leaving? Right away, that very night. How long had he been seeing the other woman? Seven years. Seven years? *Seven years!* I said something along the lines of "What took you so long to tell us?" He pushed back hard, reminding me that my own marriage was a failed one: "Who are you to judge me? You're full of shit." Then, with a trembling but clear voice, I did the unthinkable—the much fantasized but, until that moment, the un-thinkable. "Dad, you've been telling me my whole life that I'm full of shit. Well, I just want to tell you that you're full of shit, too." It was my "Fuck you, Dad!" moment, and it had taken thirty years to get there. The world didn't end. We went back in the house. But I do re-member Faron doing figure eights around our ankles, there in that bucolic but ferociously emotionally charged setting, when my old man and I faced each other off on Tarleton Road.

MY MOTHER HIRED cleaning ladies when we lived in Bedford. These part-time, but in no way unskilled, employees were black women, who, like my mother, had migrated up from the South. Unlike her, they lived in the poor neighborhoods of Harlem or the South Bronx. On the designated morning, the cleaning lady would board the Metro-North train at 125th Street in Manhattan, and an hour or so later she would be picked up at the Mount Kisco station by my mom in our green Rambler station wagon. My mother's demeanor with these women was not unfriendly, but it was somewhat curt and always detached. This had to do with her upbringing in Georgia, where being white was considered—by white people—superior to being black.

It was the 1960s and things were boiling between the races. I remember my father coming home, taking his Tandberg reel-to-reel out, and excitedly playing for us a tape recording of an interview he'd just done with Martin Luther King Jr. I imagine that Martha must have had conflicted feelings while she sat there listening to this determined, articulate, southern black man expound on life in general and civil rights in particular. She would have been hesitant to share those feelings with her young children, and perhaps even more so with her Yankee husband. I also wonder what her thoughts and emotions were when she watched the TV news broadcasts covering lunch counter sit-ins, George Wallace harangues, and freedom marchers being fire-hosed and attacked by police dogs in cities and college campuses all over the South. The word "Negro" was in the general parlance back in the sixties, but, try as she might, Martha wound up pronouncing it "Nigra," which was awfully close for comfort. At the end of one sweltering summer day, I rode with her when she dropped the cleaning lady off at the train station. I must have been quite young, maybe ten or eleven, and would have been sitting in the backseat. There was a strange, musky odor in the car, one that I didn't exactly recognize, and on the way home I asked my mother about it. When she told me that what I had smelled was the woman we'd just dropped off, naturally I asked her "Why?" "That's just the way those folks [meaning black folks] smell," she gently explained to me. It wasn't until years later I realized that what I had gotten a whiff of then was simply undeodorized human perspiration, the natural result of eight or nine hours of plain old hard, down-on-your-hands-and-knees, sweat-producing labor.

I was raised here in Westchester County
I was taught in a country day school
We were richer than most, I don't mean to boast
But I swam in the country club pool

With a father from Hewlett, Long Island
And a mother from Tifton, GA
During the war, in the Marine Corps
They met and then married one day

And I was raised here in Westchester County
My brother, my sisters and I
Oh, our dad went to work every day in New York
On a train, in a suit and a tie

I remember those coming-out parties
Where us country club kids had our fun

Steal a kiss, cop a feel off a girl in high heels
Oh, we all came in our cummerbunds

And I was raised here in Westchester County
Tennis courts and golf courses galore
At the country club pool at the country club school
I learned manners and oh so much more

I remember those big Sunday dinners
Around that dining room table we all sat
Carve a turkey, a ham, a roast leg of lamb
Dinner finished in ten minutes flat

—"WESTCHESTER COUNTY," 1983

In 1961, I finished at Harvey and was sent away to St. Andrew's boarding school in Middletown, Delaware, the same place my father had been exiled to in 1938. The student body was mainly composed of white Episcopalian boys, many of whom seemed to be from Maryland. There were no girls, no blacks, and two Jews, who were hazed with regularity. The folk boom had begun, and the hair wars intensified again. We'd heard Bob Dylan, and some of us were believers. All of us wistfully watched the free, happy, sexy public high school kids our age dance every afternoon on Dick Clark's *American Bandstand*. Every day we were glued to the black-and-white television in the Common Room, trying to pick up their moves. Actually, I already had the moves. I had learned them in the summer of 1960 from Pat O'Boyle, a tough, soulful Irish kid from Armonk, New York, who had been a neighbor of one of my Harvey classmates. Pat's older brother had taught him how to do the Pony, the Stroll, the Jerk, and the coolest dance of all, the Slop. Pat showed me all the steps, slowing them down, highlighting their subtleties, and, as we went along, critiquing my stabs at them. Conveniently, each dance had its own accompanying song. I picked up plenty from O'Boyle that summer, and when I arrived at St. Andrew's in the fall, the word quickly got out that there was a new third former who could really dance. I was duly summoned from my lowly dormitory alcove and escorted upstairs to a senior's room where, to the strains of Ray Charles's "What'd I Say," I strutted Pat's stuff for a group of senior prefects. They were amazed, as if, somehow, an alien from the planet American Bandstand had been smuggled onto the campus. I wasn't trying to curry favor, I just had the moves they wanted and was happy to show them off. They practically took notes. Once the knowledge was imparted, I was summarily dismissed and sent back down to the third form dorm. Knowing how to dance has always been essential to getting laid, which is what every teenage boy is obsessed with. At a boys' boarding school, with the exception of a few faculty daughters, there were no girls. A few times a year, girls were invited to the school for dances, but most of the time we practiced our moves with each other—think the "There Is Nothing Like a Dame" number from *South Pacific*.

One or two years later, however, once the Dylan ethos had really taken hold, some of us had tired of all this Chubby Checker–esque nonsense. It started to seem insipid, much tamer than the original rock and roll we'd first heard and loved six years earlier—the Elvis, Jerry Lee, and Little Richard stuff. *American Bandstand* lost its edge when it started pushing Connie Francis and Herman's Hermits. Bob wouldn't be caught dead lip-synching and was evoking something riskier, cooler, and more detached. We got hip to Kerouac, the French New Wave, and alienation. Kids started wearing sunglasses. I suppose

The Cardinal

VOLUME XXXV, No. 6   ST. ANDREW'S SCHOOL, MIDDLETOWN, DELAWARE   SATURDAY, JUNE 12, 1965

Loudon Wainwright Gives Valedictory At Commencement

The class of 1965's valedictorian at today's commencement exercises was Loudon S. Wainwright of Bedford, New York.

Loudie entered St. Andrew's in his third form year, and his address today marked the close of an outstanding four years begun at that time. His popularity with his formmates was evident at once, and his leadership abilities caused him to be a form officer twice.

Loudie stayed on an undefeated J. V. football team in his fourth form year, gained a starting position on the varsity the following season, and as a sixth former led the Independent Conference in scoring, from his position at halfback.

Above all, Loudie was, and is, an entertainer—and the best entertainer in a class that had several. Today's graduating class was responsible for a surge of student interest in singing and drama, and Loudie was in the midst of both movements. A highly skillful folk singer and guitar player, he has led various groups on performances anywhere from the garth sun-deck to New York coffee houses, and particularly at S.A.S. dances.

Loudie began his S.A.S. acting career in his third form year with a quick double-take in *Teahouse of the August Moon*. His roles increased in importance in *My Three Angels* and *Billy Budd* and this year he climaxed his student dramatics with a brilliant portrayal of Shakespeare's hilarious Falstaff in *Henry IV, Part I*. Loudie hopes to make acting his career, and will specialize in drama at Carnegie Tech beginning next fall.

There is an interesting parallel between Loudie's prep school career and his father's. Mr. Loudon Wainwright, who graduated from St. Andrew's in 1942, and now writes the popular "View from Here" for Life Magazine, was also a fine actor, and—not at all surprisingly—the valedictorian of his graduating class.

On the front page of
The Cardinal, 1965.

the Beatles and the Rolling Stones brought back a bit of the danger. Well, the Stones did.

Every year at St. Andrew's there was one theatrical production put on by the drama society, which was called the Criss Cross Club. In my first year at the school, I was cast in *The Teahouse of the August Moon* in the small role of a "villager." For me, it was pivotal. There were only two performances of the play, but both nights I got a big laugh by employing some strenuous mugging. The collective guffaw given out by the three hundred people in that school auditorium in 1962 was more than just approbation. It was life affirming in the sense that now there really was a reason to live. After that, being in the school plays became the single most important thing for me. In my senior year I was the high scorer on the varsity football team, but that distinction paled in comparison with my receiving the drama prize at graduation for my portrayal of Sir John Falstaff in Shakespeare's *Henry IV, Part 1*.

Now, for sure, show biz was to be my life.

In Delaware, when I was younger, I would live the life obscene
In the spring I had great hunger, I was Brando, I was Dean
Blaspheming, booted, blue-jeaned baby boy, oh how I made them
*   turn their heads*
The townie brownie girls they jumped for joy, and begged me bless
*   them in their beds*

In Delaware when I was younger, I would row upon the lake
In the spring I had great hunger, I was Keats, I was Blake
My pimple, pencil pain I'd bring to frogs, who sat entranced
My drift dream ditties I would sing, the water striders danced

In Delaware when I was younger, they thought St. Andrew's had
*   sufficed*
But in the spring I had great hunger, I was Buddha, I was Christ
You wicked wise men, where's your wonder? You Pharisees one
*   day will pay*
See my lightning, hear my thunder, I am truth, I know the way
In Delaware when I was younger

—"School Days," 1968

3.
the picture

There are pictures on the piano
Pictures of the family
Mostly my kids, but there's an old
Picture of you and me
You were five and I was six
In 1952
That was forty years ago
How could it be true?

—"The Picture," 1992

I wrote "The Picture" in 1992, and since then plenty of time has gone by, so I've been bumping up the number in the last line. These days I'm up to "that was sixty years ago," and I suppose we just might make it to "that was seventy years ago . . . ," but I doubt it, since seventy has an extra syllable, and it would be tough to make the line scan properly. The song may not be the most requested number in my show (for the last few years people have been calling out a lot for

"Daughter," a song I recorded but that was written by my friend Peter Blegvad), but it's surely one of my "hits," and after a gig, when I come in contact with people at the CD sales table, I'm reminded of just how much impact "The Picture" has had. Brothers tell me all about their younger sisters and, even more often, sisters talk about their older brothers.

The sister in "The Picture" is my sister Martha, whose real name is Teddy, because that's what everyone has always called her. I guess my parents thought their first daughter was as cute as a teddy bear. But she wasn't cute, really, not in the way my brother Andy, sister Sloan, and I were cute, with our fair, freckled skin and the same button noses that my mother's family had. Teddy's looks came from our dad's side of the family; she wound up with grandmother Eleanor Wainwright's elegant straight nose, dark eyes with accompanying long lashes, and lovely complexion. As a child, Teddy wasn't cute, she was beautiful.

Teddy and me, Katonah, New York, 1951.

We were sitting outside drawing
At a table meant for cards
And it must have been in autumn
Fallen leaves in the front yard
With a shoe box full of crayons

Full of colors oh so bright
In a picture in a plastic frame
In a snapshot black and white

In our first few, all-important years, Teddy and I were together much of the time—back to front in bathtubs, sitting side by side on our parents' bed, unbelted in the backseat of the car, across from each other at card tables, and clinging to each other at the edges of swimming pool deep ends. "Loudie and Teddy" were a twosome, a sort of little-kid couple, at least until our brother, Andy, came along in 1950. My mother always firmly instructed me to keep an eye on my sister, or "susta," as she pronounced it, and I did the best I could for as long as was possible. I held Teddy's hand, taught her to do things, and led the way for both of us. I dutifully kissed her when told to, even if I wasn't so sure that I wanted to. I always played with her, though sometimes I was too rough; once I chased and tackled her from behind and she fell and broke her leg. Of course, she forgave me; she was so thrilled that her big brother was the first one to sign her heavy plaster cast. She worshipped and adored me, so the day I rode away from her on my bicycle when I was ten years old to go meet Donny Noble and Mike Barry, disobeying my mother's decree and leaving Teddy crying in the front yard, was a terrible day indeed. I left her because I'd found friends, other boys my own age, pals to ride bikes with. Like Marlon Brando explains to the girl in *The Wild One*, "You got to put something down." But in spite of my compelling reasons, I've never truly been able to forgive myself for riding away from Teddy. It was a traitorous act and it haunts me.

You were looking at my paper
Watching what I drew

It was natural, I was older
Thirteen months more than you
A brother and a sister
A little boy and girl
And whoever took that picture
Captured our own world

When puberty struck, some rough things happened to Teddy—she got glasses, she got braces, she started taking pills prescribed by a doctor so that she would lose weight. But the hardest thing for her happened earlier and was more psychological in nature. I've always felt our mother found it difficult to love her eldest daughter. Maybe Mom felt that this perfect, beautiful child wasn't quite hers, but was, in a kind of fairy-tale sense, a threat, someone who might steal her husband's affection away from her. As a little girl, my mother had to compete with her three sisters for the attention of their emotionally distant, mostly absent father. Maybe my mother's insisting that I look after my "susta" was really a command to fill in for her, to be a surrogate parent and perform a job she herself didn't want, one she was emotionally unable to handle. Of course, all this might be shrink-wrapped bullshit, some half-assed theorizing from a guilt-ridden brother who's read too much Freud, who left his little sister crying under a tree, and rode off on his Schwinn bicycle with playing cards clothes-pinned to the spokes, clicking.

A brother needs a sister
To watch what he can do
To protect and to torture
To boss around, it's true

But a brother will defend her
For a sister's love is pure
Because she thinks he's wonderful
When he is not so sure

When you are well-reviewed in the *New York Times*, get called "a genius" in the *Village Voice*, and then suddenly have a hit song on the radio, it's a heady experience. You've made it big, and this can have a powerful effect on your friends and your family. Your friends are impressed, but some are also pissed off and resentful because it didn't happen to them. Your success can make them feel like failures, and so, after a while, they decide you were just lucky and they weren't. With your family it's trickier. They *have* to be happy about what's happened to you—or at least they have to pretend to be.

When I had my first commercial success in 1972, it was tough on Teddy. Suddenly, her big brother was some kind of a star, moving even farther away from her, flying off into a different galaxy. It was the occasional limo, not just a bicycle, that whisked me away from her. Once, in the mid-seventies, Teddy turned up drunk and crying in my dressing room at the Bottom Line in New York City, minutes before I was about to go on. I don't believe it was an attempt to derail my show as much as it was an expression of her fear and pain that we were now so very far apart. My mother, on the other hand, would always arrive backstage delighted and full of pride, basking in her first son's glory. My success was also hers, and that is the way it should be.

My father's feelings about my career can best be described as ambivalent. But, hey, I get it. I'm almost always uncomfortable waiting in line to congratulate and hug Rufus after his gigs. In that setting, I'd much prefer the spotlight and adulation to be on me.

. . .

BY 1978 there were no more limos. I'd been dropped by three labels, fired my manager, and needed to restart my career almost from scratch. It wasn't so much a question of making it big at that point as it was holding on to a job. Teddy had just gotten sober, and I proposed that she become my manager. She accepted, and suddenly it was her turn to look after me. She did so for seventeen years.

Teddy and I are living in different parts of the country now, but we're together again in the bathtub of advancing age, both clinging to the edge in the deep end of something or other, possibly oblivion. I take a handful of pills every day and hobble around New York with a hip that's been operated on twice. She's down in Florida recovering from a liver transplant. How could it be true?

And just the other night, I watched my daughter Martha's two little boys, ages five and two, playing together on my living room floor. Five-year-old Arc was trying hard to get his toy train lined up, but his baby brother, Francis, inexorably—almost magnetically—drawn to his older sibling and whatever he was doing, kept falling all over Arc's miniature world, destroying it like a drunken, oblivious, toddler Godzilla. This frustrated and angered Arc, and so his wise old grandfather reminded him to be patient with his baby brother and include him in the game, to look after him the way a big brother should. After a halfhearted stab at that, Arc just walked away from the wreckage and went looking for a book.

> *In the picture there's a fender*
> *Of our old Chevrolet*
> *Or Pontiac, our dad would know*

Surely he could say
But Dad is dead and we grow old
And it's true that time goes by
And in forty years the world has changed
As well as you and I.

4.
swimming

This summer I went swimming, this summer I might have
drowned
But I held my breath and I kicked my feet and I moved my
arms around
This summer I swam in the ocean and I swam in a
swimming pool
Salt my wounds, chlorine my eyes, I'm a self-destructive fool

—"THE SWIMMING SONG," 1974

It's not unusual for me to smell of chlorine, because many mornings, roughly between 6:30 and 7:00 a.m., I am in the pool at the Trinity School on New York's Upper West Side, dutifully freestyling my forty laps, covering the same half mile of watery distance each time. Not long ago, I had to share a lane with a man who, for some reason, I don't like, probably because he's a guy my own age who wears little sawed-off flippers and does his laps in a rather pathetic fashion, alternating between a sloppy, slow backstroke and an even slower, lame, girly sidestroke. The lanes at the pool are narrow, and no one really likes to share, although if the athletic, hardworking, forty-something Korean woman happens to be my lane mate, that's just fine, because I always enjoy watching her underwater. She has my number, though, and if space in another lane becomes available, she quickly gathers up her kickboard and ankle flotation device, ducks under the floating plastic lane marker, and scoots the hell away. Such are the vagaries of my early-morning swimming pool life. Ostensibly there to get some exercise, but due to the near-nakedness of others, I sometimes fall prey to my superannuated laddish tendencies. From the beginning, though, a lot of my life has been about me in the water, and it's stayed that way for decades, in pools, ponds, reservoirs, rivers, oceans, and bays.

My father, growing up on Long Island and spending summers in Rhode Island and Maine, was a superb swimmer. When sufficiently lubricated, he could be graceful on the country club dance floor, but on dry land he was, for the most part, an awkward, hesitant biped. As a kid, one of his nicknames had been Skinny, but once he got into his late twenties and settled into his sedentary lifestyle of smoking, drinking, reading, writing, and worrying, he put on the extra weight he always hated but could never lose. Watching him swim, however, was to witness a metamorphosis. In the water, with most of his body hidden and buoyed beneath the surface, he became a boy again, seemingly shedding not only pounds and decades but also anxieties and doubts. His Australian crawl was not so much a crawl as a glide, his strong strokes propelling him forward in quick little lurches, allowing him to cut through the water the way a rowing shell does. Johnny Weissmuller never looked so good. Conversely, my mother spent her childhood in a landlocked part of south Georgia and could barely swim a stroke. She had a fear of the water that went all the way back to a terrifying experience she'd had when she was baptized at age eight in a cold muddy river. It was a full-body immersion, a kind of sacramental precursor to waterboarding. Dressed in a coarse white linen smock, her eyes tightly clenched, arms crossed in front of her, with one thumb and forefinger squeezing her nostrils, she was forcibly dunked backward into the water by a gruff no-nonsense preacher. He held her submerged for a few seconds that must have seemed like an eternity. Then she was pulled back out, coughing, sputtering, and gasping for air. As a young married woman living in the Northeast, literally out of her element, my mother tried to conquer her water phobia. There are old home movies of her nervously pretending to swim and frolic at the East Beach in Watch Hill, Rhode Island, but she never goes in over her head. Perhaps because of her anxieties about water and drowning, Mom made sure her kids could swim, and we started classes early. I remember a boys-only class at a YMCA. For some reason we swam naked, our little hairless balls and peckers undulating in the water. That would never happen today, except maybe in Scandinavia.

This summer I did the backstroke and you know that that's not all
I did the breaststroke and the butterfly and the old Australian crawl
This summer I swam in a public place and a reservoir to boot
At the latter I was informal, at the former I wore my suit

When you're learning to swim, one of the things you're taught is to turn your head to the side to take a breath, and then, returning your face beneath the surface, to exhale by blowing bubbles. Eventually this maneuver becomes second nature to the swimmer. But even now, six and a half decades on, I'll occasionally breathe in a bit of chlorinated water by mistake, and my childhood returns to me in a Proustian moment.

When we were preteens, my sisters, brother, and I were on the

Bedford Golf and Tennis Club swim team. We learned flip turns and racing dives and garnered blue, red, and white ribbons at meets with other clubs, especially Teddy, who had a real talent for the backstroke. I was okay at the breaststroke and was a fair to middling freestyler, but where I really excelled was on the one-meter diving board. In the summer, I spent hours bouncing up and out as high and as far as I could to impress girls and irritate grown-ups a few free-falling seconds later with my explosive cannonballs and cascade-producing one-legged can openers. Even back then I knew it was all about making the biggest splash possible.

> *This summer I did swan dives and jackknives for you all*
> *But once when you weren't looking I did a cannonball*

LW3's Top 10 swimming spots—not in any particular order of preference

1. *The Forty Foot in Sandycove, just south of Dublin.* It's been around more than 250 years, and the first section of *Ulysses* ends with Buck Mulligan taking a dip there, plunging into "the scrotum tightening sea." Originally a men's-only nude bathing spot, it is now frequented by swimsuited crazies of both genders. It's open year-round, and some maniacs go in every morning. Forget the nonsense about the warming effects of the Gulf Stream in the Irish Sea. I've been going to the Forty Foot for about thirty years, and it's always really cold. For the every-once-in-a-while visitor, it's not really a swim as such, but rather an in-and-out experience, often punctuated by a bloodcurdling scream of *"Fuuuckk!"* upon submersion. There's a frantic tread in the icy brine, followed by a hasty retreat, and

afterward, during the toweling off and dressing, quick little deferential twists of the head are proffered, as if to mutely indicate to others, "Ah, it wasn't so bad."

Me and my daughter Lucy at the Forty Foot, 2006.

2. *The Andrew "Boy" Charlton—an eight-lane, fifty-five-yard heated outdoor salt-water swimming pool on the shore of Woolloomooloo (bet you can't say it three times in a row) Bay in the Domain, Sydney, Australia.* Charlton was an Aussie swimming prodigy who, in a 440-yard race, whipped Arne Borg's Swedish ass in January 1924, in front of six thousand spectators. He also kicked Bill Harris's Hawaiian butt a year earlier at age fourteen, in an 880. The great swimmers, gymnasts, and mandolin players all seem to be kids.

3. *The Highgate or Hampstead Ponds—three freshwater ponds fed by the headwater spring of the River Fleet in Hampstead Heath,*

North London. When I first started going to the men's-only pond in the early eighties, what you saw in the open-air changing area were either wrinkly, tanned nudists or pasty, out-of-shape Hasidim from Golders Green with their adolescent sons in tow, hastily changing into their swimming trunks, using the wraparound-towel maneuver. Then word got out about the nude sunbathing aspect of the place, and the men's pond became a gay cruising spot, a veritable scrotum-tightening sea of dicks on display. Now there's a special enclosed area for all that. I still go there, because the swimming is great. The Hasidim have gone elsewhere.

4. *The Western Baths Club—an indoor Victorian-era private swimming and leisure club, founded in 1876, in Hillhead, Glasgow.* The first thing that grabs your attention are the period trapeze and exercise rings that hang over this marvelous pool.

5. *Deep Eddy Pool—in Austin.* It is the oldest swimming pool in Texas, featuring a bathhouse built in 1936. The pool served as the centerpiece of a resort called the Deep Eddy Bathing Beach. Lorena's Diving Horse was a popular attraction. As seen in historic photographs, a ramp led to a fifty-foot diving platform over the pool's deep end, from which the horse and rider would dive. Fed from deep cold springs from the Colorado River and chlorine-free.

6. *Barton Springs Pool—also in Austin and chlorine-free.* In 1837, William "Uncle Billy" Barton settled the area and named the three separate springs after his daughters, Parthenia, Eliza, and Zenobia. Not great lap swimming, but it's in swinging Austin, so topless sunbathing is permitted.

7. *Lake Waccabuc*—I've been making ablutionary pilgrimages to this lovely little northern Westchester County body of water for much of my life, having been dunked and swished around in it as a toddler when my parents were members of the Waccabuc Country Club in the early fifties. In 1804, an elephant called Old Bet was brought to the United States and was a star in Hachaliah Bailey's circus in nearby Somers. One frigid winter, Old Bet caught a chill and died, and, due to frozen ground conditions, they had to cart the three-ton pachyderm out to the middle of iced-over Waccabuc. They left her there, and waited for the spring thaw. Old Bet's bones must be resting somewhere on the bottom to this day.

At one end of the lake is Castle Rock, which is not so much a rock as a cliff that rises from the water's surface. From its summit, generations of beer-chugging teenagers have leapt straight out into midair, to savor and hopefully survive the thrilling three-second, fifty-foot plummet. I jumped off Castle Rock as a kid, and then again on my thirtieth birthday in 1976 when I was looped on champagne and showing off for friends. When my fortieth rolled around, I did it alone and sober. There were repeat jumps for my fiftieth and sixtieth, despite pleas from loved ones to stop already. My seventieth came and went on September 5, 2016, and wisdom prevailed at last—I stayed the hell away from Castle Rock.

8. *East Beach*—This was the ocean beach of my childhood, located in Watch Hill, Rhode Island, where my grandmother lived. My father taught me how to ride waves at East Beach.

9. *Palm Beach*—A beautiful swimming spot forty kilometers north of Sydney. The first time I went to Australia was in 1982, and my dad

came along on that tour. We rode waves together for the last time at Palm Beach.

10. *Aquatic Park, San Francisco*. Facing the Golden Gate Bridge and Alcatraz, the Dolphin Swimming and Boating Club (1877) and the South End Rowing Club (1873) are next-door neighbors that maintain a fierce but friendly rivalry, although my friend at the South End tells me it's a tad more ferocious than friendly. Day guest privileges at both facilities are ten dollars and allow you to swim from the shared private beach. The water in the San Francisco Bay in summer (September and October) is bracing, and it has a real snap to it in February. Strong tides are always a major factor—it can take three-quarters of an hour to get out to a seemingly close buoy, while the return journey back might take you seven minutes. The funky, ancient changing rooms and saunas of the clubs are appealing, and framed historical photos and news clippings on the walls make the price of admission a real bargain. In addition, the beautifully made and meticulously maintained wooden rowing boats are a sight to behold.

A note to my grieving survivors: Kindly sprinkle my ashes at all the above locations.

5.

the endless waves

by Loudon Wainwright Jr.; appeared in *Life* magazine,
July 1988, five months before his death

My respect for waves developed early. I have memories of a summer
beach and standing at the water's edge as a child of four or five, howling
while my parents, one or both of them, frolicked just a few yards from me
in what surely were gentle rollers. Now and then they looked back toward
the beach, smiling and waving to reassure their frightened child, whose
fantasy was nothing less than that the waves would take them away from
him forever.

Over the next few years my relationship with waves improved greatly.
We lived near good Atlantic Ocean beaches, and I learned how to swim,
first in a pool, then more or less simultaneously in the surf. When my
friends and I were 10 years old, or 12, or even on into the teens, until a
growing fixation with girls took precedence over most everything, we
spent hours of every passable summer day in the water riding the waves.

Getting out only after stern parental orders or to gobble sandy peanut-
butter-and-jelly sandwiches, we reveled in the waves. We learned from

experience to avoid trying to ride those crushers that rise up steeply and almost immediately smash down and grind unwary riders into the sand. We learned to dive deeply to escape a bad rolling and to tumble as loosely as possible along the bottom when we got caught in the wrong kind of wave. We learned how to get into just the right position in the line where the surf broke, just a stroke or two behind the curl so that we could start swimming and then suddenly be picked up and catapulted down the face of a breaking wave and then hurled momentarily out in front of it.

We thrilled at the water's rough pummeling, at the sense of terrific speed that came only with being inside a really good wave, caught just right. We often shouted in plain exuberance when, at the end of one ride, we scrambled to our feet in water inches deep and ran back to catch another. Best of all, we loved to ride the towering combers, driven up by a distant storm, that few of the adults would dare to try, and we surely swaggered a bit when we walked from the surf to the bathhouses at the cooling end of a great day, cocky princelings of tide and wind and summer.

Still my ease with waves disappears as I am out of sight of land. Much as I'm drawn to the ocean and want to be near it, I'm always awake to its potential for sudden and violent change. And with the shifts in weather, the waves often rise, the mesmerizing, terrifying waves packed with power and mystery full of contempt of creatures who dare to float upon them.

Coming home across the Pacific on a troopship in 1944, I can recall standing in a protected place near the stern and watching as the huge seas ran up beneath us. We were on the edge of a great typhoon, crew members told us, and these sullen gray giants seemed to be pursuing us. One after another they rose up out of wake almost as high as the deck I was standing on, and they lifted the stern of the ship so far that the big metal screws that drove us through the water shuddered alarmingly as they beat the open air.

Many years later, seven of us, including a daughter of mine then about 10, were sailing across the Gulf of Maine one night when the weather abruptly deteriorated. The boat was a sturdy 45-footer; as the winds increased we had to take down all the sail. Even so, we planed along at an amazing speed, driven by the wind against the hull and the masts and by the waves that rose out of the blackness behind us.

It is those waves I remember best from that scary night full of heavy rain and thunder and lightning that turned our world an awful silver. On an invisible, tumbled parade they reared up, much higher than we were, braced and life-jacketed in the cockpit. Each one was capable—or so I thought in a near panic that did not begin to diminish until dawn showed clearing skies—of engulfing us, of simply overwhelming us and then leaving us awash and helpless in the night.

All this somehow makes me think I should be on the lookout for new waves this summer. Perhaps not to ride, and certainly not to exacerbate old terrors. It would be more to reflect on waves and their possible meanings and the messages they might send me now. Just to see how they call, as they have called to all of us who left their primordial, nutritious soup for life on the beach aeons ago.

6.

shoot off the fence & liza

One of my second-grade classmates at Warner Avenue grammar school in Westwood, California, was Liza Minnelli, and we were in love, or at least *I* thought so. Like everybody else, I knew that her mom was Dorothy from *The Wizard of Oz*. Having the daughter of Judy Garland as my friend in 1954 was a pretty big deal, though not quite as big a deal as living on Hutton Drive, because that was the same street in Benedict Canyon that Davy Crockett (Fess Parker) and his sidekick Georgie Russell (Buddy Ebsen) lived on. Gene Barry (Bat Masterson on TV) had a house on Hutton Drive, too, and his son Mike was in the second grade with me and Liza.

Davy Crockett was a Disney show and a huge hit in the mid-1950s. Millions of Davy Crockett coonskin caps were sold during the show's two seasons. What were those hats really made of? It couldn't have been real coonskin. In addition to the headwear, toy Winchester rifles

King of the Wild Frontier.

and cap pistols were flying off the shelves, since pretending to mow each other down was just about the most fun we kids had back then. Of course, on TV, the bad guys were mostly the ones getting shot, usually winged in the hand or shoulder, so as to be mercifully and somewhat miraculously disarmed, their six-shooters flying off in all directions. But it was on the big Technicolor movie screen that truer life was portrayed. Up there we saw Alan Ladd blow that grinning motherfucker Jack Palance away in *Shane* and Burt Lancaster take out the crazed, callow Dennis Hopper in *Gunfight at the O.K. Corral*. For some reason, I identified not with Ladd and Lancaster but with the more tragically complex and interesting bad guys, Palance and Hopper. Getting shot and dying, being on the receiving end, had much more appeal to me than being the vanquisher who metes out justice, the dispenser of comeuppance. I dreamed of being a movie and TV stuntman, and back when I was eight, my favorite game was Shoot off the Fence. My pals and I would stand or sit on a wooden split-rail fence or a stone wall and pretend to get shot, performing balletic falls to the ground, which included intense writhing, phantom wound-clutching, and death-throe moans. We rated these falls on their degree of difficulty and danger, and points were given for grace, realism, and breadth of imagination. Death-wish fantasies began early in my boyhood and have continued throughout my life.

Recently I had a small role in a movie in which I played a grandfather suffering from dementia. Toward the end of the film, he sits down on a front porch and quietly expires. No wound-clutching or agonized moans this time around, but it nevertheless felt quite familiar, a sort of shoot-off-the-fence redux. There I was, pretending and practicing for the real thing all over again.

I thought Liza was so beautiful. Like me she had freckles, but she also had her father Vincente Minnelli's big dark haunted eyes. Once, she came over to my house on Hutton Drive for what is now called a playdate. I have a memory of the two of us outside, up on a neighborhood hilltop, watching an episode of the television show *Highway Patrol* being filmed in a vacant lot below. I can't remember if we actually caught a glimpse of the show's star Broderick Crawford or not. My desire, my need, to be a performer began back then in L.A., where all life seemed to be lived out against a background of the movies and television. I had classmates whose fathers worked in the business. Donny Noble's father was a prop master, so Donny shared some of his dad's amazing professional secrets with us: swords in movies were really made of flimsy, very bendable aluminum, and the rubies and emeralds embedded in the sword hilts and scabbards were not really jewels at all. They were colored plastic! Donny's father had some of that stuff right in his garage. Andy Frank's dad was Melvin Frank, a famous movie director and producer. For Andy's eighth-birthday party, a bunch of us were taken to a soundstage on the Paramount lot to watch a scene from *The Court Jester* being shot. The stars were Danny Kaye, Angela Lansbury, and the greatest movie villain in tights ever, Basil Rathbone. That afternoon we watched Andy's dad direct the same little fifteen-second sequence over and over again. Every take seemed exactly the same to us and it almost got to be boring, but then, just in time, we were whisked away by Andy's mom and taken to another soundstage, where we got to meet and shake hands with an extremely friendly and outgoing Jack Benny, one of my parents' favorite comedians. Benny, like all movie actors, was just killing time, waiting to work. He was holed up in a kind of makeshift dressing room alcove, wearing an old bathrobe and a pair of worn brown leather bedroom slippers that I couldn't stop staring at. I think I must have been blown away by how something so completely ordinary and mundane as a man's pale white feet in old slippers could be present in such an exotic and magical setting.

One day after school I was invited over to Liza's house in Beverly Hills and her mother was home. I remember Judy Garland as being a nice person but someone who didn't look like Dorothy at all. She had short hair and was much older and quite a bit fatter than the girl in *The Wizard of Oz*. Liza's baby brother, Joey, was there that afternoon, as was her five-year-old sister, Lorna Luft. Their father, Liza's stepdad Sid Luft, was conspicuously absent. Liza's mom seemed to really like me, at least that's what I remember. She was very taken with my freckled pug nose and said it was "cute." I also distinctly recall big green peas on the plates that were put in front of us for our early supper. There must have been other things, but all I remember are those peas. Perhaps I unconsciously connected the greenness of the peas with the Emerald City.

After dinner, Liza and I went outside to play, not Shoot off the Fence but a game just as fabulous, and in a way even more so, since it sprang from a more realistic premise. In a shed at the end of the house's long driveway were Liza's Thunderbird Junior convertibles, battery-powered kiddie cars made of molded fiberglass; T-Bird replicas almost down to the last detail, with actual rubber tires. The cars were about six feet long and two feet high. One foot pedal served as an accelerator and the other as the brake. The Thunderbird Junior, manufactured by the Powercar Company in Mystic, Connecticut, could travel up to three miles per hour. This was a toy only the parents of rich kids could afford. Lee Iacocca's daughter had one. Liza had two. The game we played was chauffeur/starlet. I was the former, she, of course, the latter. I drove up and down the black-topped driveway while she lounged on the back of the T-Bird Jr. convertible and waved to an imaginary throng of adoring fans. Apparently she had witnessed something similar in her real life.

Our family moved back east in 1956, and not long after we arrived I wrote a letter to Liza. It was newsy and a little lame, what you would expect from a ten-year-old. I talked about living in Westchester and how different that was from L.A., how there was cold winter weather and even snow. I asked her what she thought of Elvis in particular and rock and roll in general. With a sense of excitement and expectation I mailed the letter at the Bedford Village post office. Weeks went by, and then months, but still no word back from Liza. I was inconsolable. My mother tried her best to soften the blow, telling me that perhaps the letter hadn't been delivered, or that somehow it had gotten lost in the mail. I didn't buy it, though, and considered Liza's not writing back a cruel rejection.

Eighteen years later, in 1974, right after she won the Oscar for her performance in *Cabaret*, I wrote a song called "Liza."

After school we two engaged in prepubescent play
At your house afternoons were spent cruising your black driveway
In your Junior Thunderbird electric kiddie car
I chauffeured you, you lounged in back, back then you were a star
Your mother, she was famous, and so you were famous, too
Call me groupie, call me gigolo, I fell in love with you
I asked you once what will you be and you quickly said "a nurse"

But the way you sparkled way back then I knew you'd caught
  the curse
Everybody has got a block off which they are a chip
But some chips grow to be great blocks, so Liza let it rip
This is your ex-chauffeur who speaks: indeed you've caught the curse
Now you've got that Oscar, I don't think you'll be a nurse

—"LIZA," 1974

Of course, I hoped Liza would hear my song somehow, and I fantasized that she might want to get in touch with me. But again there was no response. Then, about a year after I wrote the song, I did an interview with a guy from Danish national radio. A few weeks earlier he had been granted fifteen minutes with Liza while she was in Copenhagen for a big sold-out concert. During their taped interview, which was held in Ms. Minnelli's luxurious hotel suite, he played her a recording of my song on his cassette machine and recorded her reaction to hearing it. The Oscar-winning actress's comment was something along the lines of "Oh yes, I remember Loudie Wainwright. If he keeps singing that way he's going to ruin his voice."

7.
empire sand
& stone

Whenever I see horrible news items about adolescent boys going crazy and dropping bricks off bridges onto passing cars, I shudder and remember some of the early teenage insanity I got up to with my friend Peter Case (not the singer-songwriter) in the leafy, affluent environs of Bedford Village. Near his house, from a bluff above Route 22, we chucked sticks and rocks at motorists below, just to see what would happen. We even tried rolling a rotting piece of a dead tree, which could easily have killed any number of people, but, thankfully, we couldn't physically pull it off. We'd seen this kind of exciting violent stuff in the movies, in Westerns, where the bad guys roll a boulder off a cliff to halt and then rob the stagecoach, and we could not resist the temptation to reenact our own variation, having no sense whatsoever of what the consequences might be. Peter and I also staged fake emergencies just for the thrill of it. We would lie down on the grass alongside Route 22 with catsup smeared on our faces. When drivers would jam on their brakes and screech to a halt to come to our assistance, we'd jump up and run away, howling with laughter, into the woods. If it wasn't a death wish, it was, at the very least, messing with death.

A few years after this roadside Russian roulette phase, one Saturday morning, four or five of my sixteen-year-old friends and I trespassed onto a lot belonging to Empire Sand & Stone, a construction machinery and equipment outfit that used to be located in northern Westchester. The pack of us peer-pressured and dared ourselves into commandeering some large dump trucks and bulldozers, the keys still in their ignitions, that had been left unattended over the weekend. Our collective driving skill was poor, with maybe one or two of us having actual learner's permits, but we were undeterred, and for about an hour we went crazy, careening around the lot in the dangerous heavy-duty vehicles, stripping gears we had no idea even existed, plowing into, knocking over, and breaking through anything in our way, which included signs, large mounds of dirt and gravel, and a chain-link fence. Somebody, I can't remember who, crushed and then flattened a smallish shed. I personally bulldozed an eight-foot-tall pine tree, uprooting and killing it in the process. Miraculously, no one was hurt, and when the spell of temporary testosterone madness wore off, we sort of returned to our senses. Like any good gang of criminals, we decided to split up, taking off to our various homes on bikes and foot, amazed at all the fun we'd just had and thinking we'd gotten away with murder.

We hadn't. On Monday morning a police car pulled into my parents' driveway. Through the living room picture window I saw the cruiser pull up, and I hightailed it down to the hall bathroom, where I shut the door and waited for the shit to hit the fan. It didn't take long. "Loudie," my mother called out to me in a voice that had a controlled urgency to it but was tinged with anger. Screwed, blued, and tattooed, as we used to say, I was summoned to join my mom and the officer, who were seated at the dining room table, where all interrogation and upbraiding usually took place at our house. But now it wasn't my pissed-off father reading me the riot act for some minor infraction but rather a cop in uniform, with a badge and a Smith & Wesson strapped to his hip, confronting me with a charge of felonious trespass and egregious destruction of private property. The burly, somewhat bored-looking policeman told me I'd been identified as one of several hooligans who had been spotted wreaking havoc at Empire Sand & Stone on Saturday. "Were you there?" he asked me. "Yes, sir" was my immediate timorous reply. Tough guy. My mom muttered a deeply disappointed "Oh, Loudie" under her breath. The cop then told us that one of my fellow marauders had squealed, so it didn't take long for me to follow suit and rat everybody out. The fingering of my friends felt worse than anything else.

There was a hearing at the end of the week in the Bedford Hills courthouse, where we juvenile delinquents (JDs!) and our parents appeared before a judge. It was an exercise designed mostly, I think, to scare the hell out of everybody. My friends and I were minors and Empire Sand & Stone chose not to prosecute, but there had been considerable damage done, all of which was carefully itemized and ran up to several thousand dollars. I distinctly remember that the cost of the pine tree I bulldozed was eighty dollars. I mowed a lot of lawns that summer.

I got the black belt, you got the gun.
Let's team up tonight—have some fun.
Let's drink some drinks, find us some fights.
C'mon, c'mon, c'mon, c'mon: it's Saturday night!

I'm very angry, you're hopping mad.
Let's hurt some people—let's hurt them bad.
Let's break some heads, let's bust some teeth.
C'mon, it's Saturday night: let's get some relief!

We'll get our rocks off.
We'll rape a co-ed.
Beat on a wino 'til he is dead.
I'll slug a hippie, you'll plug a cop.
We'll go on a rampage and we won't wanna stop.

Now they say he's helpless. I do not care.
Let's get the guy in the wheelchair.
God, I hate women: they mess up your life.
I'll kill your mother, you kill my wife.

It's a hard day at the office, one needs to unwind.
Let's mix up some cocktails . . . the Molotov kind.
Burn down the high school . . . the synagogue.
Let's burn down McDonald's—let's go whole hog!

Now I know a rooftop, don't you say nope.
Let's try out your rifle, the one with the scope.

Tomorrow is Sunday, there's gonna be some parades.
Back at my house, I've got some grenades.
I've got the black belt, you've got the gun.
Hey, we're gonna team up tonight: have some fun!

—"CLOCKWORK CHARTREUSE," 1973

8.

i remember sex

Days of the week used to have importance individually, and to a kid the most important day was Saturday. Obviously, its principal distinction was that there was no school that day. Something special or at the very least fun had to happen on Saturday. For me, Saturday was all about getting away from the rest of the family, hanging out with my pals, going out to play, escaping the strictures imposed by parents and teachers. Spending Saturdays with my friends in Bedford meant exploring graveyards, reservoirs, fields, woods, snow-covered golf courses, building sites, and vacant lots. Also, there were figurative explorations, through the means of dialogue and cross-examination. You held forth or questioned your friends about the rumors having to do with girls, sex, fame, success, and all the mysteries of the great big unfathomable world that lay in wait. Neither you nor your buddies were really sure about anything important, but there were plenty of theories flying around. You didn't talk seriously to one another about God, or ethics, or what might happen after death. You might have timidly asked your parents about that stuff, or, more likely, just left it to rumination.

Saturday, after morning chores, was more or less yours, whereas Sunday was when you had to get your homework done and, often as not, there was a sit-down family meal. You might even have to check in with God on Sunday morning. There were phases when our parents made us go to church and other times when they didn't bother to drag us there. When we got to be teens they mostly left us alone, though my mother, raised a Southern Baptist, could never resist her cheerful, gently sarcastic parting shot as she walked out the door alone: "Well, I'm off now to save your souls." My father's faith seemed to always be wavering. He appreciated the idealized concepts of redemption and forgiveness in religion, along with some of the tasteful pomp and ceremonious circumstance that goes with it, and he loved the uplifting experience of singing the hymns. But he also deplored the sanctimony, condescension, and phoniness that could emanate from the pulpit. However, that didn't stop him from sending me to the same Episcopal boarding school he had attended, where boys were required to go to chapel five evenings a week for Vespers, with an even longer service on Sunday morning. Four years under that regime pretty much finished me off as far as church attendance goes. I sit in on marriages and memorial services out of a sense of duty now, but I'm more or less closemouthed when it comes to the call-and-response prayers and the hymns. Even a muttered "Amen" sticks in my craw. I can't remember the last time I took Communion.

ONCE YOU HIT PUBERTY, it's all about the serious business of getting some version of sex. In terms of reaching first base, kissing—even French kissing—got old pretty fast for me. When I was up in the loge section of the Bedford Playhouse, smooching with my Saturday night movie date, what I was really going for was some bare tit. In this pathetic rite of passage, getting anything below the belt, that is to say third base, wasn't easy in those formative years. A movie theater is a public place and not really a suitable venue for finger fucking. You needed to be in a car or on a recreation room couch for that kind of action. I know that oral sex is casually practiced by young people today, but that would have been a wild and impossible dream in 1960, only becoming a reality as a way to up the ante after "going all the way." I also remember, during make-out sessions with girls, meekly asking them to "touch it," which, in those days anyway, was asking quite a lot. Well, as they say, if you want something done, do it yourself, and I certainly did: beating off, whacking off, jerking off, and cuffing it, as if I were some crazed male mental patient in Peter Brook's movie *Marat/Sade*. My father once caught me "at it," and to alleviate our mutual embarrassment, he confessed that he, in turn, had been caught in flagrante by his old man. Then he told me how boys used to be warned by teachers and clergymen that masturbation causes hair to grow on the palms of the hands. We both laughed about that.

"Scopophilia" is a term used to translate Sigmund Freud's *Schaulust*, or the pleasure of looking, and it's something the eminent doctor considered to be "a regular partial instinct in childhood." Like young guys everywhere throughout the ages, I scoped out (pored over, really) "men's magazines"—certainly *Playboy*, but also grittier down-market porn like *Swank* and *Dude*. The naked models on view in those magazines were not so tastefully airbrushed, and they seemed convincingly real to me, looking much more experienced and dangerously willing. Even the paper the salacious material was printed on had a cheaper, more porous quality, making the overall experience feel dirtier, which, of course, was the desired effect. I was too young to buy these magazines, so I did what any self-respecting teenage boy would do—I stole them. I would go to Trela's Candy Store in Bedford Village after school, where I would loiter with intent in the magazine section, casually thumbing through the comic books. Then, when it seemed safe, I would grab a few dirty mags and surreptitiously slip them down my khakis or blue jeans, zipping up my windbreaker to hide whatever remained visible. Heart pounding, I would exit the premises, or if I was feeling particularly ballsy, I might go up to the cash register, buy a candy bar from Mr. Trela, and then take my leave. It was all pretty exciting. In addition to being a pervert I was a brazen thief. One afternoon, on a dusty shelf on the second floor of Trela's, I found an especially exciting item of erotica, a hand-drawn pornographic pamphlet version of Chic Young's *Blondie* comic strip, in which the eponymous blonde and her sandwich-loving husband, Dagwood, were portrayed doing it on the living room couch and, even better, on the kitchen table. At some point we miserably horny, teenage scopophiliacs got hip to the nudist magazines that you could somehow send away for, and that certainly was a game changer. These were pre-*Hustler* times, so shots of actual female pubic hair were at a premium, desperately sought after and hard to come by. There was, however, a level of discomfort seeing photos in the nudist magazines of the prepubescent hairless girls who mostly reminded me of my younger sisters. And the sight of naked male sun worshippers wearing only sneakers and socks while playing tennis and badminton was a real turnoff.

One of my good friends at the Harvey country day school was a kid named Mike. His twin sister was my date at a few Westchester dances and coming-out parties in Manhattan, and was also one of the girls I made out with up in the loge at the Bedford Playhouse. Mike, his sister, and their parents were all strikingly good-looking. The dad's line of work was something straight, like business or banking, but he was so ruggedly handsome that he also got work as a print model. When we were thirteen, Mike and I had a brief, exploratory homoerotic dalliance consisting of some mutual masturbation and a bit of oral sex. It was interesting, I recall, but ultimately much more enjoyable for him than for me. It was because of Mike, though, that I hit the scopophilia jackpot. In his parents' bedroom bureau drawer he had found some black-and-white Polaroids of his naked mother that his dad had taken. When Mike showed them to me I was completely blown away. This was the very same sexy mom who had served me bologna sandwiches for lunch, for God's sake! She was a real person in my life, and there I was, suddenly checking out her nipples, not to mention—hallelujah!—her actual snatch. No encounter with her would ever be the same again. From then on, the mere greeting of "Hello, Loudie" to me from Mike's mom would instantly result in an attack of terrified blushing and, to go with it, a fierce hard-on.

I remember sex—that thing we used to do,
Where you'd lay down and usually I'd lie on top of you.
Sometimes you'd lie on top of me, we tried that out a bit.
But it didn't work as well, I guess something just didn't fit.

I remember sex—we had it at night.
A few times in the morning, and after we would fight.
And on special occasions when we'd had too much to drink,
Once in a Morris Minor—a convertible I think.

I remember sex—it was such a big deal
And we'd worry where it would come from,
Much more than our next meal.
And we were always hungry, often we overate
And it was up and down and back and forth
and hurry up and wait.

I remember sex, and when we went to bed,
Sometimes we didn't sleep at all, we just had sex instead
And having it was heavenly, not getting it pure hell.
And it was either great or bad—few did it merely well.

I remember sex and how it made us feel:
Completely realistic yet totally surreal.
A thing that we all thought about and all that we thought of,
The distant crazy cousin to the scary thing called love.

I remember sex—I started on my own.
When you and I stopped having it I tried it on the phone
But that was so expensive and sex is just a crutch.
And since I kicked the habit I don't think about it much.

But . . . I remember sex—something that we did,
And we always used to worry that we'd end up with a kid.
Then we'd have to get rid of it or else we'd have to wed.
These days sex can kill you, kids, so stay awake in bed.

—"I Remember Sex," 2012

9.
letter to ches baum

(Written in 2000, and originally appearing, in slightly different form, in *Songs Without Rhyme*, a collection of prose pieces written by singer-songwriters. The book was conceived of and edited by Rosanne Cash and published by Hyperion.)

Dear Mr. Baum,

Thank you for your kind letter and open invitation to visit St. Andrew's. I enjoyed your random observations and vignettes. They were sharp, funny, and interesting. I had no recollection that Dad was visiting S.A.S. on the day of the JFK assassination. Of course, we all remember where we were on that day, but it's strange I should have forgotten such an important personal detail. I hope you'll forgive me for using the formal greeting in my reply, but starting off with "Dear Chester" or "Dear Ches" somehow doesn't seem right to me. Not only am I writing to my former teacher and the former chair of the school's English department, but it's been over thirty-five years since you and I have seen or spoken to one another. This is my fault entirely, since I've stayed away from St. Andrew's pretty much since

my visit in 1968, three years after graduating, when I showed up
on campus with long hair and a red beard, carrying a guitar case.
Mr. Washburn, my old football coach, was friendly that day. Mr.
Cameron was more than happy to see me. He seemed genuinely
pleased that I had begun to sing and, even more important, write
songs for a living. "Bull" Cameron, that towering fearsome figure,
able to freeze a fifteen-year-old slacker at twenty paces with his deep
guttural growling "You, boy!" turned out to be extremely kind, even
solicitous, toward me. Messrs. Schmolze and Hillier were not
so welcoming; huffing and puffing, unable to hide their deep
disapproval of the hippie I'd clearly become. Mrs. Schmolze, right
out of Dickens with that prissy name and her antiquated bobbed
red hair, was especially cold. I suppose I expected unconditional
approval from one and all, sensitive and naive young man that I
was. At any rate, I left Middletown that afternoon vowing never
to return, yet determined that one day I'd show them.

Offering up another excuse for my long absence, let me say that
my last year at St. Andrew's was an unhappy one. A recent look at
the 1965 yearbook confirmed that you were away on sabbatical that
year, so you may not have known this. I did well enough at football
and enjoyed being in the school play (starring as Sir John Falstaff in
Shakespeare's *Henry IV, Part 1*, with a very bad English accent, à la
Dick Van Dyke in *Mary Poppins*). But almost everything else went
badly. Academically I scraped by, somehow passing Spanish. I was
bored, itching to get out into the world, not the big wide one we
were being prepped and groomed for, but the one I'd glimpsed on
American Bandstand and at the Newport Folk Festival. It was a
world of guitar-playing, truth-telling guys with long hair and
sideburns, wearing blue jeans and work shirts, dudes on motorcycles
tightly clung to from behind by the likes of Tuesday Weld in tight

toreador pants or a sandaled and tanned Joan Baez. I had
discovered the trouble with boys' boarding school. There were
no girls there. I was fed up with fantasizing about Mr. Hillier's
fourteen-year-old daughter, Patsy, or Coach Reyner's wife with her
muscular calves and Doris Day haircut, and there was next to no
excitement anymore at the prospect of twisting the night away with
some poor little rich girl from the Shipley School or Miss
Whatever's.

The others in my senior class seemed intent on getting into the
colleges of their choice. I didn't even want to go to college. Instead
I was "ready to go anywhere," as Dylan (Bob, not Thomas) sings
in "Mr. Tambourine Man." It was only after unending parental
pleading and threats and a long emergency meeting with the
headmaster, Mr. Moss, that I agreed to a compromise. I would
apply to Carnegie Tech, where I would study acting, have actual
sex with aspiring ingenues, and look and dress as I damn well
pleased. I was accepted there, but spent only a year and a half in
Pittsburgh. There was something happening in San Francisco
involving grateful dead and a Jeffersonian airplane, so I dropped
out of college in 1967, wriggled out of the draft (psychiatrist's
letter), and headed to the West Coast for the Summer of Love. I'm
sure my parents wanted to kill me. Mrs. Schmolze undoubtedly
would have.

My father once told me the story of how, in 1941 or '42, he ran
away from S.A.S., sneaking out of his dormitory late one night and
setting off on foot for Wilmington, there to get a bus or train up to
New York. Back then this would have been a serious disciplinary
offense, punishable by immediate expulsion. However, his advisor
and dorm master, Mr. Voorhees, who was probably tipped off, took
notice of his absence and went after him in a car. He found Dad a

few miles down the road and convinced the tearful escapee to
return to school. My father claimed he'd always been grateful to
Voorhees for this, but I never quite bought his cautionary tale with
its implied moral.

Now I've come to the last of my excuses. I'm afraid it's another
long-held resentment. It was my father's decision that I go to St.
Andrew's, his alma mater. Like many if not most kids who are sent
away to boarding school, I felt I was being gotten rid of, exiled from
mother and home; farmed out. When I arrived as a third former in
1961, my adviser was none other than the elderly and soon-to-retire
Mr. Voorhees. This couldn't have been a coincidence. We're always
in the shadows of these titans, our parents, and there I was at my
father's old school, stuck with his somewhat strange name
(pretentious roman numeral III, to boot), eating at the same long
polished wooden dining tables he had eaten at, daydreaming and
bored as he had been in the same stuffy classrooms. Please don't tell
me the faded map of South America is still up on that wall. It's even
possible I chucked my socks, jock, T-shirt, and towel into some
ancient iron gym locker that he might have used twenty-two years
earlier. Maybe my father thought that I would like going to his old
school, that I would enjoy the legacy aspect of it all, carrying on the
tradition, etc. I didn't. Things were already competitive enough
between us. I sent my own son Rufus to the Millbrook School, and I
like to think he appreciates my decision now—that and the one not
to name him Loudon IV.

So there you have some reasons why I've stayed away, why I've
never attended a reunion or put in an appearance on alumni
weekend. Now you know why you haven't seen me there, standing
outside in a seersucker jacket on a fine mid-June evening holding a
napkin-wrapped vodka and tonic and recapping my touchdown and

two extra points in the Tower Hill game with some old and frighteningly older-looking teammates. When Mr. Washburn retired, I sent a small contribution for his going-away present, and more recently I succumbed to your mighty powers of persuasion, coughing up a few hundred bucks for the annual fund. But aside from these meager gifts, I've ignored every appeal from the school for money—all because I'm still pissed off at poor Mrs. Schmolze! Well, she's not the only one.

In the spring of 1965, my senior year, my father received the Headmaster's Award, which is given, as you know, every year to an alumnus and friend of the school who has "made a mark in the world." Dad, as an editor and widely read columnist for *Life* magazine, most certainly had done just that, and he came down to Middletown to receive the award and address the entire school. I recall the speech he gave as being very straight and extremely positive. It was full of wonderful things to say about the old place and how it had prepared him so well for the outside world. As appropriate as that was for the occasion, his seventeen-year-old son sitting there in the auditorium, angry, rebellious, and perhaps a little embarrassed, thought it was a cop-out, a kind of betrayal. I knew my father had been unhappy at St. Andrew's, as unhappy as I was. He had told me so. Perhaps I'm blocking it out, but I don't think he even mentioned the Voorhees incident in his speech.

I suppose this all sounds petulant. I know I'm carping. Maybe it's easier to hold on to these grudges, or perhaps it's simply that I've always been jealous of my father's success. For the last forty years I've been fantasizing about my own acceptance speech, for surely it's just a question of time before I, too, am given the Headmaster's Award. I'll go down there to Delaware on a chopped Harley wearing a black leather jacket and engineer boots with what's left of my hair and a long white beard flapping behind me, and I'll tell it like it was.

All the best,
Loudie Wainwright ('65)

P.S. In truth I must admit that I caved on my policy to stay away from the school. I drove up to New York from Baltimore recently and, seeing an exit for Middletown, I pulled, or perhaps was pulled, off Interstate 95. Driving the rental car through town I was amazed to see the old movie theater and barbershop were still standing, much less in operation. Now I nose the Caprice toward St. Andrew's. Suddenly I'm there. Aside from the new gym and the even newer science building (neither of which were built thanks to any contribution from me), the campus looks as it did forty years ago. I park, get out of the car, and walk into the main building. I feel slightly furtive, like a man slipping back into a room to retrieve a wristwatch he's left on a bedside table, not sure if the woman in the bed is sleeping or pretending to. This feels like running away in reverse. It's spring break, so aside from a custodian or two, the place is empty. I climb some stairs, heading to what was once the third-form bathroom. It's still there. Pushing open the heavy swinging door I belly up to a cracked and familiar-looking urinal. I pee, marking this old territory. In 1961, after lights, I sat cross-legged and bathrobed on the black-and-white-tiled floor of this can and, while finishing a paper or cramming for some exam, suddenly would look up, startled and amazed by the loud, cutting blare of the night train's horn. It was a sound expressing everything that was beyond the school, the whole empty world that was waiting for me.

Now I'm down in the basement, which to this day still houses the tuck shop, school store, and school bank. I'm searching the darkly stained pinewood paneling, for somewhere among those hundreds of crudely carved, scratched, and branded sets of initials and dates there should be an *LSW III '65* or *LSW jr '42*. But I can't find us. Maybe we were never here.

I'm in the auditorium now, remembering Saturday nights thirty-five years ago. Watching the weekly movie, I was "Wainwright" then, always insisting on sitting alone, away from my chatty goofball friends, so as to concentrate on the flick, hunkered down in the dark watching *Forbidden Games*, *Odd Man Out*, *Mr. Hulot's Holiday*, and, so appropriate for a boys' boarding school, *The Great Escape*.

Now I'm standing outside the old gym, scanning the thick, ugly plastered walls. The school's team pictures hang there in honor and remembrance. There's "Bull" Cameron in his early thirties, fierce, martial, and magnificent as he poses in street clothes with his young wrestlers of 1935. Among them is a scowling crew-cut twelve-year-old Chester Baum. I find my varsity football team picture. I'm number 22. Left halfback. Bad skin. Then, thirty feet away, there's a picture of my father standing on the gym steps in 1942 with his varsity baseball team. The word "Saints" is stitched across the chest of his grayish, scratchy-looking button-up jersey, and there's a cap perched on the back of his head, its brim pointing up and off at a ridiculous thirty-degree angle. On his left hand, looking for a moment like a very mild case of elephantiasis, is the beat-up, fat, cartoon-fingered mitt. Certainly you couldn't call such a thing a glove. He and I, father and son, are connected by our same sad expressions. We're glum young men, unhappy Loudons. I don't care much about any of this school history after 1965. My time and before is what concerns me. It is interesting, though, to note the few young black faces that begin to pop up in the team pictures of the late sixties and early seventies. Then, suddenly, in 1973, there's proof of the miraculous invasion from the other planet—a photo of a girls' field hockey team. I go outside and stand in the center of the football field, recalling the horrific sight of Andy McNair's knee being driven the wrong way by the vicious clip he received in the 1964 Tatnall game. Then I experience the memory of my father seated in the stands watching me play. Now he's up, and cheering. I've got the ball. Then I imagine him on that same field in 1940, or maybe '41, in next to no shoulder pads, shod in mud-caked high-topped cleats, wearing an ancient face-guardless helmet, searching those same stands for his own father.

10.
bright college days

In the winter of 1964 I informed my parents that I didn't want to go to college. Boarding school had mostly been a frustrating and boring experience for me, and I had decided I just wasn't cut out for higher education. My father suggested a compromise. He reasoned that if I was interested in acting, why not go to a college that trains actors—a drama school? In the end I relented and applied to the drama school at Carnegie Tech (now Carnegie Mellon) in Pittsburgh, which had an acting program considered by many at that time to be the best in the country. To be accepted, applicants had to audition with a monologue. My audition was held in a conference room at a hotel in midtown Manhattan, and, though I had no plan to play it, for some reason I brought my guitar with me, almost as if to say to the powers that were, "This is who I really am." Sitting here now, I can't recall what my audition piece was, but I must have impressed somebody, because I was admitted.

The emphasis at Carnegie was to train the young actor, so there were no academic courses per se, except one required, boring English class called Thought and Expression, which many of us wound up cutting. Voice, stage makeup, movement, and speech were all deemed essential and absolutely mandatory, but for me they were a pain in the ass, especially speech. The speech department was headed by the legendary autocratic Edith Skinner, who in the late 1940s formulated something called American Theatre Standard Speech and was the author of *Speak with Distinction*, a giveaway title if ever there was one. Her mission at Carnegie (and later at Juilliard and NYU) was to train nineteen- and twenty-year-old acting students to sound vaguely British, like Franklin Roosevelt, Katharine Hepburn, or, even better, that paragon of American Standard Speech, Arlene Francis of *What's My Line?* fame. Always referred to by her first name, as befits a grande dame, Edith was the doyenne of her field, and she intimidated and instilled fear in the hearts of us "dramats." When I meekly told her my name in class one day, her withering reply was "'Lou . . . don' . . . What a beautiful name. Such a pity you can't pronounce it."

As far as theories about acting went, there was a schism at Tech in those years, a kind of outside-in versus inside-out dichotomy. Some of our teachers were more traditional and believed in performance grounded in external technique, while others were proponents of the exploration and use of the actor's inner life and personal psychology—the doctrines and so-called methods of Lee Strasberg, Stella Adler, and Sanford Meisner. To oversimplify, the latter camp accused the former of being phony, while the traditionalists considered method acting to be self-indulgent and undisciplined. In 1965, self-indulgent seemed to many of us the cooler way to go, since disciples of Strasberg and Adler included Marlon Brando, Montgomery Clift, and James Dean. Edith wouldn't have dared tell Marlon how to pronounce his first name. Actually, she probably would have. Being able to cry on cue was a big deal for us organic, truthful types, since it was outward proof that we were feeling something or other inside. In acting class, improvisations often began with pretend requests for car keys, and would end in tearful, hysterical rages about having to get and/or pay for an imaginary abortion. I remember being in a freshman studio production of the eighteenth-century Restoration comedy *The Recruiting Officer* and trying to whip myself into a frenzy in the wings by thinking about some ancient childhood trauma so I could "make the emotional moment" upon my entrance. The idea of just being in a play—that is to say, just playing—often went out the window in acting school.

Brooke and me in *The Recruiting Officer*, 1966.

At the beginning of my freshman year I was housed in a dorm called Donner Hall and my roommate was a square engineering student. We had nothing in common, and the next semester I roomed with a fellow dramat, a sophomore directing major who liked to do hatha yoga in the nude before going to bed. This curious, outgoing habit of his got to be an annoying distraction, and in the spring I managed to get my own single room across the street at Hamerschlag Hall. In that dorm was a room we called the Malt Shoppe, where my classmates David Lander and Michael McKean were creating and honing the Lenny and Squiggy shtick that would become famous a decade later on the sitcom *Laverne & Shirley*. Other illustrious Carnegie alumni who were there when I was include Steven Bochco, the creator of *Hill Street Blues* and *NYPD Blue*; Stephen Schwartz, the composer of *Pippin* and *Wicked*; and the comedy original Albert Brooks, who was in the class below mine and at that time went under his given name of Albert Einstein. I also met an acting student there named Peter Ostling, who later changed his name to Peter Jason. Jason remains one of my dearest friends to this day.

I had been cloistered in boarding school, and going to Carnegie was a big change, an upheaval, really. Suddenly there were girls, wannabe beatniks, black kids, gay kids, and gay black kids. At St. Andrew's there had been a few carefully closeted teachers and students, but in drama school, people were flamboyant about who they were. There were factions, but they were not warring ones—they mingled. The gay show-tune crowd got along just fine with the rock and roll beatniks. Beards, long hair, drinking, pot smoking, sex, LSD, and more sex were all on the menu at college. I certainly had had an erotic life at boarding school, but it was all in my head, and satisfaction was self-administered. The summer before I went away to college I lost my virginity in about fifteen minutes, having been set up with a young lady who was rumored to put out for just about every boy in the town of Bedford.

Once I got to Pittsburgh, I started to fall in love and get laid in earnest and with regularity. My first girlfriend at Carnegie was Dede, a beautiful brunette who was shy about her acne. I had a fling with Mary, a free-spirited, foulmouthed, uncorseted painting major with a funny, crooked smile. And then there was Brooke. She grew up in

Manhattan, the daughter of lefty, bohemian parents. She had long, thick brown hair that hung down to the middle of her back, unshaven legs and armpits, and a modern dancer's supple, strong body. She carried herself like a sexy earth goddess in an R. Crumb cartoon, and she also recalled those scary female man-eaters in Fellini films, though her voice was squeaky and small, which, of course, drove Edith nuts. Brooke's best friend was Amy, who was considered to be the most talented actress in our class, mostly because of her ability to get in touch with her inner life, which meant she could burst into tears at the drop of a hat. Brooke and Amy were very tight and hung out a lot, and some of us wondered (and I worried) that they might be secret lovers. Brooke and I were lovers, but I never really felt confident in that role, always unsure that I could satisfy her. She brought out all my not-so-dormant fears and anxieties about sex, and our afternoon trysts in my room in Hamerschlag became unhappy and anxious tests for me about my prowess and performance. In my insecure boarding school mind, Jean-Paul Belmondo needed a Jean Seberg type, not an Anna Magnani.

My fretful relationship with Brooke was one of the reasons I would eventually drop out of college after a year and a half. To quote the old Jimmie Rodgers song, "When a woman gets the blues she hangs her little head and cries / But when a man gets the blues he grabs a train and rides." At the beginning of my sophomore year I switched my major to directing, perhaps to escape the clutches of Edith Skinner. Really, though, I was just miserable and lost in Pittsburgh. Clutching for straws, I tricked my parents into lending me some money, supposedly to buy an electric guitar. Instead, I bought a 1956 Triumph Thunderbird 650 motorcycle, thinking, I guess, that tooling around town on it might improve my feelings about my masculine self-worth. But I was no Steve McQueen, and Pittsburgh's streets back then were cobblestoned and trolley-tracked, providing less-than-ideal conditions for motorcycling. After taking a few scary spills, I sold the Triumph.

The most essential person I met at Carnegie was an acting classmate from Port Washington, Long Island, named George Gerdes. George, like me, played the guitar, and he said that when he spotted me at the audition in the New York hotel conference room with my Martin D-28 in tow he knew we were destined to be brothers-in-arms. George was a particularly important influence because he had done something that I hadn't yet. He had written songs. They were goofy, funny, rockin', existential ditties like "Will You Love Me When I'm Dead?" and "I'm Just a Paranoid, Schizophrenic, Lover Boy, Baby, and It's All for You." I'd been playing and singing other people's songs for some time, but until I met George, the idea that anyone could write his own material seemed a fantasy beyond reach, a thing that only my heroes Bob Dylan and Richard Fariña could accomplish. Along with Jeff Boverman and Mike Schwartz, Gerdes and I formed the Illumicron Fab Tabs, lifting the name for our group from Tom Wolfe's *Electric Kool-Aid Acid Test*. At St. Andrew's, I'd performed on campus at dances and school functions in folk and jug bands, but the Fab Tabs actually gigged in bars and clubs in the Shadyside section of Pittsburgh. We were happening. George was also a terrific mimic, doing spot-on takes of Elvis Presley, Muhammad Ali, Howard Cosell, James Dean, and countless others. My one and only slightly passable impersonation is my impression of George Gerdes's impression of James Mason. George was a devotee of the Beats and in particular *On the Road*. He would often say he considered himself a sort of Neal Cassady to my Jack Kerouac, though my self-identity as a Westchester WASP was a little too entrenched to buy that comparison. George was my guide on my first LSD trip. As he succinctly puts it in the liner notes he wrote for my 1979 album, *A Live One*: "I prevailed upon him [me] to have a rendezvous with a paisley lightning bolt that was going around at the time."

Having gotten a glimpse of the Void, suddenly acting, my affair with Brooke, even the fun of being in the Fab Tabs, all seemed rather meaningless. I dropped out of Carnegie a few weeks after the acid trip, right in the middle of my sophomore year, and went home to live with my parents, not knowing what the hell to do. Unbelievably, I almost enlisted in the airborne division of the U.S. Army, which in 1967, at the height of Vietnam, would have been a risky move. The morning I was supposed to be sworn in at Whitehall Street in lower Manhattan, I miraculously overslept and missed the train into town. That afternoon I phoned my recruiter in Peekskill and informed him I would take my chances with the draft. By the time I was classified 1A, I had seen my father's shrink, who was good enough to diagnose me as a sociopsychopath. He might have gotten that impression because, before our final therapy session, I took a shitload of speed and maniacally babbled at him for forty-five minutes. Anyway, a letter was written and sent to the draft board, and I was reclassified 1Y, ineligible for service. Next stop: San Francisco, and the Summer of Love.

Pennsylvania's western daughter with your tubes of liberty,
Princess of pig iron slaughter with your boyfriend Carnegie.
Oh you were stain-glassed, you were smokestacked, you were laid in
*   cobblestone.*
You were trolley car tracked, and for you the red sky shone.

And while thieves and black-sleeved buccaneers pitched and kicked
*   their orbs,*

It was for you I cheered my wild cheers at the field of Mr. Forbes.
I sent sentiments from Shadyside, I paid homage from the Hill.
Oh no, it cannot be denied—un-cola coke can't kill.

Let the trees in Schenley Park grow strong, may the bagpipes never
    burst
Let the Allegheny roll along, may I thirst the Duquesne thirst.
May your steel mills stand forever and your Learning Tower, too.
May Mellon remain clever. Good luck and God Bless you.

—"ODE TO A PITTSBURGH," 1970

11.
the summer of love

It's been fifty years since the Summer of Love took place, and everybody knows the place it took was San Francisco. At the beginning of 1967, I was living with my parents in Westchester, painting houses and assisting a local carpenter, but I'd been hearing about the hippie scene in Haight-Ashbury for almost a year and had been working pretty hard at growing my hair. On a humid June day, after ingesting a tab of LSD on an East Village rooftop, I wound up at a free Grateful Dead concert in Tompkins Square Park. My lysergically soaked mind was blown, not only by the swirling, spacey music, but also by the striking appearances of the musicians in the band—in particular, the glowering, aloof Pigpen on keyboards and his opposite, the willowy, boyishly beautiful rhythm guitarist Bob Weir. During the Dead show, like many a privileged suburban kid before me, I had one of those epiphanies we heard so much about in classrooms and at chapel services: I realized I needed to travel to the place from whence all this happening energy came. So a few days later, I started hitchhiking across the country with a knapsack, a guitar, a sleeping bag, and one hundred dollars I'd made selling pot. It was a half century ago, so I don't recall much about the trip west, other than that I was hassled by the police in Flagstaff, Arizona, but that in itself felt pretty cool, because Flagstaff is one of the towns mentioned in Bobby Troup's iconic song "Route 66." (Perhaps this is the place to admit that, for many years, I thought Chuck Berry was singing "Don't forget Mona" as opposed to "Don't forget Winona.")

Letter to Mom and Dad, 1967.

In those days I was going out with a game blond girl from Yorktown Heights named Nicole, and I'm pretty sure we got the weed to bankroll the San Francisco escapade from her older brother. Nicole traveled across the country to meet me that summer, but her parents bought her a plane ticket. She and some friends from Bard College

had rented a big shambling apartment on McAllister Street in the
Fillmore District, and that's where I landed when I got to town. Donald Fagen, who a few years later would form Steely Dan with Walter
Becker, was crashing there, though at that point he was just a quiet,
geeky wannabe hippie. But then one day, at the Good Karma Café at
Eighteenth Street and Dolores, while we were waiting for our rice
and veggies to arrive, Donald sat down at an old, out-of-tune upright
piano and proceeded to bang out a soulful version of a Ray Charles
hit. Minds were, again, blown.

Our days during the Summer of Love were not filled with activities, because nobody had a job or was even contemplating getting
one, although there were rumors that the post office was hiring hippies as letter carriers. An entire day, it seemed, could be taken up by
nothing at all in particular, or perhaps something as mundane as a
visit to the Haight-Ashbury free clinic for a hepatitis shot and some
barefoot broken-glass removal. A few times a week we would wake
up, drop acid, and then walk around the crazy, up-and-down city,
often meandering three miles through Golden Gate Park all the way
to the ocean, always stopping to commune telepathically with the
iconic, majestic buffalo in the Bison Paddock. There was plenty of
free music, as well as outdoor agitprop theater from the San Francisco Mime Troupe, the ragtag and vociferous collective whose po-
litically charged outdoor plays sprang up in the public parks all over
the city. Along with thousands of others, I attended Hells Angel
Chocolate George's* wake in Golden Gate Park, where the Dead and
Janis Joplin's Big Brother and the Holding Company performed, as
did lesser-known acid rock outfits of the era like Blue Cheer and

---

* Wikipedia once again to the rescue. Hells Angel Chocolate George got his name
because of his addiction to chocolate milk.

Mount Rushmore. I don't recall that I did any of that embarrassing, goofy, free-form, stoned-hippie dancing you see in archive footage from 1967; I think I mostly sat there on a hillside in a half lotus position with my eyes closed and a beatific grin on my face.

As for my own music, that was put on hold, so much so that I eventually sold my guitar to pay for yoga lessons at the Himalayan Academy on Sacramento Street. As the summer wore on, I drifted into the subset of hippies who were interested in Eastern spiritual disciplines. My doors of perception had been chemically cracked open, but now the idea of getting high naturally seemed much more appealing. In the late 1960s, Asian swamis, mystics, and monks with names like Bhaktivedanta, Satchidananda, Chögyam Rinpoche, and Vishnudevananda started to appear in American towns and cities, offering up their various takes on traditional methods for enlightenment. These self-proclaimed "Masters" seemed benign, wise, and accepting to us stoned-out middle-class kids, and we were attracted to them and their promises not only because we were young and gullible but also because, to a certain degree, our frightened, disapproving parents had, along with the rest of straight society, disowned us. There were also homegrown gurus on the scene who, like ourselves, had begun their spiritual journeys as enthusiastic drug takers—Bubba Free John, Mel Lyman, Ram Dass (Richard Alpert), and, the most notorious of all, Timothy Leary. Toward the end of the Summer of Love, I began to think of myself not so much as a dropout but as an all-American-boy bodhisattva, capping off my all-night acid trips with early-morning chanting and free vegetarian Prasad (breakfast) at the Hare Krishna temple on Frederick Street. I made excursions to the City Lights bookstore in North Beach and to the San Francisco Public Library near the Civic Center to pore over exotic, timeless texts like *The Tibetan Book of the Dead*, the *I Ching*, and the

Bhagavad Gita. Being just a hippie seemed like a stupid waste of time; now I aspired to escape the futile birth–death cycle, and was anxious to open up my third eye and get my thousand-petaled lotus chakra spinning.

Eventually, the Summer of Love morphed into an autumn of discontented weirdness, and the peace and love vibe, based on a philosophy of freedom and sharing, and fueled by pot, LSD, DMT, mescaline, and psilocybin mushrooms, was replaced by the paranoia and sickness that accompany the proliferation and use of speed and heroin. The serious drug dealers who started coming over from Oakland were significantly more mercenary and violent. There were several grisly murders in the Haight, and by the time the November rains began in San Francisco, it all had become a bummer. Nicole and Fagen and the other McAllister crash-pad kids had returned east to college and/or the comforts and safety of their parents' homes, but I stayed behind, spending more and more time at the Himalayan Academy, studying with Sivaya Subramuniyaswami (Robert Hansen). At the academy, I took hatha yoga classes, chanted mantras, learned breathing techniques, and practiced meditation. Then I upped the spiritual ante by retreating for a few weeks to Subramuniya's ashram in Virginia City, Nevada. Technically, I was in training to become a monk, but most of my time there was spent working fourteen intentionally mindless hours a day in the ashram's printing press, cutting paper and assembling pamphlets and instructional Raja yoga manuals. After ten long days and short nights, I started to experience a profound interior alteration. My personality—that is, who I thought I was—seemed to be slipping away. My fellow novitiates excitedly assured me that this was a good thing and something to embrace, since the ancient wisdom tells us that personality, like damn near everything, is merely an illusion and therefore must die in order for self-realization to occur. To some that might sound like a beautiful idea, but now that it was actually happening to me, I started to freak out. A voice in my head (My ego? Common sense?) was screaming, "What about sex, fame, wealth—my *destiny*?!" I requested and got an emergency audience with my guru. In his sparse, darkened, sandalwood-reeking office, Subramuniya sternly asked me what I wanted to do in this lifetime, and, after some hesitation, I replied meekly, "Be an actor, I suppose." From the look of disdain on the Master's face, I realized that was the wrong answer, and then I was summarily excused. I said my good-byes to the junior monks, gathered up my knapsack and sleeping bag, and trudged up the hill into Virginia City to wait for the bus back to the material world. Since I now had entire lifetimes in front of me to kill, I ducked into a touristy saloon, bought myself a pack of Lucky Strikes, and ordered a beer.

When I got back to San Francisco, there suddenly seemed no real reason to be there, so I decided to hightail it back east. In those days, one of the ways hippies got themselves back and forth across America was by means of the "drive away"; people or companies who needed their cars transported would advertise on health-food-store bulletin boards or in the classified sections of alternative papers like the *Village Voice* and the *Berkeley Barb*. All a prospective driver needed was a license and the means to pay for gas. I saw an ad somewhere and connected with a hippie couple a few years older than I was, who already had a car lined up and were looking for an additional driver. We set off, once again traveling the Mother Road, Route 66, and the three of us had a fine old time tooling east in a long late-model Chevrolet Impala until, halfway across the country, we ran out of gas money. We stopped in Oklahoma City, found the Western Union office, and wired friends for funds. The dough took several hours to get there, which was quite nerve-racking for three counterculture freaks stranded in *Easy Rider* country. Laying as low as possible, we mostly stayed in the car, the other guy and I cautiously tucking our ponytails under baseball caps. Finally the money arrived, and we gassed up and headed out of OKC. But on the outskirts of town, at a stoplight, sure enough, a police cruiser sidled up beside us. The light changed, and a few hundred yards later the cruiser was joined by two others and we were pulled over. We were told to step out and stand away from the vehicle, and then four cops searched the car and found a plastic baggie full of pot that we had stashed in the glove compartment; a "lid," as it was called in those days, or about thirty dollars' worth. Then we were read our rights, handcuffed, and bundled off to the county jail. During the day, my partner in crime and I milled around with thirty other guys in a large holding area called a tank. At night, each man shared a bunk bed with a fellow inmate. I spent five pretty scary days and nights there, and although I wasn't sodomized, I suspect it would have just been a matter of time. My favorite fellow con was a wise-cracking DJ with a deep, mellifluous voice who was serving time for grand larceny. He had been fired by the local AM radio station, and in a fit of pique and stupidity he broke into the station after hours and stole six thousand LPs, thereby cleaning out the entire listening library. His dulcet tones and larger-than-life presence kept us lowlifes entertained for hours. When I was arrested, my one allotted phone call was to my sister Teddy, knowing that she would contact my parents, who were living in London at the time. Once he got the news, my extremely pissed-off father took two very long and expensive flights in order to come and bail my soon-to-be-pounced-on ass out of jail. The authorities in Oklahoma City, once they realized they had busted the son of a famous *Life* magazine writer, were licking their chops, and the prosecutor was talking about a prison sentence of up to ten years for me. My fellow travelers, the older hippie couple, had previous drug-related arrests on their records, so they were really up shit's creek. I have no recollection of what happened to the drive-away car. Once my father paid $2,500 in bail, he and I flew back to New York. He hired a lawyer recommended by a judge friend of his. A few weeks later, I returned to appear in court in Oklahoma City, where the wheels of justice had been sufficiently lubricated, and I got away with probation and a suspended sentence.

In a sense, I had come full circle. At the beginning of the summer of 1967, I had dealt some weed to get out to San Francisco, and less than a year later I was busted for the possession of that same illegal substance and my life as a hippie was over. I was several thousand dollars in debt to my father and finally had to get a job. I went to live with my father's mom in Watch Hill, Rhode Island, and found work in a boatyard there. Then, using a borrowed guitar at a friend's Ellery Street apartment in Cambridge, I wrote my very first song, and within a year I had a record deal and a publishing advance. In no way was I enlightened or self-realized, but a career had miraculously dropped in my lap. Things were looking pretty good. Good karma, I guess. Far out.

Once I got locked up in a dirty old jail.
The coffee was cold and the cornbread was stale.
But I didn't cry, I tried to be brave
Until the warden tried to give me a haircut and a shave.
"Warden, you can hold me for a year in your jail,
But don't shave off my beard, don't cut my ponytail.

"All you really found was stems and some seeds.
I'll give you my earring and I'll give you my beads.
I don't mind wearin' one of your prison suits.

I'll give you my bell-bottoms and my cowboy boots.
Don't shave off my beard, don't cut off my hair
It took me two years to grow it and it just isn't fair.

"Listen to me, Warden, won't you listen to me beg?
Chop off a toe, a foot, or take a whole leg.
I'm down on my knees. Man, you're robbing my strength.
Take it easy, Warden, won't you leave me some length?
I want a lawyer, Warden. I want a priest.
Take it easy, Warden. Leave the mustache, at least."

But the warden didn't hear a single word that I said.
He chopped off all my hair on my face and my head.
But one day someone's gonna come and gonna put up my bail.
And I'm gonna walk out of this dirty old jail.
And the warden, who's the reason I'm shedding my tears,
I'm gonna mail him a snapshot in two . . . or three . . . years.

—"SAMSON AND THE WARDEN," 1971

Every time I return to San Francisco, the smell of the eucalyptus trees brings the Summer of Love back to me, and sometimes, when walking through Golden Gate Park, I've even thought I recognized a few of my long-ago hippie brethren, now grizzled, blown-out old men with vacant eyes, staggering around with fifty-year-old sleeping bags draped over their shoulders. There but for fortune . . .

12.
watch hill
back pages

Watch Hill, Rhode Island, and I go back. In 1900, my great-great-grandfather Park Painter, a Pittsburgh steel magnate, built a wood and stone mansion called Graydon in Watch Hill, and his granddaughter, my grandmother Eleanor Sloan, had houses there, albeit much more modest ones, until her death in 1985. It's a rich town, maybe not quite as wealthy as Newport, but there's still plenty of money. If you've got a couple of million you can pick up a studio apartment at the Ocean House. Taylor Swift bought the Harkness Mansion a few years back and had the Army Corps of Engineers re-landscape her private beach. As you might imagine, security is now tight. Watch Hill also has the oldest carousel in America; its wooden horses are suspended by chains. My people have been riding that merry-go-round for years and years.

Every August in the early sixties, my sister Teddy, my brother Andy, and I were driven by our mom to Stamford, Connecticut, and put on the train to Westerly, Rhode Island, which is just a short distance from Watch Hill, where we stayed with Nanny, as my grandmother was called, for a few weeks.

Nanny was a long-standing member of the Watch Hill Yacht Club. Her husband, Loudon, had been a serious sailor, but for some reason, their only son, my dad, wasn't interested in sailboats. We were WHYC members, but for my father the club was primarily a place to socialize, which is to say, to drink with his friends, his mother, and mine. The members-only bar was and still is on the second floor of the old wooden clubhouse. There used to be a nicely lettered, painted sign at the foot of the bar stairs with a stern warning about having to be nineteen years or older in order to ascend and imbibe. By the time I was nineteen we'd stopped summering there, so I never made it upstairs. In 2013, though, I sailed my Cape Dory 27 from Shelter Island to Watch Hill. I dropped the Wainwright name at the club, was granted admission, and enjoyed a few glasses of sauvignon blanc up in the bar.

For Teddy, Andy, and me the yacht club was our summer social hub. We hung out there with the other rich kids—Peter Calder, Palmer Chapman, Perkie Orthwein, and Mary Scott—and we all goofed around the little town, having club sandwiches at the Olympia Tea Room, playing pinball and eating grinders at the St. Clair Annex, swimming at East Beach, waterskiing behind Richie Panciera's Boston Whaler, sneaking cigarettes, and trying to get older kids to buy us beer.

On Saturday mornings there were races with other yacht clubs, and all our pals grabbed their sail bags and were taken in launches out to their Wood-Pussies and Blue Jays. Teddy, Andy, and Loudie, however, stayed behind, killing time waiting for the junior mariners' return, picking on one another or playing ping-pong downstairs at the yacht club. For some weird reason, my dad, who had a general apathy when it came to his kids' activities, hadn't arranged for us to have sailing lessons.

In 1968 I wrote "Edgar," a slight and forgotten first song about a craggy unfiltered-Camel-smoking lobsterman I'd met when I was working at the nearby Avondale Boat Yard. My grandmother had gotten me the job, having taken me in after the Oklahoma City bust.

"Edgar" wasn't a very good song, but it got me going. I started to go out and perform at open mikes and "hoots," where the audiences seemed to be mostly composed of other singer-songwriters and a sprinkling of Japanese tourists. It took about a year of playing the folk grottoes and coffeehouses in New York and Cambridge, Massachusetts, before I was "discovered" by Milton Kramer, the vice president of Frank Music. I signed a publishing deal with Frank and immediately paid back my father all the money that he'd spent getting me out of the jam in Oklahoma City. That felt good. Then things started to happen fast, beginning with a rave review in the *Village Voice* of a 1969 show I did at the Gaslight on MacDougal Street, opening for John Hammond Jr. That led to a bidding war between two record labels—Atlantic and Columbia. Columbia's head of A&R—coincidentally John Hammond Sr.—was rooting for me to sign with his label, but Nesuhi Ertegun at Atlantic came up with more money, and my first album, *Loudon Wainwright III*, was released on that label in 1970. Nobody bought it, but the critics were generally kind and occasionally overly effusive. I was dubbed, among other things, the new Bob Dylan, the Charles Chaplin of Rock, the Woody Allen of Folk, and, my favorite, the male Melanie. Somehow, I had stumbled into a career.

My grandmother was like no other. Too bad you didn't meet her.
Every day at three, she'd have a G&T. At Bridge you could not
  beat her.

Christmas time she'd end up crying, listening to Chevalier.
And I got ten bucks in a card each year in September for my birthday.

My grandmother didn't much bother too much about bein' a granny.
She didn't bake or knit, she didn't give a shit. Us kids called her Nanny.
In the summertime we'd visit her, take the train up to Rhode Island.
Westerly, Ollie's taxi would pick us up, we'd all pile in.

My grandmother, my sister and brother and me all went to the ocean.
In her cabana there, in that big beach chair, she'd survey our
*   commotion.*
At the yacht club we got our grub; we had grinders and grape sodas.
What a dream: popcorn, ice cream—two weeks, no junk food quotas!

My grandmother would light up another, you know that cough of
*   hers was chronic.*
She didn't drink wine, but she was just fine with that nice tall gin
*   and tonic.*
Nanny had opinions, Nanny wasn't prissy.
She said men were queer who just drank beer, and ginger ale was for
*   sissies.*

My grandmother provided cover for me when times got tricky.
She took me in despite my sin, when I was busted in the late sixties.
She found me a job in a boatyard.
In her kitchen I cooked my brown rice (vegetables, and hijiki seaweed).
Wasn't too long before I wrote my first song, and pretty soon I'd done
*   it twice.*

—"NANNY," 2005

13.
milt

After seeing me perform one night at the Gaslight, Milt Kramer decided I had all that it took to become a star, and for almost ten years he tirelessly worked at trying to make that happen, despite my own ambivalence about stardom—an ambivalence that at times resulted in outright resistance to Milt's dreams for me and his machinations on my behalf. The publishing contract Milt signed me to was with Frank Music, the company owned by the songwriter Frank Loesser. That was an especially big deal for me, because the original cast recording of *Guys and Dolls* was just about the most played LP in our household when I was growing up. In 1968, Loesser was dying of cancer, and Milt kept saying we should visit him in the hospital because the legendary songwriter would appreciate knowing that, despite all the long hair and electric guitars on the scene, there were still kids out there who could write good songs. I had short hair and played an

Me and Milt Kramer, 1969.

acoustic Gibson Hummingbird, but never mind. Sadly, Frank Loesser died in July of 1969, before I got my chance to meet him.

Milt then got me a recording contract in what seemed like next to no time. It was the 1970s, when male singer-songwriters were in vogue and such a thing was still possible. In the offices of record company executives, Kramer cut an imposing figure—stout and barrel-chested, with a shaved head and a conspicuously large handlebar mustache, which he waxed and combed and, on special occasions (as when extolling his new young client's remarkable talents to Clive Davis or Nesuhi Ertegun), would go so far as to actually twirl. Underneath his elbow-patched tweed jackets, Milt packed his leather-holstered heat, a .38-caliber snub-nosed revolver. He was always more than happy to let people know that he had a license to carry a handgun. Once or twice I tagged along with him to his indoor shooting range in Chelsea and watched him pepper and perforate the heads and torsos of the snarling paper-target bad guys. Pity any poor would-be mugger or psychotic autograph hound, because Milt was a hell of a shot. He also bred and raised Doberman pinschers at his place upstate, and he drove around Putnam County in what had formerly been a New York state trooper patrol car. I wouldn't say my first manager was paranoid, but he certainly believed in self-defense.

Milt Kramer grew up a chubby Jewish kid in Brooklyn. His father owned a mannequin factory in Manhattan but was also a bigwig in the Yiddish Folksbiene Theatre, and Milt trod those boards as a child actor. I think that might have been how he was initially bedazzled by and then drawn into show business. Kramer was convinced that, most of the time, he knew the solution to any problem. "I know what's wrong" and "I can fix that" were two of his favorite sentences. It has to be said that sometimes he did and he could. When I needed dental attention, Milt found me a dentist, and when I admitted to him that I was suffering from depression, he found me a psychiatrist. Oddly, both these doctors also had the first name of Milton. My manager had plenty of ideas about writing songs, too, and when I pushed back and resisted his suggestions, his argument was that he had worked with some of the very best—Mike Todd, Jule Styne, Meredith Willson, Stan Daniels, and of course, the greatest of all, Frank Loesser.

At the beginning of a career, a young performer needs someone who believes in his talent to imbue him with confidence, to convince him he's better than all the rest. This person often serves as a paternal figure for the performer, and that was certainly true in the case of Milt. My own dad somewhat grudgingly appreciated my talents but could be, as they say in therapy, "withholding." Since he was trained as a journalist and editor, my father avoided hyperbole, and firmly resisted the use of superlatives like "genius" and "brilliant."

Milt, enthusiastic, effusive, and larger than life, heaped on all that stuff. Along with "I know what's wrong" and "I can fix that" was "You're the best" and "You're going be a star." When he would excitedly tell my parents his predictions for their son's success, my mother ate it up, but my old man cringed. So, in a certain but crucial sense, early in my career Milt Kramer was a surrogate father for me. Milt doted on his daughter, Jeanne, but he never had a son of his own, and I'm sure that was one of the reasons why it was so painful for us both when we parted company in 1978. The arguments we had over my career and how to conduct it had intensified to the point where we could no longer work together. I think Kramer wanted me to be not so much the new Bob Dylan as the next Glen Campbell, with lots of hit records and my own prime-time TV variety show. Next lifetime, maybe.

But Milt and I remained friends. In his last years, he was wheelchair bound, but Jeanne still managed to get him to my gigs in Annapolis and the Washington, D.C., area. Milt's parting words on those happy but wistful occasions were always the same. After my show he would gently take my elbow and, pulling me down to his level, would whisper in my ear, "You're still the best."

14.
kate

I got a brand-new lover and her name is Crazy Kate.
Kate is from the country that is north of New York State.
And if I die in Canada, don't divide my estate.
Just give it to my killer, my new lover, Crazy Kate.

—"CRAZY KATE," 1969

That's the opening verse of a song I wrote about Kate McGarrigle. I never recorded it, nor am I sure I even finished it, but that doesn't really matter, because those four lines say plenty. There was a sense of danger, doom, and excitement about Kate, and I was inexorably pulled toward her from the get-go. I saw her for the first time in 1968 at the Gaslight, on a night when she was performing in Jerry Jeff Walker's backup band. She and her duo partner at that time, the guitarist Roma Baron, were just sitting in with Jerry Jeff, but I was knocked out, blown away, and pretty much floored by Kate's chops as a singer and piano player. A few years later, Kate would begin to write her amazing songs, thus becoming a triple threat. I

Kate, 1970.
Photograph by David Gahr, courtesy of the Estate of David Gahr.

mean that in a good *and* a bad way. Good for her and the world, but ultimately bad for me—too threatening to my fragile ego. After I introduced myself that night at the Gaslight, Kate and Roma and I went barhopping in the West Village, hitting the Kettle of Fish, the Lion's Head, and the Corner Bistro. We even made it over to the White Horse Tavern on Hudson Street. I had originally set my sights on Roma, the more conventionally pretty one of the two, but as the evening wore on into the morning, I found myself being drawn to the strange, funny chick with slightly buck teeth and the sharp, somewhat out-of-line nose. By the time (about 3:30 a.m.) that Kate dashed across Sixth Avenue against the light, laughing at the hurled epithets and honking from the oncoming traffic, I was pretty much a goner. Serious romantic contact was established a few nights later, when we had sex four times in a row.

IN 1970, Kate and I were living together in a small apartment at 4 Franklin Square in Saratoga Springs, New York. The nicest feature in our little pad was the lovely old fireplace in the living room. We wound up in Saratoga because it was the home of Caffe Lena, "the longest continuously running folk music coffeehouse in America," as Lena Spencer, the Caffe's founder and reigning queen bee, liked to remind people. Lena was a kind of den mother superior to young up-and-comers on the acoustic music scene at that time. Rosalie Sorrels and Utah Phillips lived in Saratoga and were part of that scene when Kate and I were there. Don McLean and Arlo Guthrie were regular performers at the Caffe early in their careers, and Dylan even stopped by, though there is some question as to whether he ever did an actual gig. Lena is long gone now, but the Caffe is still there on Phila Street, right next to Hattie's Chicken Shack.

Used to have a red guitar. I smashed it one drunk night
Smashed it in the classic form, as Peter Townshend might.
Threw it in the fireplace and left it there a while.
Kate, she started crying when she saw my sorry smile.

—"RED GUITAR," 1972

Kate and I played music together in those days, recording old-timey classics like "Weave Room Blues," "Little Birdie," and "If I Lose" on my Sony reel-to-reel tape recorder. She taught me how to "frail" on the five-string banjo, and for that I owe her a debt of gratitude. We were in love and having plenty of the fun, romance, and sex that goes with all that. Then, due to our hit-and-miss birth control practices, Kate got pregnant. We decided we weren't ready for a family yet, so she got an abortion. But then, a few months later, there was another pregnancy, and this time we chose not only to have the baby but also to get married. We didn't really know what the hell we were doing, but in 1971 we tied the knot at my parents' house in Bedford. After the ceremony and reception, we drove to my little rental in nearby Katonah and had our first night alone together as husband and wife, except we weren't exactly alone, because my buddy Keith Sykes wound up crashing on the couch. Keith, a Memphis singer-songwriter friend, had traveled up from New York City for the wedding, and he and I spent most of my wedding night in front of the tape recorder, drinking beer and listening to mixes of my soon-to-be-released second album, while my bride softly cried herself to sleep in the bedroom down the hall. It was a fraught and inauspicious beginning to the marriage, and I'm sure you're thinking, *What a selfish bastard!* But wait a minute, it gets worse.

The decision to honeymoon in Copenhagen was not, in hindsight, a great one, because once we got there I couldn't stop, speaking of hindsight, wistfully ogling the beautiful blond Danish girls who seemed to be on every street corner. The town was crawling with them. Naturally, this kind of behavior didn't go down well with Kate, and when, on the third day of the honeymoon, during a big fight, I confessed that I had never really wanted to get married in the first place, that pretty much did it. She took the blue Volvo station wagon we'd bought in Gothenburg, drove to Amsterdam, and then ferried on to England. Of course, as soon as she left, I realized how idiotic I'd been and, completely racked with remorse, I bade good-bye to Copenhagen, "that friendly old girl of a town," and went looking for my heartbroken, four-months-pregnant new wife. I got to London and found her staying with her Montreal friend Chaim Tannenbaum at his flat on Percy Street. I was expecting Chaim to play the role of the aggressively protective older brother. I worried about getting a punch in the nose or at the very least a forceful "Fuck off," but instead, Tannenbaum was quite pleasant to me. He seemed mostly embarrassed about the situation, and right away it became clear that he was rooting for a reconciliation, ready, I suppose, to have his brokenhearted friend off his hands for a while.

Kate and I tearfully made up, and a few days later we started living together in a bedsit in Kennington. But soon we were fighting again, and Kate went home to her mother and sisters in Canada. Looking back, I freely admit I was a lousy husband, way too young and completely unprepared for the job. She, in turn, was "crazy Kate"—headstrong, volatile, competitive, and at times downright combative. But we were married, expecting a baby, and still in love, and so, after another reconciliation by phone, she flew back to London. We set up house again, this time in a flat I'd rented on Holland Park Avenue, and things were okay there until one terrible afternoon Kate began to miscarry. I called 999, and she was rushed by ambulance to the Harley Street Clinic. At five and a half months, the baby, a boy, was born, but lived only about an hour. Kate was discharged from the clinic a few days later, and it wasn't long again before she flew back home alone to Montreal.

Now, I expect you're thinking, *Thank God that's over.* But wait! We reunited in Saratoga and moved to Boston, which is where Kate got pregnant again. Then we rented a little cottage in Mount Tremper, New York, near Woodstock, and Rufus was born in July of 1973, across the river in Rhinebeck. Our landlord in Mount Tremper was a seemingly kind old gentleman, a former scientist named Albert Fellows, who claimed he had worked on the development of the atomic bomb in Princeton, New Jersey. When we first moved into the cottage, Fellows was exceedingly friendly, frequently dropping by unannounced for visits and the occasional game of chess. But that spring, two-thirds of the way through Kate's pregnancy, I went on a European tour for a few weeks, and by the time I got back a sort of war had broken out between my wife and Albert. Kate had understandably grown tetchy and impatient with what she perceived as Albert's oversolicitousness, and had made it clear she didn't want him coming around anymore. Rebuffed and hurt, our landlord decided we weren't the nice young couple he'd imagined and he began a campaign to evict us, complaining about noise and showing up to take pictures of our garbage cans. Things escalated, and soon after Kate came home from the hospital with Rufus, we fled to my parents' house in Bedford. After a few months there, our little family unit relocated to New York City at 604 West 115th Street. Our superintendent and next-door neighbor was a large Slavic woman named Anna who wore her hair in a tight bun and resembled the terrifying gimlet-eyed prison camp commandant in Lina Wertmüller's movie *Seven Beauties*. In addition, Anna had two aggressive German shepherds who raced to the door, ferociously barking whenever anyone knocked. Completing the Diane Arbus–like picture was Anna's niece, a thirteen-year-old girl who was born a thalidomide baby and had deformed arms that somewhat resembled flippers. Kate, always bohemian with a penchant for the dramatically bizarre, took a real shine to Anna and her niece and often used them as babysitters for Rufus. This always made me, the cautious and conventional square that I am, very nervous. I have a memory of Anna's niece carrying around our grinning, drooling one-year-old in their apartment by hooking her shortened arms underneath his, with the two excited, barking German shepherds nosing and licking our little baby boy's chubby face. To be honest, I would have preferred the day care to be provided by the annoying Albert Fellows.

Kate and I had some happy times as young parents on West 115th Street, but eventually I returned to my philandering ways, and our fighting and drinking resumed and intensified. In 1975, Kate and her sister Anna's first album was released to great acclaim, and that shook things up in terms of my previously mentioned frail ego. My wife's career suddenly was in ascent, while mine, as it so happened, was in decline. My conjugal misbehavior spiked and we split up yet again that year, but then (you're not going to believe it) we got back together for one last round. In May 1976, Martha was born in Mount Kisco. Our family of four lived in a cottage on Lake Waccabuc in Westchester County, but after a few unhappy months in that idyllic setting, Kate left with the kids and went back to Montreal, this time for good. The marriage was over, though the battles, with our kids acting as foot soldiers, raged on, long- and short-distance, for thirty more years. I assumed the roles of despised shit-heel ex-husband and guilt-ridden long-distance father. The fallout from the marriage and divorce was traumatic for all four of us. However, crass as it may sound, it resulted in plenty of good songs. Hers: "Kitty Come Home," "Go Leave," "I Eat Dinner," "Kiss and Say Goodbye," and "Talk to Me of Mendocino," and mine: "Mr. Guilty," "Whatever Happened to Us," "Reciprocity," "Unrequited to the Nth Degree," "On the Rocks," and "Our Own War." When Rufus and Martha grew up and began to write their own family songs, the battle of the bands intensified.

They got drunk last night,
Had a knock-down, drag-out fight.
He was determined, she saw it her way.
He threw a tantrum, she threw an ashtray.
They got drunk last night.

How's this for a how do you do?
He's unfaithful and she's untrue.
They're their own masters and they're their own bosses.
They reserve the right to employ double crosses.
How's this for a fine how do you do?

You'd need a chair and a whip to control their relationship.
Once they were lovers and practically best friends.

Now he's into bondage, she's into revenge.
You would need a chair and a whip.

And if one of them should die,
I suppose that the other might cry.
There would be tears of sorrow and great grief,
Or else there would be tears of release and relief,
If one of them should die.

—"Reciprocity," 1976

February 4, 2015: Rufus, Chaim, and I are driving on the New York State Thruway, just past Exit 19, the turnoff for Woodstock, where forty-two years ago Kate and I were living in our little cottage, waiting for number one son to make his entrance into the world. Pretty soon we're past Albany and on the Northway, passing the exits for Saratoga Springs and 4 Franklin Square. Rufus is behind the wheel of his leased Land Rover, and we're listening to Russian opera. It's loud. Chaim is in the backseat, and he's an opera buff, so I'm outnumbered. I just look out the window and wait for it to end. Since I'm in the shotgun, I finally pull rank, reach over and switch Sirius to the soul channel. Marvin Gaye trumps Beniamino Gigli. We're driving to Montreal to celebrate my grandson Francis Valentine's first birthday. His mother, my daughter Martha, is throwing a party.

February 5, 2015: Martha bakes a big chocolate cake, which Francis gets all over himself and absolutely loves, though he's blissfully in the dark about the concept of the presents, the song, et cetera. His older brother (by four years), ArcAngelo, leads the singing and blows out the candle on the cake. Five years before, I was in this same house in the Outremont neighborhood when it was still Kate's house. I was there the night she died from complications of the clear cell sarcoma she had been battling for two years. She died in her own bed, the same bed that I slept in last night. By the time I'd arrived for the visit five years ago, Kate had been unconscious and in a coma for some days. I'd come up at Rufus's urging, though some months earlier his mother had quietly extended an invitation to me on the phone to visit her, an offer I'd been too scared to accept at the time.

During Francis's birthday party I survey the living room, taking note of relics from his grandparents' long-gone marriage that are scattered around—vinyl records, posters, a rug, dusty books, pictures of Rufus and Martha when they were babies. The forty-five-year-old Sansui stereo receiver is tucked into one of the lower shelves of a bookcase. The orange light of the on/off switch is lit up. It's likely the appliance will outlive me, too. Kate would have been sixty-nine tomorrow.

February 6, 2015 (Kate's Birthday): Rufus, Chaim, and I drive seven hours from Montreal to Toronto to do a benefit for a cancer charity that Kate was affiliated with. I do most of the driving, so today there's a lot of Willie's Roadhouse on the box. Things get tense in the last hour when Rufus wants to override the route the GPS lady is telling us to follow, but we finally get to the venue. We open the show with "Come a Long Way," a song of Kate's that I recorded in 1974. Chaim and Rufus then sing some of her French songs. After that, Chaim and I duet on "Over the Hill," the one song Kate and I wrote together way back before we were married, when we were just two out-of-control young people in love. Rufus does a mournful rendition of "The

Walking Song," another of his mother's songs from that earlier time. Then the three of us perform my tune "The Swimming Song," which was on Kate and Anna's first album. Next, Chaim takes the guitar and rips the room to shreds with "I Eat Dinner," a Kate song about being a single mother. I've always hated the song, because it's so beautiful and terribly sad and always makes me feel deeply ashamed of all the shitty things I did to her and to our kids and to myself. We finish the set with Richard Thompson's "Down Where the Drunkards Roll." Rufus is the main event at the benefit, so he comes out solo for the encore and does his song "Dinner at Eight":

No matter how strong, I'm gonna take you down
With one little stone I'm gonna break you down

I'm the "you" he's singing about and it's okay—tonight I'll just take the shot and be Goliath.

Then the audience brings us back for one more and the three of us finish with Marty Robbins's "At the End of a Long Lonely Day":

With the world locked outside, I just hang my head and cry
At the end of a long lonely day.

15.
scrambled eggs

wrote this sometime in the early eighties:

Yeah, I've got kids. Back home. In the homes they share with their mothers. Homes without fathers, husbands, or boyfriends. Sounds sad, doesn't it? Well, it is if you want it to be. It's sad when I see them. When they come and see me. When they come and visit me. Sounds like I'm in jail. Jail for once-wed bachelor fathers.

My kids are curious about me, and I really believe they need me, but as all the studies have shown, kids are very strong and flexible. They can adapt to a bad situation such as a broken home. For a while, anyway. But then, as all the studies have also shown, kids from broken homes sometimes get screwed up later on. That's a terrible expression—a broken home. Like a machine that doesn't work properly. Or a vase that's fallen off a mantel and then is badly glued back together.

At this point, the kids are young, and my biggest fear is that they're going to hate and blame me for their unhappy lives. It will be my fault, because I couldn't stick it out with their mothers, that I wasn't around when I needed them (Freudian slip—when they needed me). My own father stuck it out, but he wasn't really around, even when he was in the same room. He was certainly a presence at least, which is something I can't say for myself. Except for these filial visits.

Usually I pick them up at the airport, handed off at the gate by a smiling stewardess. They are unaccompanied minors and tagged as such. I suppose some day there might be an unaccompanied-minor strike. After an awkward hug, there's the strange long walk to wait at the baggage carousel, which, unlike a merry-go-round, is a fairly serious place. The drive into the city is pretty nice. We're going to my apartment, and there's an anticipation about that in the car or taxi. Do they remember what it looks like? Dad's place? Has it changed since the last time? I'm excited about what it will feel like to have my children in my house. Will they transform the place from a lonely bachelor pad into a happy home? In the vehicle we talk about what's taken place in our lives since we last saw one another. Nothing important: "I finished a record." "School is fine."

Then we get there and everybody's excitement wears off and we settle into the job, down to the real problem of what the hell we are going to do together.

ME: Did you eat on the plane?
THEM: Yeah, but we could eat again.
ME: What would you like?
THEM: I don't know.
ME: Some eggs?
THEM: Okay.

ME: Scrambled?
THEM: Okay.

Then they watch television while I try to make great scrambled eggs—scrambled eggs that they will never forget, scrambled eggs that they will remember when they're eighty. My father used to make good scrambled eggs. And every once in a while linguine with white clam sauce. Those were his specialties. By that I mean they were all he could cook.

It's not easy to cook, and thank God for the television, for without the television what would they do while I was cooking? Read? Draw? Maybe for a while, but this is not the 1930s. It's the early '80s. And in New York City you don't suggest to your kids, "Why not go outside and play?"

Pretty soon even the television lets me down, and they start to fight with each other. Now, what this is, truly, is an effort on their part to get something really happening. Something really cooking. Not just eggs. Because they know that when they start to argue, bicker, fight, I get crazy, because fighting is wrong and I have to fix it. But fighting is also their job, the job they've been sent to do by their mother. Their job is to come visit me in New York and make me fucking crazy.

I try to control the fighting with a wimpy, imploring "Kids . . ."

Doesn't work.

Soon it shifts into "Kids, cut that out!"

No dice.

Next comes "Okay, I'm warning you!"

Wow! A warning!

Then it peaks with "Goddammit, I told you!" Et cetera.

If I'm angry enough, they stop fighting, because miraculously we've made contact with one another. There's a connection between them and this total stranger. Their father. And it's just like the yelling they get at home from their real parent, their mother. Lower lips quiver, tears well up, sinuses clog. The crying starts.

Now something interesting happens. I feel terrible, too, but I can't let up. I've got to follow through with the punishment. Maybe a little more angry reprimanding. When they were younger, maybe a spanking. Turning off the TV. Separating them, exiled behind closed doors. It's all damaging, but I don't hesitate to use any of it. Sooner or later, though, my anger and outrage subsides and I change back into the kind, receptive, affectionate, sheepishly recalcitrant father.

I explain why they shouldn't argue, fight, and torture each other. Of course they understand. They understood before I yelled at them. But we needed the ritual yelling and punishment. Nodding of heads, wiping of more tears. The snorting and snuffling of warm wet snot. The return to watching TV—peacefully, blissfully coexisting. I return to the scrambling of eggs, thinking I have accomplished something. Unfortunately, this batch of scrambled eggs will never be great.

When a ship is sinking, and they lower the lifeboats
And hand out the lifejackets, the men keep on their coats
The women and the children are the ones who must go first
And the men who try to save their skins are cowards and are cursed
Every man's a captain, men know how to drown
Man the lifeboats if there's room, otherwise go down

It's the same when there's a war on, it's the men who go to fight
Women and children are civilians, when they're killed it's not right
Men kill men in uniform, it's the way war goes

When they run they're cowards, when they stay they are heroes
Every man's a general, men go off to war
The battlefield's a man's world, cannon fodder's what they're for

It's the men who have the power, it's the men who have the might
And the world's a place of horror because each man thinks he's right
A man's home is his castle, so the family let him in
But what's important in that kingdom is the women and children
A husband and a father, every man's a king
But he's really just a drone, gathers no honey, has no sting
Have pity on the general, the king, and the captain
They know they're expendable, after all they're men.

—"MEN," 1992

16.
disguising the man

1965

LONDON—At last I am properly dressed. That is, on some occasions I'll be properly dressed, because any fool knows that a man can't wear his new English suit every day. But on the good days, when the suit has been well brushed and its fibers adequately rested after a decent period in the closet, I will wear it with pride and the confidence that I fit all over.

Of course, all this has probably happened too late. A man should really have his first London-tailored suit in his speedy years, sometime in his early James Bond period. And he should certainly have more than one. Still, if a single Savile Row suit does not make a new man, it has at least made this one feel splendidly redecorated, a miracle of waistcoat and good gray worsted. When I choose it over the less distinguished American models on my rack, I can be sure that its $170 elegance covers up a substantial secret.

Much of my feeling about the suit undoubtedly comes from the experience of buying it. It was the most lingering, pleasurable purchase I have ever made, and I'll remember it long after the trousers are out at the knees. During the five meetings I had with my tailor over a period of two months, the conversation was delightfully single-purposed. We talked about MY requirements, MY measurements, MY appearance, and we seemed always to be progressing toward a triumph that would be totally mine.

I selected my tailor because he was nice about a button. With a friend I had been looking at suit materials in several London shops, and we finally wound up in a small establishment where the friend had bought a suit earlier. He introduced me to the tailor, a short gentleman named Mr. Perry who was dressed in a double-breasted black waistcoat and striped trousers. A tape measure was draped around his neck. Mr. Perry was entirely courteous, but as he showed us bolts of cloth he kept glancing in the direction of my middle. At first I thought he was registering some kind of understated astonishment at the cut of my American ready-made suit and then I thought he might be wondering about the problem of dealing with my shape. I was beginning to not like Mr. Perry when he spoke.

"I think you have a bit of a problem there, sir," Mr. Perry began. "That is, if you don't mind my saying so, sir." He approached and delicately touched the center button on my coat. "The button, sir," he said. "I doubt if it will last out the day. We'll have it tied down properly for you in a moment." I felt relieved and ridiculously grateful and decided that a man so discerning about buttons would have to be marvelous about suits.

We selected the material rather quickly. When I kept returning to a swatch of a light-colored tweed and said I liked it, Mr. Perry said, "It's very nice, but if I may say so, sir, I believe you'd look a bit massive in it." Appalled at the thought of being any more massive than necessary, I selected a darkish gray with a very faint stripe. "That's a cloth that suits you, sir," Mr. Perry said firmly. "It's not flashy, not pretentious and it makes up smart. We should get a good result." The matter was settled.

Until the measuring session that followed I'd never realized how many crucial dimensions I have. From the nape of the neck to the armpit (11 inches), from the center of the back to the elbow (22 inches), from the inside of the leg—known in London as the fork—to the seam of the shoe (32¾ inches), the circumference at the trouser seat (breathtaking). There are 25 vital measurements, and Mr. Perry took them all, calling them out like depth soundings to an assistant who wrote them down on a large pad. These were necessary to cut the pattern, Mr. Perry advised me, and they would then be placed in the company files. How agreeable to reflect that this catalogue of specifics would be kept in a safe place.

Weeks elapsed before I returned to London and Mr. Perry. Looking for the first time at my new suit, I felt much the same horror I'd felt at the first sight of my eldest son. He'd looked very raw to me through the nursery window, and so did the suit, the jacket scarred with basting thread, the pockets missing or sewn shut. Mr. Perry did not reassure me entirely when he found some fault with the shoulder of the jacket and simply clipped some threads and removed one complete sleeve. In the wreckage we agreed and disagreed politely about details. Mr. Perry persuaded me that the jacket should have more shape at the waist and not be like an American suit ("reasonably tidy but lacking in character"). I persuaded him that the trousers should be fitted to accommodate a belt and not suspenders. Mr. Perry did not really like that at all, but he cheered up considerably when we settled on the waistcoat. It would depart somewhat from the straight conservatism of the rest of the suit and have little lapels of its own. "The step-collar vest is coming into fashion, sir," he said approvingly. "I think we're quite right to just go ahead and take the chance." Flushed with risk-taking, I proposed two side vents in the jacket. But Mr. Perry coolly checked me.

At the next session the suit was almost finished, and Mr. Perry offered some guidance for the future. "I suggest you wear it in regular rotation with your other suits, sir," he said. "Once a week would be about right. If you give it fair treatment and rest between times, it should last five years or more. Brush it regularly, sponge it a bit if need be, and don't get it cleaned unless there's been some sort of an accident." I tried not to think of the accidents that regularly befall my suits. "And let me remind you, sir," he finished, "look after it for moths."

The next morning was our last, and much as I wanted the finished suit, I was reluctant to stop buying it. Mr. Perry held each trouser leg clear of the floor as I put on the pants. The lapels on the waistcoat were magnificent. The jacket fit perfectly across the shoulders. I gazed appreciatively at myself in mirrored quadruplicate. Mr. Perry smiled slightly. "I don't think we'll find the belt bothers at all, sir," he said. "You're well turned out."

When I paid Mr. Perry, I asked him if there had been any special problems in making the suit for me. "Oh, no, sir," he began. "Some might say that tailoring is the art of disguising the man, but it's only if a man has a bad appearance that there are any problems. If he has a good figure we come off trumps."

I felt that he had not quite answered my question and repeated it. "The only thing . . ." Mr. Perry said. "Oh, I don't know if I should mention it." I urged him on. "Well,

"I think you have a bit of a problem there, sir..."

sir," he continued, "you have a rather long body, and that's the thing we had to try to minimize. We had to lengthen your legs, so to speak, and shorten your body. Nothing serious, really, and it worked out quite well." This was the first time I'd heard of this particular defect in my structure, and I took another look in the mirrors. Mr. Perry was right. It was impossible to tell now where my short legs ended and my long body began.

In a postoperative glow at his sartorial surgery, I said goodbye to Mr. Perry and set off down the street, trying to make my strides long enough to keep the secret of my suit.

17.
bands

Fifty-something years ago I saw and heard some great bands at the Deercrest Inn in Banksville, New York. Back then the drinking age for kids from the Empire State was eighteen, but it was twenty-one just across the border in Connecticut, so a lot of the Deercrest's younger clientele drove over from towns like Greenwich and New Canaan. The acts at the club were mostly unknown R&B cover bands, but occasional known entities like Mitch Ryder ("Devil with the Blue Dress On"), Bobby Hebb ("Sunny"), or the Duprees ("You Belong to Me") would grace the stage, if a stage is what you could call an eight-inch-raised wooden platform. One night in 1964, I went with some friends to hear the legendary Isley Brothers, and featured in their backup band was a skinny young black left-handed guitar player who was dressed in a tight-fitting Eleganza suit ("For the man who knows style when style is so right") and sporting what used to be called a fifty-dollar process. Even more noticeable than his flashy threads and conked hair, though, was the way this kid could play, effortlessly squeezing, almost shaking, the riffs and fills out of the electric guitar, and doing it behind his back if and when he chose to. The expression on his face was haughty and gleeful, and a particularly powerful sexual charge went through the room—packed with affluent white suburban kids for whom the height of style was tasseled Bass Weejuns, no socks, and madras Bermuda shorts—when the southpaw actually went down on, or as we used to say back then, "ate out" his Fender Stratocaster. Just a few years later, in 1967, I saw this amazing musician at a rock festival in London. By then he was fronting his own band, and I'm sure you've figured out by now it was the Jimi Hendrix Experience.

Like a lot of my generation, I "dabbled in psychedelics," which is just a euphemistic way of saying I took a fair amount of acid. One of the side effects with that kind of fooling around is that it can lead to an interest in Eastern spiritual disciplines. At least that's what happened to me. Eventually I was lured away from the ancient spiritual texts of India and China and wound up fixating on things Japanese. I "discovered" macrobiotics. Actually, Jewell Walker, my movement teacher in the acting program at Carnegie Tech, started the ball rolling in 1967 by touting a book to some of us called *You Are All Sanpaku*, written by William Dufty and based on the teaching and writing of Nyoiti Sakurazawa. Sakurazawa wrote under the pen name of George Ohsawa and was the founding father of macrobiotics. According to him, health, peace, and spiritual realization could be achieved by balancing the opposing oriental principles of yin and yang, thus establishing what he called "The Order of the Universe." The balancing act was facilitated by adhering to a strict traditional Japanese diet of whole grains and vegetables. Meat, drugs, dairy, alcohol, caffeine, and sugar, in particular, were the big no-no's. Cigarettes, oddly enough, were okay. Anyway, I got swept up in all this from about 1968 to 1970, and looking back now I think it had a positive effect on me, initially at least, because after cutting out the booze, sugar, and meat, and sticking mostly to brown rice and vegetables, I started to feel pretty cleaned out and focused. I also began to write my own songs around this time, several of them referencing my immersion in macrobiotics. There was "Bruno's Place," which starts with the line "Several stars played guitars and were backed with feeling by a chopstick-wielding rhythm section." Also "Glad to See You Got Religion": "Glad to see you've gotten careful about the things you eat and drink. / Glad to see you've gotten choosy about the things you do and think." And who could forget "Cook That Dinner, Dora" with its cringe-inducing lyric "Dora, you can do it with all your pots and pans / And your ageless old friend fire and your magic woman hands." "Bruno's Place" and "Glad to See You Got Religion" were on my debut album, which was recorded in 1969 and released in 1970. Check out the striking, stark black-and-white photograph taken by Lee Friedlander on the cover of that record. Yes, it's true I was going for a preppy psycho-killer look, but the short hair, sports jacket, and button-down shirt were also de rigueur for the young male macros of that era. I was living in macrobiotic study houses in Brookline, Massachusetts, then, learning cooking, acupuncture, and massage; just generally boning up on the Order of the Universe with Michio Kushi, who was a direct disciple of Ohsawa and the East Coast macrobiotics head honcho. As far as Michio was concerned, groovy long hair and bell-bottom trousers were way too ostentatiously yin, whereas short hair, jacket, and, ideally, tie were yang. Men were supposed to be yang; women, yin. The gals, like the guys, were strongly encouraged by Kushi to dress conservatively. Come to think of it, we all went around looking and, to a degree, acting like Young Republicans, Mormons, or Seventh-day Adventists. Basically, I was caught up in a food cult.

Meanwhile, my first record had gotten glowing reviews and there was a career in music waiting for me if I wanted it. But there was a problem—I wasn't sure I wanted it. Being in a cult creates an Us versus Them situation or, if you will, our world versus the outside world. Fame and wealth with all the trappings might seem alluring, but its pursuit was, as Michio would have put it, "too yin." According to him, along with steak and ice cream, one of the biggest killers out there, and an absolute must to avoid, was the sin of pride, or what he called arrogance. Of course, Scientology, Bono, and the Reverend Ike have shown us that spirituality can comfortably go hand in hand with unbridled ambition, but for me in my benighted post-psychedelic-truth-and-enlightenment-seeking days, making it big felt wrong, something to be ashamed of and guilty about. I had released a great album and people wanted to see and hear me play, but I was hiding out in those macrobiotic study houses in Brookline. But then, luckily, or perhaps as my destiny would have it, the firm of Robertson, Hudson, Danko, Helm, and Manuel came to town, and one of the Laws of the Universe kicked in big time. As Michio was always reminding us, "Everything changes."

On June 23, 1970, the Band was the first act to perform at Summer Thing, an outdoor concert series held at Soldiers Field, the old concrete Harvard Stadium in Cambridge. Wikipedia reminds me that the event was sponsored by the flat, tasteless, and now thankfully long gone Schaefer Beer. We didn't quite sneak out, but let's just say a few of my macro pals and I slipped away from Brookline to see the show that evening. I felt a little like Pinocchio, foolishly lured to Pleasure Island for my transmogrification into a donkey. I remember sitting at the back of the stadium in the dark, waiting for the show to begin, surreptitiously sipping my oh-so-yin Schaefer friendly frosty. Below us in the distance the stage was pitch-black, the only thing visible on it the piercing red lights on the guitar amps. The stadium held thirty thousand and it was packed. There was no announcement or introduction offered when five shadowy, indiscernible figures in hats strode onstage all at once. Still shrouded in darkness, Garth Hudson began his soaring, arpeggiated B-3 organ intro, which seemingly would go on forever, until Levon Helm joined in, hitting the shit out of the drums. Then the stage lights came up as the three others from Ontario joined the glorious and convulsing ruckus that was "Chest Fever." Danko, Manuel, and Helm sang the nonsensical lyrics as one straining but totally pure vocal entity, and that night everyone at Soldiers Field shed their sprouted donkey ears and were transported way beyond Pleasure Island, to a place that brown rice, umeboshi plums, headstands, and even LSD could never have taken them. We had been knocked sideways by art, but art that wasn't previously owned and handed down by our teachers and parents. It was Art that seemed to be our very own.

The next day, I left Brookline and went back to New York City. I'd had enough. I told my manager I was ready to go out and do some gigs to promote my record. Then I went down to McSorley's on East Seventh Street and treated myself to a draft beer and a liverwurst and cheese sandwich.

18.

in your street

A year after my first record came out on Atlantic in 1970, I happened to be in London, and one morning I decided to drop by the offices of Polydor Records, the company that distributed my album over there. I didn't have an appointment, and nobody from the label even knew I was in town. I said something to the receptionist like "Hi, my name is Loudon Wainwright. You guys put out my record over here." She walked back into the offices, and a few seconds later four very excited people rushed out, exclaiming things like "Oh my goodness, you're here!" and "I can't believe it!" and "This is incredible!" The reason for all the hubbub was that John Peel, a DJ on BBC Radio 1, had been playing the hell out of my album. Peel was the coolest, most-listened-to guy on the radio at that time (and for many years to come), so lots of people were wondering who Loudon Wainwright III was. The people at Atlantic went into high gear, arranging interviews with the music press and an exclusive on-air radio interview with the great Peel himself. I owe John a lot. He almost single-handedly created my career over there, by playing and praising my songs to his faithful, avid listeners.

I began to tour Britain regularly, including a stint as the opening act for the English rock-and-jazz fusion band Soft Machine. We traveled by train on British Rail, riding in those cushy first-class carriages you see in movies like *The Lady Vanishes* and *A Hard Day's Night*. In those days, in addition to the dailies like the *Guardian*, the *Times*, and the *Telegraph*, there were the music papers, the big three being *Melody Maker*, *Sounds*, and the *New Musical Express* (*NME*). My career was in rapid ascension then, and I used to buy all the papers at the station newsstands and then greedily read and reread reviews and articles about myself on the train journeys. My carriage mates, the somewhat older guys in Soft Machine, having been around the block a few times, mostly stuck to the soccer and cricket results.

On October 12, 1971, I had the scary privilege of opening for the Everly Brothers at the Royal Albert Hall. The place was packed, seven thousand strong, when I walked out onto the stage with my red Gibson Hummingbird to start my set. It was supposed to be thirty-five minutes long, but it only lasted about twelve. Andrew Bailey wrote about the gig in the *London Evening Standard*: "It was plain to see that the bulk of the audience had come to see the Everly Brothers. The nostalgic atmosphere was enriched by the presence of a large bunch of Teddy Boys and their carefully coiffured chicks." Then Bailey went on to say some very nice things about me. "But I thought Wainwright's solo performance was one of the most stunning I have ever seen. No one can sing his songs like he does. His thin, high-pitched voice forces you to listen to his lyrics, which is where his special talents lie. His songs chronicle with succinct and witty imagery the progress of young America. I especially liked his droll and tastefully jaundiced view of the subject." I'm not sure about my chronicling the progress of young America, but it was a pretty nice write-up. My section of the notice, however, ends on a sadder note, as Bailey remarks, "My admiration was obviously not shared by the large section of the audience who clapped and jeered when Wainwright announced his last song." What the man from the *Evening Standard* did not mention was that, just prior to my announced departure from the stage, some Teddy Boy in the stalls threw a heavy pint mug at my head; fortunately it shattered at my feet, and that emphatic act of protest sent me skittering to the wings. Speaking of throwing things, some years later at an outdoor festival held in a hurling(!) stadium in Cork, I attempted to entertain several thousand Irish teenagers, who had been drinking for hours in the hot summer sun. The headliners were the rabble-rousing IRA favorites the Wolfe Tones and, like the Teddy Boys at the Everly Brothers show, the audience could be characterized as impatient. I was the first one sacrificed on the bill. At one point as I was singing, my peripheral vision picked up something flying through the air, end over end, heading my way. A split second later, my Martin D-28 guitar took a direct hit from a half-empty liter plastic bottle of hard cider, and an early exit/escape was once again precipitated. Kris Kristofferson was on deck, and when he and his band came out, the drunken louts threw shit at them, too. To quote Mr. Congreve, "Musick has charms to soothe the savage breast," but not on that day.

19.
stinkin' to high heaven

My obituary, coming much too soon to a newspaper near you, will certainly include a mention of "Dead Skunk." In spite of all my many and varied accomplishments, the skunk thing, I fear, will be the lead item in my obit. Certain people take great pleasure in reminding me about my hit song, like the idiot at the YMCA check-in desk with the bad toupee who cheerfully proffers his pithy "I think I smell a skunk" each and every time I see him. Throughout my career I have been asked ad infinitum how I feel about the success of "Dead Skunk," and my glib answers include "It paid for a lot of child support" and "Better a song about roadkill than one about getting high on a mountain in Colorado." I'm told it was banned by the BBC, but I consider that an honor, since in 1953 they axed ten out of the twelve tracks on *Songs by Tom Lehrer*. In Little Rock, Arkansas, home of the Arkansas Arts Center, Arkansas Repertory Theatre, Arkansas

Symphony Orchestra, and Ballet Arkansas, the single was number one for six weeks, and I've often wondered if Bill and Hillary ever made out to the tune way back in their courting days. A few years ago I actually met and shook hands with our forty-second president, and I couldn't resist asking him if he remembered "Dead Skunk." Always the waffler, he was noncommittal in his glassy-eyed response of "I'm not sure." Every once in a while I play the damn song, but mostly in uncomfortable situations where there is an understanding or obligation that I do so, for instance when I'm the ridiculously overpaid surprise musical guest at a very rich drunk person's seventy-fifth-birthday party. I've also been known to cave if I get a handwritten request to sing it from a child in a wheelchair. It's not that I'm ashamed of the song—as the composer of "I Wish I Was a Lesbian" and "I'm Saving My Black-heads for You," how could I be? I just grew weary of cranking it out every night and pandering to my audience's expectation that I sing it. But if you don't play the hit, be it "Alice's Restaurant," "Year of the Cat," or "Baubles, Bangles, and Beads," people will be pissed.

Major Skunk-age.

However, I really shouldn't lose sight of the fact that "Dead Skunk" has given people a great deal of enjoyment. Adam Sandler and I met in

2001, when he guest-starred with me in an episode of Judd Apatow's TV show *Undeclared*. Adam, himself the purveyor of many fine novelty songs, called me recently and thanked me for "Dead Skunk." It turns out he plays my hit for his two young sons every morning when he drives them to school. "It's their favorite song ever," he told me.

20.
nashville

This morning my old college buddy George Gerdes sent me another of his obit e-mails. I often get the news that yet another show biz luminary has died from the Double G. He's had his antennae up for the final rite of passage for quite a while. Gerdes made two albums in the 1970s. The first was called *Obituary*. That was followed by *Son of Obituary*. This morning's note from George was short and sort of sweet. Referencing my fourth record, *Attempted Mustache*, he wrote, "I am starting to grow a mustache in honor of the man who precedes us into the Great Unknown." The record producer Bob Johnston had died at the age of eighty-three, ten days after Billy Sherrill bought the farm at seventy-eight. Two of Nashville's greatest, down for the count in a single fortnight. Billy produced and

wrote for George Jones and Tammy Wynette. Bob produced records
with Dylan, Cohen, Cash, and even did one with me.

IN 1972, after *Album III* and the strange, confusing success of
"Dead Skunk," I wasn't sure what to do. I was now pegged as "the
Skunk guy" and was feeling like I'd sold out. My first two Atlantic
LPs had been voice-and-guitar affairs, critically successful but commercial duds. After being dropped by Atlantic, I was signed by Columbia. The powers that be (Clive Davis) decided that I had to stop
goofing around and make a record that actually got played on the
radio, so I was paired up with the producer Thomas Jefferson Kaye
and a band called White Cloud. It worked. "Dead Skunk" got airplay
and *Album III* did well. But, always ready to indulge in self-loathing,
I now felt guilty, ashamed of a commercial success, so when Bob
Johnston came calling, in 1973, I got excited. This was the guy who'd
produced *Blonde on Blonde* and *John Wesley Harding*. How could I
not go there? "There" was Nashville.

Just a few weeks after Rufus was born in July of 1973, Kate and I
set up camp with our newborn at Roger Miller's King of the Road
Motel in Music City. That's where we stayed while I made *Attempted
Mustache*. There was a very talented blind singer-songwriter pianist
working in the motel lounge bar every night named Ronnie Milsap.
As long as I'm name-dropping, my album was recorded at Ray Stevens's Sound Laboratory. That's Ray Stevens of "Ahab the Arab"
fame.

I don't know if they still make records quickly in Nashville, but
Attempted Mustache was recorded in four days and mixed in two.
We were out of there in less than a week. The players were some of

the legendary cats of that time—Kenny Buttrey, on drums, and Tommy Cogbill, on bass, are both now dead. There were a clutch of great guitar players—Johnny Christopher, Mac Gayden, Ron Cornelius, and Reggie Young. The piano player was Hargus "Pig" Robbins, who also happens to be blind. Doug Kershaw plays fiddle and yelps on "The Swimming Song." Kate and I play banjos on that one, and she duets with me on "Dilated to Meet You," a song written for Rufus when he was in utero, waiting in the wings, so to speak. Bob Johnston plied us with lots of red wine, as I recall. Rufus cried a lot in the motel at night, and we didn't get a lot of sleep.

THE RECORD WAS A FLOP. Radio stations wanted to know why there wasn't a funny animal song. The reviews were mixed, though Robert Christgau of the *Village Voice* gave it an A minus. In my opinion, a number of my best songs are on it, including "Down Drinking at the Bar," "Lullaby," "The Man Who Couldn't Cry," and "The Swimming Song." A lot of people I played the record for, including my parents and my manager, Milt Kramer, felt *Attempted Mustache* was overproduced and mixed badly. "It's hard to hear the lyrics," my father complained, and looking back, I think that's a fair criticism. Still, the album has a loose, ramshackle feel to it, and some people like it a lot, including my daughter Martha, who has discerning taste. The photo on the front cover is pretty cool. We were driving around Nashville with the photographer Marshall Fallwell, looking for a location to shoot in, when suddenly we drove past a funeral home—and there on the front lawn were a pair of plaster polar bears, each one holding an armful of plaster snowballs. I kicked off my shoes and posed next to one of them, flashing a stupid

Me and the polar bears.

grin underneath the half-assed mustache I was attempting to raise at that time.

We're wondering when you will arrive
We're wondering what you'll be
We're wondering if you'll be a her
Or if you'll be a he

Maybe you'll arrive today
Perhaps tomorrow night
We're hoping you won't hurt too much
And that you'll be all right

Life has a few unpleasantries
We may as well confess
We suppose you'll cry a lot
And that you'll be a mess

There is one thing you should note well
Of this there is no doubt
You cannot get inside again
Once you have come out

Even though there's trouble
Even though there's fuss
We really think you'll like it here
We hope that you like us

—"DILATED TO MEET YOU," 1973

21.
suzzy

Suzzy Roche was sixteen when we met. It was at a party at some-one's West Village apartment. I noticed the quiet, black-haired teenage girl, but it was her oldest sister, the brilliant, mercurial Maggie, that I was interested in. The most notable thing about Suzzy was her gap-toothed smile.

A few years later, in 1976, after the many splits, reconciliations, and all the drama, my wife, Kate McGarrigle, packed up our kids and moved back to Montreal. Rufus was three and Martha a few months old. I was twenty-nine and suddenly living alone in a house in Waccabuc, New York. I knew that Suzzy, by then a college sopho-more, was studying acting at SUNY, in nearby Purchase, and one spring day, on a strong impulse, I showed up at her apartment. I came with a gift, or really what amounted to a kind of calling card. It was a vinyl copy of Kate and Anna's first album. I probably said something like "You might like this." Suzzy shyly thanked me, but I could tell that what she was thinking was *This is weird.*

We walked around Lake Waccabuc, looking at the fall foliage, and I took pictures of Suzzy with my Canon 35-millimeter camera. You see smitten guys on the make doing this all the time, thinking they're David Hemmings in the movie *Blow-Up*, photographing/seducing Vanessa Redgrave. Suz was a willing and photogenic model, and I sensed that in addition to her being beautiful and funny, she was a good performer. That was borne out when I saw her onstage at Purchase in a production of Arthur Miller's *The Crucible*. She played Mary Warren, John Proctor's maid and one of the accusers in the play. The role is relatively small, but Suzzy gave a remarkable performance. She made the daring choice of giving Mary protruding buckteeth, and as a result, all her lines were spoken with a crazy Jerry Lewis nutty professor lisp. Her commitment to her character was so specific and complete that no one in the audience could take their

Young Suz in Waccabuc.

eyes off her. Suzzy wasn't upstaging anyone. She was just better than anybody else. I was a goner.

We began spending more and more time together, and I found myself becoming a sort of Svengali/Henry Higgins figure, exposing my new girlfriend to my firmly held tastes and prejudices, especially in music and film—"I've got to take you to see *Juliet of the Spirits.*" "Wait until you hear Paul Brady!" It was under my tutelage that Suzzy tried lobster. She seemed eager to absorb all I was imparting, often responding to my enthusiasms with a demure "That's great." Perhaps what she was really thinking was, again, *This is weird.*

My career was at an all-time low. I'd been dropped by my second major label, Columbia, and was struggling to stay on my third, Arista. The record I was making for them at the time was called *Final Exam*, which was a prescient choice, since I was booted not long after its release in 1978. Suzzy was a beautiful younger performer, full of talent and just starting out, so in addition to my being a sort of Svengali, there was a bit of a Norman Maine/*A Star Is Born* thing going on.

In 1975, Maggie and Terre Roche, as a duo, made *Seductive Reasoning*, a fairly well-received album. Paul Simon was one of its producers. The record sold poorly, however, and soon after its release, Maggie and Terre's career stalled. About a year and a half later, Suzzy joined forces with her sisters and that trio became the Roches. They quickly burst onto the scene, playing to packed houses and receiving rave reviews in the *New York Times* and the *Village Voice*. Onstage, Suzzy always performed in the center position, Maggie and Terre on either side of her. She was a mesmerizing presence: funny, spacey, angry, sexy, and sorrowful all at the same time. In 1979, Robert Fripp produced their Warner Bros. Records album *The*

Roches and it was a critical hit, making many of the Top 10 lists that year. I was beginning to feel out-Svengalied. There were also inevitable comparisons to that other singing-sister act signed to Warner Bros.: Kate and Anna McGarrigle. Now it *was* getting weird.

Kate had the mistaken impression that Suzzy had stolen me from her, so the success of the Roches, not to mention the comparisons in the press between the two groups, made her furious. I'm sad to say that for the next thirty-five years, Kate waged a kind of psychological war of attrition on me and Suzzy, and also, by extension, on our daughter, Lucy. The hostilities continued even after Suzzy and I split up in 1985. But Suz and I remained very close friends. Maybe that, in addition to the hell-hath-no-fury stuff, was what Kate found so painful.

I guess it's been weird, but, more important, it's been beautiful. Suzzy has been more than just a close friend. She has been a constant. When I have been at my absolute lowest, often at three or four a.m., she is always the person I call. In addition to making solo records, Suzzy has written two novels, a children's book, and for the last twenty years has been an essential contributing member of the theater company the Wooster Group. She is also one half of another dynamic family singing duo, and her partner is our daughter, Lucy Wainwright Roche. Suzzy has been a loving mother, not only to Lucy but to my other kids, Rufus, Martha, and Alexandra. She has always been in my corner.

Unhappy anniversary, it's one year since we split.
I walk and talk and get around, lie down, stand up, and sit.
I eat and drink and smoke and sleep and live a little bit.
Unhappy anniversary, it's one year since we split.

Unhappy anniversary, it's ten years since we met.
There is no need to remind me, no way I could forget.
We fell in love, then we fell out, both times there was no net.
Unhappy anniversary, it's ten years since we met.

Unhappy anniversary, I cannot count the days
And nights that I have thought of you since we went separate ways.
I tell my mind to forget you, but my heart disobeys.
Unhappy anniversary, I cannot count the days.

—"Unhappy Anniversary," 1986

22.
snafu

Lucy was born in 1981 on December 16, sharing her birthday with, among others, her grandfather (my dad) and Ludwig van Beethoven. Early in 1982, Suzzy and I, after several weeks of intense and watchful newborn parenting, decided we needed a night out. We overbriefed Lucy's first-ever babysitter, and then, with excitement tinged with anxious guilt, we kissed our lovely innocent good-bye and set off into the night. The familiar frisson of carefree young coupledom felt good as we walked out our door and down the street. Suz's brother Dave was playing with his band at a long rectangular-shaped club called SNAFU, which was walking distance from where we lived in Chelsea.

It was mostly a friends and family affair that night. Among those at the gig were Suzzy's sisters, Maggie and Terre, and my sister Teddy. Everyone seemed to know everyone else. There were thirty of us there at the most, and the atmosphere was relaxed. At the appointed time,

Dave and his little rock combo took the stage, plugged in, and began their set. They got about two minutes into the first song when one of the thick wire-wound strings on the electric Fender bass snapped with an amplified pop. This almost never happens. Guitar strings break all the time, but bass-string breakage is highly unusual. Everyone waited while the bass player began changing his string. Suddenly another pop was audible, though this one sounded completely different from the first one. It was more like a crack. Then a shouting, urgent voice silenced the room. *"All right, everybody, shut the fuck up! This is a robbery. Do what we fucking say and nobody will get hurt!"* The overwrought speaker was a strung-out-looking man in his twenties and he was brandishing a handgun, waving and pointing it at the crowd. The second pop had been the report produced when he fired a warning shot into the ceiling to get our attention. Then another young man, his accomplice, assured us in a firm but much more reasonable fashion that this was indeed a robbery and we were to follow instructions, because his crazy friend was willing and entirely capable of shooting us if we didn't. The guys in the crowd were told to line up and enter the men's room one at a time, divesting themselves of wallets, watches, and rings as they went in. A small table was placed in front of the bathroom door to receive the surrendered valuables. There was to be complete compliance and absolutely no talking. Another table was set up in front of the ladies' room, and the women were given the same orders: pocketbooks, wallets, rings, bracelets, necklaces, earrings, et cetera, were to be turned over in an orderly fashion. As we were herded into our lines, the crazy gunman kept screaming things like *"Keep fucking quiet and do as we fucking say or I swear to God I will fucking kill you!"* and *"We are not fucking around with you fucking assholes!"* Everyone was impressed with the seriousness of the situation and did as they were told with the exception of, I found out later, my headstrong sister Teddy, who decided that she was not a *"fucking asshole"* and would therefore keep her valuables in her possession. Somehow she managed to get away with it.

The scene inside the men's room was confused and somewhat comical, and the detainee's demeanors ranged from Steven Seagal–like steely determination for revenge to Wally Cox shaking-in-your-shoes timidity. There were about fifteen of us in there, intensely debating in hushed voices the best course of action. Should we risk our lives, rush out, and overpower the duo with our sheer number? Or rather, should we, like mice, continue to do as we were told? The second course of action seemed the wisest one, especially whenever the crazed psycho-killer gunman threw open the men's room door and wildly waved the gun around. When someone is just a few feet away and points a gun at you, you begin to wonder what it will feel like to have a bullet enter your body and tear through your viscera. Will it hurt? How *much* will it hurt? In addition, I was thinking that Suzzy and I would never see Lucy again, that our primal, intense, loving acquaintance with her was about to be cruelly cut short after just a few weeks. Why, in God's name, had we gone out that night? It was about then that one of the mouse-types started to sob quietly next to me. Then something happened that managed to alleviate the seriousness of the situation. A newcomer appeared in the men's room, brandishing a vanilla ice-cream cone. He clearly hadn't grasped what was happening. "This is some kind of a joke, right? A TV movie, *Candid Camera*–type thing, right?" he inquired between licks. We quietly assured him that it was not a joke, and then urged him to *Shut the fuck up.*

The robbery probably hadn't lasted ten minutes, but to us it felt much longer. The gun-toting madman finally stopped appearing at the men's room door, and after a minute or two of silence, one of us (I wish I could say it had been me) stuck his head out and called to his wife over in the ladies' room. She meekly answered back that she was all right, and very slowly and cautiously we all emerged from our segregated holding pens. At this point, it wasn't so much fear that we were experiencing as shock. All of us had been traumatized by the event; we were physically safe but psychically assaulted. I remember wandering around in a daze, looking for Suzzy. It wasn't at all like in the disaster movies; there wasn't any crying or hysterics. Almost in slow motion, people, friends, siblings, and spouses began to quietly confer, and a few hugs were exchanged. Suz and I found each other at last, stunned and relieved but anxious and terribly guilty about leaving behind our infant. Teddy, pissed and proactive as ever, went outside and found a phone booth to call the cops. That was when we realized the robbers had taken two women with them as hostages. Now the traumatic event seemed even more sinister, and we were thrown back into crisis mode. The police arrived, and we were detained for what seemed like another eternity for all the necessary questioning and law enforcement rigmarole. Suzzy and I were allowed to leave first so we could hurry home to Lucy. Later that night, at home, we somehow found out that the two kidnapped women had been released somewhere near the George Washington Bridge. They had been molested before they were let go.

By the next day the shock of the incident had begun to wear off, and my anger started to kick in. It wasn't the stolen watch and wallet so much as the feeling of being violated. All my liberal leanings concerning crime and punishment suddenly went out the window. I wanted those thugs caught, and I wanted them locked up for life. A few weeks later we found out that they had indeed been apprehended. It turned out they had been committing robberies all over

Manhattan, using the same wild modus operandi, and finally their luck ran out. I don't know if they ever wound up shooting anyone, but I hoped they would die in jail. It was quite some time before Suzzy and I went out and left Lucy alone after that.

NEW YORK POST

THURSDAY, MARCH 18, 1982   **25** CENTS   © 1982 News Group Publications Inc. Vol. 181, No. 105
AMERICA'S FASTEST-GROWING NEWSPAPER

Bandits foul up SNAFU club — rob 50 patrons

By DAVID NG

TWO gunmen invaded a packed Chelsea nightclub last night and methodically robbed about 50 patrons before leaving with two female hostages.

The women were later released unharmed.

The gunmen entered the SNAFU club at W. 21st St. and Sixth Av. about 9 p.m., stood by the club's door until a break in the music and then fired a shot into the floor.

"We heard one gunshot at the floor and turned around," said Teddy Wainwright, who was in the club.

"They said 'everyone get out your money,'" said Miss Wainwright.

The holdup men separated the women and men customers and ordered them one-by-one to empty out their pockets and walk into the bathrooms, she said.

The bandits also forced the bartender, Steven Circles, to open the cash register.

"They ordered me to put the money into a woman's pocketbook and told me if I tried anything funny they would blow my head off," he said.

Circles was forced into the mens' room with the other male victims.

They waited until they heard the gunmen exit through a side door. The men then freed the women and called police.

But before leaving, the robbers had ordered two women customers, both in their 20s, into their car as they made their getaway.

The unidentifed women were driven to the Upper West Side underneath the George Washington Bridge and released, police said.

The suspects, described as Hispanics in their 20s, appeared nervous, witnesses said.

SNAFU *New York Post* clipping.

23.
sir walter raleigh syndrome

My dad was a ladies' man—he liked them and they liked him. He was tall, smart, funny, miserable—all that good stuff. And he was famous, which is gunpowder with women. He never wrote about his addiction to romantic danger, since he knew it would be unsuitable for *Life* magazine. I, on the other hand, have written plenty of songs about fooling around with the fairer sex and the heartbreak that can ensue. Like multitudes of guys before me, I primarily went into show business to meet and, hopefully, get girls.

But the freest I ever felt was when I was a prepubescent ten-year-old and getting girls didn't matter.

There was a time I didn't have any power, but the world was an oyster to me.

No short days, just long ones, right times, not wrong ones, happy as a clam or a kid can be.

—"10," 2012

What mattered was getting outside and playing—building forts, riding bikes, climbing trees. When girls suddenly became an irresistibly alluring part of the equation, everything got more complicated. In my sorry little mind, females—whether wives or girlfriends or groupies—were primarily to be pleased, and whenever I worried that I'd failed in that regard, I felt resentment. This idea (ideal) of being a masculine caretaker was instilled and reinforced in me at an early age by my mother, who often made me feel like I had to function as the man of the house. At least that's what one shrink told me.

Sometimes I think many of my skirmishes with women are the product of what you could call Sir Walter Raleigh Syndrome.

The night had been rainy, and just where the young gentleman stood a small quantity of mud interrupted the Queen's passage. As she hesitated to pass on, the gallant, throwing his cloak from his shoulders, laid it on the miry spot, so as to ensure her stepping over it dry-shod.

—*A partial description of the Sir Walter Raleigh/Queen Elizabeth I cloak legend from* Kenilworth, *by Sir Walter Scott*

If I'm with a woman and we come upon a metaphorical mud puddle, off comes the proverbial cloak, which then is spread over said puddle. Lots of women still like this chivalrous behavior. It makes them feel like . . . well, like a queen. And guys like to think of themselves as "gallants" like Sir Walter Raleigh or his cousin Sir Galahad. The problem is, mud is not so great for cloaks, and after a while the guy starts to think, *Hey, why doesn't she just step around the puddle?* But another problem is, the whole setup with men and women often seems to be predicated on this chivalry shit. You can't question the rules and conventions, not if you're a guy—at least a guy of my generation. You've got to open the door, pick up the check, pull out the chair, and throw down the cloak. At this point you might say, "But that's not the way things are now. Women are liberated. They don't want to ruin your cloaks." That might be true, and I have always, with a few exceptions, been attracted to self-reliant women. But in the end it doesn't really fly because, no matter what, all this man/woman stuff continues to run deep with me. I'm a guy with Sir Walter Raleigh Syndrome. Ringo Starr displays some of the symptoms of SWRS in Richard Lester's comic masterpiece *A Hard Day's Night* when he eagerly lays down his raincoat over a series of mud puddles for a giggly "bird." Lester employs a comic triple when the damsel in distress, much to Ringo's horror and our delight, takes a step onto the gallant's coat for the third puddle and, with a shriek, disappears down a deep hole.

It's not strange, no mystery,
That you and I are history.
I've put up my protective wall.
It's four feet thick and ten feet tall.

Ten feet tall and four feet thick.
Granite, concrete, steel, and brick.
Protection for, you understand,
The little boy, the inner man.

Boys kiss the girls, then make them cry.
It's a man's job, that is why.
And when you cry, you're just a clone
Of every woman I have ever known.

And every Harry, Dick, and Tom
Gets all of this shit from his mom,
Who was unhappy. Mom was sad
Because of a wall that Dad had.

And once it's up it won't come down.
And Mom's a queen and Dad's a clown.
And it's not strange, no mystery,
That you and I are history.
It's four feet thick and ten feet tall.

—"4 x 10," 1992

24.
the hollywood sign

You can't really get to the Hollywood sign. It's possible, I suppose, but you'd need the physical agility required to scale a serious security fence and a willingness to break the law. You can get fairly close by hiking up a path where Beachwood Canyon ends, and you can reach a point behind and above the structure if you trek certain fire roads and trails in Griffith Park. But if you actually wanted to get there, to climb or perch on the sign, deface its surface with graffiti or feces, or, as Peg Entwistle did in 1932, jump off the letter *H* to your death, it wouldn't be easy. So we all settle for gazing up in reverence or regret at those nine iconic fifty-foot-high letters. At night the sign is invisible, as it hasn't been illuminated since 1949. The sight of the Hollywood sign lit up at night like a Christmas tree would almost be unbearable. Broad daylight is enough. When it's dark, all the Hollywood hopefuls drive up to Mulholland Drive to gaze down onto the shimmering, sparkling flats below, in the beginning thinking, "One day I'll be a star." Eventually the rumination turns into "How the hell am I going to get a fucking agent?" And then, after being beaten to a pulp, it's "I've had it, I'm going back home." I suppose if you're lucky enough to be working, even as an extra on some doomed pilot, the Hollywood sign is a glorious sight. If you have a job, all the heartbreak is temporarily forgotten. And before an audition, the sign takes on the power of Mount Rushmore and can rekindle hope. Even though I have a career in music, I've always sought acting jobs. Before many an appointment with a casting director, I've trudged around the Lake Hollywood reservoir, scene sides in hand, mouthing my lines. As I round a bend I look up, and there is the Hollywood sign, a benign presence above me that seems to say, "Don't worry. You'll get it." But if, after striking out (you can usually tell before you're out of the audition room if you didn't get the job), I were to go back and walk around the same reservoir (the actual location where Andy Griffith and a young Ron Howard, as Opie, went off to fish to whistling theme music many years ago), the sight of those letters would be a cruel mockery, a rebuke. That's the kind of town it is. Millions loved *La La Land*, but, and primarily because, it's pure fantasy. I'll take Nathanael West's *Day of the Locust*.

It amazes me that I've been going back to the place for so long. I lived there for three years as a kid in the fifties, but 1974 was when I went out to make it big. Larry Gelbart, the principal creator of the TV show *M*A*S*H*, had seen me in L.A. performing at the Troubadour and had the idea of working a guitar-playing singer into his show. That's how I became Captain Calvin Spalding, the singing surgeon, for three episodes. Hollywood had called in earnest. My marriage to Kate was in crisis when I moved out to L.A. from New York and set up shop at the then fairly funky Chateau Marmont Hotel on

Sunset Boulevard. The Chateau was a step up from where I usually stayed, the Tropicana Motel, where Tom Waits famously hung out with Rickie Lee Jones. The Chateau was a better place for a guy like me, though, because it had just the right amount of old-time Hollywood decadence and was relatively quiet, clean, and affordable. This was several years before John Belushi overdosed and died in one of the hotel's bungalows, a *Hollywood Babylon*–esque event that made the place hip again, sending the room rates soaring.

When I lived at the Chateau, the most glamorous tenant was the Austrian actor Maximilian Schell, though once I shared the elevator with Donald Sutherland, the original Hawkeye Pierce from the movie *M*A*S*H*. Schell gave acting lessons to young hopefuls in his suite, and one of his pupils was a young woman named Julia Anne Robinson, who also lived at the hotel. She and I had what could best be described as an in-house flirtation: a few dinners at the Imperial Gardens Japanese restaurant next door, some conversations by the pool, and one opium-smoking session back in her room that resulted in what I recall as being a fumbling stab at sex. In 1972, at the age of twenty-one, Julia had broken through as an actress in *The King of Marvin Gardens*, Bob Rafelson's not quite as critically acclaimed follow-up to *Five Easy Pieces*. She shared fourth billing with Scatman Crothers, behind Jack Nicholson, Bruce Dern, and Ellen Burstyn, playing Jessica, the vulnerable young tap dancer who is ensnared in a love triangle with Jason and Sally (Dern and Burstyn), while also being drawn to the shy David, played with uncharacteristic restraint (no grinning) by Nicholson. Recently I rewatched the movie, which holds up nicely. Though she's overshadowed by the three dynamic leads, Julia gives a lovely performance. I'd forgotten how beautiful she was, with striking bright blue eyes, a big toothy smile, thick blond hair, and lightly freckled skin. Her performance was an auspicious beginning that sadly, but not untypically, went nowhere. When I met her three years after her big break, she was ensconced at the Chateau, waiting for her agent to call. Happens all the time. Show biz is particularly rough on young women. All actors are at risk, due to their generic narcissism, but when the phone stops ringing for an ingenue, some real internal damage can take place. Julia had clearly been wounded by her Hollywood experience. Her only other film, an obscure Jerry Orbach vehicle called *A Fan's Notes*, based on the Frederick Exley novel, also came out in 1972. She went to Cannes that year. After that, she apparently never worked again. Around the pool she spoke of packing it all in and heading back home to Twin Falls, Idaho. She died in an apartment fire in Eugene, Oregon, in 1975. It was a sad, gruesome, and awful ending, though at least Julia, unlike Peg Entwistle, managed to get out of town alive.

I am a full-fledged grown-up adult,
Trying to make a dent, I'm trying to get a result.
Holed up in a Hollywood hotel suite—
Tequila to drink and avocado to eat.

When I was ten years old I was alive
In the Benedict Canyon on Hutton Drive.
Now I'm right back in my old backyard,
Trying to get a billboard on the boulevard.

I never thought I'd see so many TV stars,
I never thought I'd see so many rented cars.
Never thought I'd see so many desperate eyes,
Never thought I'd hear so many bold-faced lies.

All kinds of victories, lots of downfalls.
Drugs in the rugs and ghosts in the walls.
Starlets in the lobby that can make a man drool,
Blood on the curtains and a phone by the pool.

I never thought I'd see the age of twenty-five.
It's twenty-nine years now I've been alive.
The panic I feel can hardly be told—
In a matter of months I'll be thirty years old.

—"HOLLYWOOD HOPEFUL," 1976

LIFE

THE
VIEW
FROM
HERE

Loudon Wainwright

25.

a vulgar tribute to greatness

An excerpt, October 1, 1965

Gift-wise, it was some affair. Many of the presents for Mickey Mantle were stacked on baggage carts near Yankee Stadium's second base, but the motorbike was driven out from the bull-pen. The outboard engine arrived late in the program without its matching boat, and the two horses pawed the dust near the third base coaching box. The big shiny car was parked at home plate. Of course there were things one couldn't see at all, like the year's supply of free gasoline for the car, the round-trip tickets to Nassau, Puerto Rico and Rome and the paid-up college educations for the four Mantle boys. But Mrs. Mantle's dark mink coat was visible, all right, when she tried it on, and it was easy enough to imagine that inside all those boxes on the carts were wristwatches, golf clubs, a rifle, clothing, a year's supply of sneakers for the whole family and— somewhere in the pile—a six-foot, 100-pound salami in the shape of a baseball bat. Thus was any real value of Mickey Mantle Day, any sincere tribute to one of the finest athletes of his time, all but buried in the gaudy display of loot.

How absurdly vulgar we can be. Over the years, as befits his great talent and courage, Mickey Mantle has been rewarded in cash money in amounts that surely make it possible for him to buy goods he doesn't even need. Yet to the man who already has almost everything we proudly present a year's supply of coffee, enough slacks to pant a platoon and something called a custom rug. To the man who has been such a splendid crowd-pleaser that more than 50,000 people will turn out to honor him near the end of a dismal season for both him and his team we gratefully offer free parking at a well-known chain of lots and a year's supply of bubble gum. Most of the presents were positively staggering in their inappropriateness—enough to dissolve the lump in a man's throat.

But in some important ways Mantle Day was not a garish bust. Even the vulgarity of the program could not really dampen the enthusiasm the fans felt for Mantle. The applause at several moments—when he first appeared, when he spoke, when he came to bat in the game following the ceremony, when he was replaced in the late innings—fractured the air with its intensity and made my eyes water at the very sound of it. The warmth and honesty of that noise was far greater than I've ever heard in a concert hall or a convention, and Mantle looked stunned at it himself. At one point he stood at his position in left field and looked up at the great crowd in the stadium around him. Then he seemed to be reading the signs hanging from the railings around the park. "There Will Never Be Another Mick," "Mickey, Most Valuable Player Ever," "We Love Ya, Mickey," they read in big homemade, homely scrawls, and he appeared so absorbed in them that I wanted to shout out at him that there was a ball game going on.

Some other nice things happened, too. Between innings, Mantle passed some of his presents along to fans whose seat numbers were drawn at random. When Mantle came up for the first time, the opposing pitcher, a Detroit Tiger named Joe Sparma, suddenly walked off the mound, strode to the plate and shook Mantle's hand. It was exactly the right thing to do and apparently it undid Mantle, for he hit an easy fly to the outfield. And Mantle's own speech was moving and straight. "A lot has been written," Mantle began, blond and still boyish-looking in front of the microphone, "about the pain that I've played with. When one of you fans says, 'Hi, Mick, how ya doin'? How's the leg?' it makes it all worth it." He swallowed and waited for the clapping to stop. "I just wish I had 15 more years to play here," he said then, and there it was, what he really wanted, the unattainable, impossible gift for the man who has everything.

26.
going for the laugh

'm heading up to do a show in Rochester, New York, today, so naturally I thought of my college classmate Tony McKay doing the following Jack Benny bit in the Malt Shoppe a half century ago.

> JACK BENNY: Rochester . . . I thought I told you to clean out
> the garage.
> ROCHESTER: I did, Mr. Benny.
> JACK BENNY: Well then . . . What's that big pile . . . of junk
> doing in the middle of the floor?
> ROCHESTER: That's no pile of junk, Mr. Benny . . . that's
> your car!

Tony does a slow JB take, fixing us with a slightly startled, pained
look on his face. His left hand ascends to the chin and rests there,
supported at the elbow by the right hand. Long beat.

Shit, it was funny.

When I was a kid I saw stand-up and sit-down comedians on TV, usually when they appeared on *The Ed Sullivan Show*. Then I'd go out and buy their albums, and at home I would play the records over and over again. *Inside Shelley Berman, Stan Freberg Presents the United States of America, The Wonderful World of Jonathan Winters*, and *The Button-Down Mind of Bob Newhart*. As a fourteen-year-old class clown/show-off, I memorized the routines on these comedy records, and performed them, first for myself in front of a mirror and then for my friends at school. I was pretty good at making people, well . . . kids, laugh. I was also aware of the so-called sick comedians of that time, the edgy mavericks Lenny Bruce, Mort Sahl, and Dick Gregory, but somehow they seemed too dangerously original to be mimicked. I suppose I wasn't quite up to speed yet on the subjects of sex, drugs, and politics. Or I was just drawn to imitating the sillier guys. Most of the comedy albums I was obsessed with were recorded live in nightclubs, and the hysterical, happy, somewhat drunken audience laughter was what got me hooked; grown-ups laughing their asses off, people in their twenties and early thirties who seemed completely transported by what the performers were doing. In real life, people in their twenties and early thirties intimidated me, I suppose because they were almost as old as my parents were. To a fourteen-year-old, someone who was, say, twenty-six seemed ancient. My dad, except when he was slightly bagged, was a rather button-downed fellow, and soon, upon reaching the stage of obnoxious teenage rebellion, I would be calling him out for being uptight. But witnessing him laugh and let go was a joyful experience for me. I couldn't help but love him when his defenses were down like that, when a Jonathan Winters routine or a Victor Borge song cracked him up and reduced him to tears. Maybe that's one of the main reasons I go for the laugh in my shows: to release the tensions the paying customers have brought with them into the room. But I'm not being selfless, because amusing people provides instant gratification for the performer as well as the audience. When three hundred or three thousand people all laugh at precisely the same moment, their validation and approval of you is immediate. In my live show, I like to mix it up by alternating between the serious and the funny. I work at unsettling the audience to a degree, to get them off guard so they're not sure what comes next—whether they'll be laughing, squirming, or maybe even crying. I also maintain that some comedians make especially interesting actors. Barry Humphries actually becomes the Melbourne housewife diva Dame Edna Everage on one night, and the next he can transform himself into his grotesque creation, the Australian cultural attaché Sir Les Patterson, who is the polar opposite. When Richard Pryor did his heart attack sketch and actually portrayed his own artery-hardened heart, you were overcome with horrified laughter at the realism of it, what they used to call in acting class the believability of it.

LW and Barry Humphries as Jerome and Claire in *Ally McBeal*.

Some of my fans and followers have expressed a preference for my more serious, sensitive material, songs like "The Picture," "Your Mother and I," and "A Father and a Son." Others like the novelty songs—"The Shit Song," "The Acid Song," and "IWIWAL (I Wish I Was a Lesbian)." A bit of a hue and cry went up from the serious camp in 1972 when "Dead Skunk" became a hit, and I found myself having to defend my novelty song to some journalists and fans who seemed to expect me to apologize for it. Someone is always going to not like what you do. But as Bette Midler used to say, "Fuck 'em if they can't take a joke." Or was that Sophie Tucker?

Like everybody, I want to be loved, but I also don't always want to just please my audience. Sometimes I like to piss them off a bit, push the proverbial envelope. In my early song "Motel Blues," which is about being lonely on the road, the protagonist sings, "When you kissed me in the club, you bit my tongue" and later on begs the girl to "Come up to my motel room, save my life." The idea that a guy would write a song about getting laid, and joke about it, was provocative in 1971, and on one occasion back then, during a live radio interview, I was threatened with castration by a feminist DJ. These days, of course, I, like everyone else, am at risk of being lynched by a Twitter mob. On my 1974 album *Attempted Mustache*, I included a live version of "I Am the Way,"* which was a parody of Woody Guthrie's

---

* Robbie Williams certainly liked "I Am the Way," so much so that in 1998 he essentially lifted my line "Every son of God gets a little hard luck sometime, especially when he goes around saying he's the way" and put it in his song "Jesus in a Camper Van." My song was a parody of Woody's, so Guthrie's company, Ludlow Music, owned the publishing on "I Am the Way" and they sued Williams. The trial got quite a bit of publicity, some of it not so great. I was characterized in the press by Robbie's legal team as an obscure, washed-up, one-hit wonder. In the end, though, Ludlow won the case and received 25 percent of the royalties "Jesus in a Camper Van" garnered. I was hoping for a taste, but got zilch.

"New York Town." The song includes the offending lines "I can walk on the water and I can raise the dead" and "Don't tell nobody but I kissed Magdalene," and it was a showstopper. Many, if not most, people dug its irreverence, even to the point of singing along with me on the last chorus. But some Christians, particularly of the born-again variety, were not so enthusiastic. I was not threatened with castration per se, but I was told on several occasions that my eternal soul would burn in hell. I guess we'll just have to see about that.

27.
the blues

I t's all there in a 1938 Donald Duck cartoon called *Donald's Better
Self.* First Donald's alarm clock goes off. It's time for him to get up
and go to school. He pulls the covers over his head, determined to keep
sleeping, but his identical Better Self—an angel with halo and wings—
magically appears and, in a controlled and loving way, urges him to
rise and shine. Suddenly the horned, pitchfork-toting devil version of
Donald shows up. "Hey, don't be a sap," Bad Self sneers. "Let's go back
to sleep." The psychic tug-of-war depicted in this cartoon has been
going on in me for as long as I can remember. I hear a positive voice in
my head that says, "You're fine. It will work out. Things are good."
Then I get the negative counterargument: "You're a piece of shit. You
don't stand a chance. Everything sucks." At the end of *Donald's Better
Self,* the somewhat annoying angel prevails and literally kicks the
kind-of-cool devil in the ass. If only it were that way in real life.

I've had the blues for about sixty years now, and I expect I'll continue having them until the day I die. Feeling down is a natural and familiar state for me, and most of the time I seem to operate on or about half-empty. When I wake up, doubt, pessimism, anxiety, and self-recrimination often kick right in, and throughout the day I spend a lot of energy fending off my own negative feelings. When I experience a moment of real happiness I'm struck by how unusual it feels. Suddenly I'm a different and, it would seem, much better person. How the hell did that happen? Surely it can't last. And it doesn't. Pretty soon I'm back to the way I usually feel, which is not so great.

My depression, which I hasten to characterize as mild to middling, as opposed to crippling or severe, is chronicled throughout my oeuvre. There are enough songs about being down for an entire album: "Motel Blues," "Muse Blues," "California Prison Blues," "Golfin' Blues," "Pen Pal Blues," "Vampire Blues," "The Krugman Blues," "Ghost Blues," "Depression Blues," and "Suicide Blues." Then there are songs that get into the specifics: "What Are Families For?," "Therapy," and "I Can't Stand Myself."

We both tried, nobody died, but I feel damn near dead
I miss you, but I'm really blue, 'cause I'm back with me instead
I can't stand myself

—"I Can't Stand Myself," 1997

It could be said (and certainly has been by ex-wives and other authority figures) that I've embraced and even nurtured my depressive feelings, and I suppose I buy the theory that artistic creativity springs from neurotic suffering. But which would you rather listen to on a desert island, "Sugar, Sugar" or "Just Like Tom Thumb's Blues"?

With the exception of a particularly hard tumble I took when my mother died in 1997, my depression has been manageable. I've never been unable to get out of bed because of it, although the need to go back there recurs with some regularity. At present I am not taking any medication, unless you count the two glasses of wine I drink every night. Although I never cop to it when I'm filling out a form in a doctor's office, these days I smoke a single cigarette upon retiring, in order, I tell myself, to gather and contain my thoughts and emotions about the tumults and agitations that have taken place that day, and the ones that await me on the morrow. But instead of deriving any relief or satisfaction from my relatively harmless nightly fix, I beat myself up about it as I stub the butt out in the ashtray. Smoking is something I'm not supposed to do. I'm misbehaving. I'm "bad Loudie." On occasion the Good Self and the Bad Self team up for a duet about my being bad Loudie. That's a real drag.

When things get unmanageable I check in with my therapist. I pay him money to remind me that I'm not a bad person. You'd think I would know that by now, and I do, really, but I keep forgetting. My shrink has my backstory, and so for forty-five minutes he and I talk about how I'm feeling by delving into the rocky psychic terrain of my past.

SHRINK RAP

So I go to the shrink and the shrink says to me
"So what's going on?" so I tell him, You see
I bitch about this one, and that one, and her
I moan and I groan and I slag off and slur
My children don't love me, my parents are Gods
He's heard this before, he sits there and nods
Friends and family aren't friendly, they treat me like shit

In England they'd say that I go on a bit
A bit's less than an hour, I'm advised to detach
"Festering itches, so try not to scratch"
I get what I came for, which was my money's worth
And the books in his bookcase laugh at us both
So I go every week, does this stuff really work?
In the waiting room on deck sits another poor jerk
I check out the Van Gogh on the waiting room wall
The print by that lunatic laughs at us all
His pipe and his chair laugh at us all

The most important people in my life—the principal players, if you will—are members of my family. To a degree, it's important to escape them in order to achieve some autonomy in the world, but the reality is that you never quite get away from your "loved ones." I'm often asked why I've written so many songs about the people in my family. The answer is: How could I not? They are the ones who have meant the most in my life, and they continue to have a hold on me, even those who have died. Especially those who have died. So I write a song about competing with a father ("Surviving Twin") or having uneasy Oedipal issues about a mother ("White Winos"). Nothing is solved or fixed, but I've got a song to sing that's about something that weighs on my mind. And possibly something that weighs on yours, as well.

I've written so many songs about you
This is the last one, after this I'm through
It's taken so long to finally see
My songs about you are all about me

—"So Many Songs," 1992

I've used therapy, jogging, aikido, macrobiotics, and yoga at different times in my life to beat back the blues and stay out of the barroom. You need to shut up that little prick Bad Self that's constantly mouthing off about how worthless you are. But having the blues has also provided me with subject matter and a modus operandi, singing about feeling like shit. And let's not forget the E, A, B7 blues chord progression I use over and over when I'm moaning, groaning, and venting in song. Where would I be without the blues? Someplace better maybe, but not of this world.

Mother liked her white wine when she was alive
And she was desperate to live and her limit was five
Carefully I kissed her and sent her off to bed
We always stuck to white wine, we stayed away from red

Mother liked her white wine, she'd have a glass or two
Almost every single night after her day was through
Sancerre, Chardonnay, Chablis, Pinot Grigio
Just to take the edge off, just to get the glow
You've got to take the edge off if you want to get . . .

Mother liked her white wine, she'd have a glass or three
And we'd sit out on the screen porch, white winos Mom and me
We'd talk about her childhood and recap my career
When we got to my father, that's when I'd switch to beer
We got to the old man and I'd always switch . . .

Mother liked her white wine, she'd have a glass or four
Each empty bottle a dead soldier, the marriage was the war
When we blurred the edges, when we drank a lot

That's when I got nervous, when the glow got hot
I always get nervous when the glow gets . . .

I still like my white wine and I'll have a glass or two
When I'm down I'll drink some whiskey, it's something I shouldn't do
And every now and then I'll take a drop of red
When I'm with a woman I want to take to bed
When I'm with a woman that I want to take . . .

Mother liked her white wine when she was alive
She was desperate to live and her limit was five
Carefully I'd kiss her and send her off to bed
Thank God we stuck to white wine and stayed away from . . .
Mother liked her white wine

—"White Winos," 2001

28.
another sort of love story

1971

Right in the middle of a long New Year's weekend full of bright weather on lovely snow and a numbing succession of televised quarterbacks, our dog died. Or to put it absolutely straight, after a family agreement rare in its unanimity, we had his life stopped by a veterinarian who agreed it was the right thing to do for such a painfully and fatally ill animal. His name was John Henry, but I'm not sure why we'd called him that.

I don't think I have ever been more sharply aware of the fine line between here and gone than I was near the end when I held him close on the vet's table. The kind doctor, her eyes floating in tears because she knew him and us, pumped something bluish into his leg, and with the calm, open-eyed patience that characterized so much of his style, he waited that briefest moment until it struck his center and killed him. A couple of polite gasps and it was over.

Slightly undone by my sentiment and for some wild reason remembering not Lassie but *Love Story* and the astounding communicative success of Erich Segal, I will risk a version of his opening question: what can you say about an 11½-year-old dog that died? That he was at least as beautiful as Ali MacGraw. And dumber. And a messier eater. That he ran shining and marvelously fast through fields and rolled snorting in snow and floated a burnt-auburn blur over stone walls. That he didn't much mind Mozart and Bach but that violin solos and harmonicas made him howl. That he could destroy six glasses with one sweep of his tail. That, when I would ask him how he ranked me among the people he liked, he would thump his tail against the floor and grin, occasionally punctuating that with a noise that became a smell. But he was half Irish setter and half golden retriever, and his manners were predictably imperfect.

There was a totally nonhuman quality in his loving. Virtually everyone was a suitable target for his affection, and unlike your one-man brute who will slobber over his master's hand and then dismember the neighbor's child, he menaced nothing, including the rabbits he chased and never got and the skunks who always got him.

Not that he was indiscriminating. He was not a tramp, and he did not follow strangers. He was a wide-ranging country dog, but his daily investigations most always brought him home at night. He liked to sleep on rugs, usually where it was convenient to stumble over him. He liked to ride in cars. Best, he liked to be invited along on walks, and he worked like a roving scout around the walker—in front, behind, alongside, often at a dead run a good distance away—and when he rested in winter during one of these wonderful dashes in all directions, he would break ice in a stream to cool his belly and his tongue.

Although he was forced to live with a succession of cats, I don't think he liked them at all. Yet in most moods but joy he was a model of understatement. The weary and wary tolerance he displayed at the cats' rude spitting or at their hit-and-run assaults from ambush beneath a chair was the closest he came to expressing real distaste.

Obviously our knowledge is limited about his relationships with other dogs. He probably had wet down bark or bush with every dog within a radius of three miles, but he didn't seem to care much for groups, preferring instead to run alone or with just one other at a time. He was alert and forward but not aggressive, and though his hair bristled splendidly, and he growled well when challenged, he had a distinct aptitude for avoiding fights and could walk away from one with a casualness that implied it wouldn't be worth his trouble. In his late years he was treated roughly by a much younger and stronger dog down the road, but he accepted this indignity in a way that wasn't cowardly, as if it were somehow in the normal order of things that the puppy he had earlier taught to play was now bouncing him around quite badly. Even when he was very feeble and old, he always trotted out to defend his home station.

I hope he had a full and happy sex life, but I only know of one affair; it was arranged and he fathered a litter from it. His partner in this matter was a female dog from a household of good friends. She, too, was sweet and easygoing and she looked more or less as if she came from a similarly mixed background. We tell a story about this match and I am no longer sure whether it is entirely true. The story goes that, oblivious of approaching delight, he was taken by car to the vet's for one supervised meeting. The vet said afterwards that he felt certain everything had gone well, but perhaps for insurance the two should be brought together again the next day. So the next day our dog was put in the car and driven to his appointment, which was once more declared a success. The affair was pronounced consummated—and closed. The dog came home. The following morning he was found ready in the car, presumably awaiting another trip and another meeting.

Unlike Segal's doomed creature, this one wasn't perfect. Now and then his taste in food would turn to garbage and he upset many cans in search of the ripest morsels. He dug holes in lawns and he liked to sprawl on young plants. He was a discoverer of mud. When he found something—often invisible and even nonexistent—to bark at, he barked hard and he utterly ignored commands to stop it and come the hell home. I am proud of one area of his ignorance. He knew no tricks at all, unless you count a sort of half-baked paw shake he employed as a last effort in his perpetual and undiscouraged search for affection.

In his last days he had great difficulty getting up; he tottered weakly on three legs and was dreadfully thin. The pain, even muffled with pills, was leaving him stupid with exhaustion, and it became clear past all reluctance that what he needed most was a push out of life. Briefly I had the conventional and outlandish thought of doing it myself, and so did one of my sons, who likely loved the dog the most. Then, with her potion that hit with such shocking and merciful speed, the doctor ended our nonsense.

That night I dreamed that my son kept calling him. The boy had a way of calling that dog. I woke. Life gets to be a series of dogs, I thought, and I ticked off those I could remember. Ghosts in the house suddenly. Old dogs. When I slept and woke again, it was cold half-light and I was almost sure I heard the dog's toenails against the hall floor and his single discreet bark to go outside. I won't live with a lot more dogs and I won't live with another dog like him.

29.

grammy chronicles

Last night I dreamed that I won a Grammy.
It was presented to me by Debbie Harry.
I ran up onstage in my tux,
I gulped and I said, "Aw shucks,
I'd like to thank my producer and Jesus Christ."

These lyrics are from "The Grammy Song," which appeared on my ninth album, 1983's *Fame and Wealth*. I'd been bouncing around in the music business for fourteen years and had experienced both success and failure, or as they used to say on ABC's *Wide World of Sports*, "The thrill of victory and the agony of defeat." At that time, it seemed highly unlikely to me that I'd ever win a Grammy Award, and for years I watched others on TV bounding up onstage to collect their little statuettes—people and groups who struck me as being from an entirely different planet than I was. Paul Simon, Stevie Wonder, Fleetwood Mac, and the like were stars in the music business, whereas I was merely a puny asteroid relegated to the far periphery of the rock and roll galaxy. Perhaps you sense some mockery

or pseudo-self-deprecation in my tone? You need to be contemptuous
of the people you envy.

The audience gave me a standing ovation.
I shed tears of joy, I shed tears of elation.
Behind the podium there,
Debbie grabbed my derriere.
I'd like to thank my producer and Jesus Christ.

Then, wonder of wonders, in 1986 they created a Grammy category called Best Contemporary Folk Album and I was nominated for
my record *I'm Alright.* I rented a tuxedo and bought two round-trip
plane tickets to the ceremony in L.A., which was held at the Shrine
Auditorium. Suzzy was my date, and we were both pretty excited.
The dinner and party for all the nominees at the Biltmore Hotel the
night before the ceremony was the best part of the adventure. At that
point everyone was equal—we were all prospective winners. Because
of the TV schedule and the time difference on the West Coast, Suzzy
and I were in our seats at the Shrine early the next afternoon. Way
early, because the Best Contemporary Folk Album award was presented a few hours before the telecast even began. The new category
was pretty low on the Grammy totem pole, number fifty-one or two-
ish, right after Best Polka Record. Suz and I were up in the nosebleed
seats, looking down on the assembled wattage in the first few rows—
Peter Gabriel, Steve Winwood, and a particularly super-tensed-up
wannabe winner Paul Simon. I admit I, too, was pretty nervous. And
the Best Contemporary Folk Album winner was . . . Steve Goodman!
Shit! Oh well, he deserved it, and he also was a friend of mine. There
was an important extenuating circumstance, too. Goodman had died
in 1984, way too early, at thirty-six, and the Grammy-winning record

was a tribute album featuring other artists doing Steve's songs. It was a beautiful thing for his widow, Nancy, and their three daughters that Steve should win that afternoon. The next day, Suz and I flew back to New York, chastened but in no way devastated. After all, I'd been nominated.

I took my Grammy and Debbie and I walked off stage.
We made the cover of Cash Box *and the "Random Notes" page.*

A few years later I put out another album called *More Love Songs*, and amazingly I was nominated again. The ceremony was held in New York City that year, at Radio City Music Hall, so at least I didn't have to spring for plane tickets. My sister Teddy, who was also my manager at the time, was my date. We both figured I was a shoo-in. *More Love Songs* was a great record, and I'd been nominated two times in a row, so it had to be my year. But there was a dark horse in the pack. Or should I say a dead horse? Yes, another posthumous Steve Goodman record was nominated and in the running, a record ominously titled *Unfinished Business*. Folks, they gave the Grammy to the dead guy *twice*!! This time there was not a scintilla of charity in my heart for the dearly departed Steve. He was dead but I was pissed.

In the weeks that followed things went fine for me,
An Oscar, a Tony, and an Emmy.
Bo Derek and Barbara Mandrell,
Meryl Streep and Tammi Terrell.
A Pulitzer and a Nobel,
Joan Rivers and Lana Cantrell.

Five gold and one bronze as well.

And I'd like to thank my producer and Jesus Christ.

—"The Grammy Song," 1982

There is a kind of happy ending/postscript to my tale. In 2010, my album *High Wide & Handsome* was nominated for a Grammy in a category called Best Traditional Folk Album. The ceremony was held back in L.A. I flew out there with my wife, Rita, and my producer, Dick Connette, and that afternoon I finally walked off with the hardware. The victory felt especially sweet because not only had it been a long and torturous journey to get the Grammy, but one of the other nominees in the category was my old Saratoga Springs buddy Bruce "Utah" Phillips. Bruce had died in 2008, and his nominated record was a tribute album. It sounds churlish and awful, I know, but I finally beat the dead guy.

Me and the hardware.

30.

me & clive & david

I dreamed about Clive Davis last night. He and I were in a nightclub, sitting on a couch, talking to each other. By that I mean he was holding forth about something having to do with the all-important business of selling records. In the dream I was paying close attention, but was still completely unable to make heads or tails of what Clive was saying. As always, he was tanned within an inch of his life, but oddly he was also wearing sandals and had a strange little handheld device that served as some sort of a fan or lubricator. Every so often he would bend down and give his protruding toes a spritz or blast of whatever was in the thing. Then a tall surly man came over to the couch and began interrupting, trying to horn in on our conversation. I wanted Clive's attention all to myself, and after a few warnings I turned on the interloper and began to beat him up. I was really just showing off, and Clive seemed to know it. He was only slightly impressed.

After all this time, it surprises me that the music mogul still has a secure place in my unconscious mind.

In 1972, Clive flew me, my manager Milt Kramer, and my then backup band White Cloud to London to perform at the Columbia Records convention. I had just made *Album III*, and Clive's plan was to get the sales, marketing, and radio promotion troops psyched up about my first album on the label. Everyone was put up at the Grosvenor House near Hyde Park. I don't recall much about the show I did with the band. I think it was okay, though not particularly great. What I do remember was being in the lobby bar of the hotel very late at night with a bunch of others, watching the legendary Cleveland promotion man Steve Popovich go at it with the great singer Harry Nilsson. They were playing a kind of quiz game. Someone would call out the name of a hit record from the 1950s or '60s and Harry and Steve would each try to be the first to shout out the name—not of the recording artist or band (that would have been way too easy), but of the writer or writers of the proffered song. Some of the songwriters, because of their careers as performers and recording artists, were well-known, like Goffin and King, Neil Sedaka, and Doc Pomus, but others were more obscure, guys like Baker Knight, the composer of Ricky Nelson's hit "Lonesome Town" and Mickey Gilley's "Don't the Girls All Get Prettier at Closing Time." Popovich and Nilsson were clearly enjoying putting on a show for all of us that night, displaying their wide and deep grasp of what some might consider mere trivia. To them, however, it was anything but trivial. They proudly considered their detailed and arcane knowledge to be of the utmost importance.

Music biz boy wonder and mogul-in-the-making David Geffen was at the London convention that summer because he managed Laura Nyro, one of Columbia's most important new artists. Geffen was also in the beginning stages of starting his own custom label for Warner Bros., Asylum Records, and at one point that weekend he cornered me at the after-hours club the Speakeasy, where lots of us conventioneers were hanging out. David spent some time in a quiet booth trying to convince me that I should jump ship and leave Columbia. He insisted that a small hip label like Asylum would be a much better fit for an artist like me. I carefully pointed out that I was signed to Columbia for a three-record deal, but Geffen implied that there were ways to get out of such contracts. Flattered by his praise and attention, I nonetheless respectfully demurred, and I told him my plan was to stay put. The next morning I had a breakfast meeting with Clive up in his suite at the Grosvenor House to discuss strategy for my soon-to-be-released album. I rang the doorbell and who should come to the door to let me in but my new pal David. He flashed me a nervous but impish smile and raised his forefinger to his lips, giving me the "Mum's the word" sign. It was all part of the game these guys played.

I made three albums for Columbia, and then, due to poor sales and no hit song, the label dropped me in 1976. Clive himself had been given the heave-ho by the boys at Black Rock* after it was alleged that a sizable chunk of the parent company's money had been appropriated by the label president to pay for his son's bar mitzvah. Davis didn't stay down for long, though, and a year later he started his own label, Arista. He was kind enough to sign me up for a two-record deal. Unfortunately, both of the records I made for Arista—*T Shirt* and *Final Exam*—were critical and commercial flops. In 1978, I was touring in support of *Final Exam* with Slow Train, a country-rock

---

* "Black Rock," aka the CBS Building at 51 West Fifty-second Street in New York City.

band that was comprised of White Cloud's drummer Richard Crooks, a Brooklyn piano player named Steve Tubin, and a trio of Oklahoma musicians—John Crowder, Ron Getman, and Glenn Mitchell, who everybody cheerfully called Sperm. The guys from Tulsa had played in a high school band together and the drummer in that outfit was Gary Busey. Clive and Arista had promised us six weeks of tour support, hotels, and expenses for us six musicians, plus one roadie and a tour manager. After just a few gigs, the tour support was pulled. I spoke to Clive in New York from Chicago when we got the bad news and asked him why he had reneged on the promise of support. His explanation to me was one befitting a successful CEO: "That was then and this is now."

I'm mentioned in a nice way in both of Clive Davis's memoirs. There's a picture in the first book of the two of us together, happy and smiling and ready to conquer the world. That, of course, didn't happen, and I always assumed I had faded from Davis's consciousness, squeezed out and replaced by others he had shepherded to stardom and tangible success, the likes of Barry Manilow, Janis Joplin, Carlos Santana, and Whitney Houston. In 2010, I was at the Grammy Awards for my record *High Wide & Handsome*, and at one point, I spotted Clive with his entourage, waiting to be seated. A scared part of me wanted to slink away, but, having just been pronounced a winner, a bolder feeling asserted itself. I walked over and addressed him: "Hi, Clive, do you remember me? It's Loudon Wainwright." "Why, of course I do," he said, and then proceeded to give me a hug and ask how I was. I blurted out, "I just won a Grammy!" He seemed genuinely pleased and hugged me again. It felt like a full-circle moment, kind of beautiful, albeit somewhat pathetic. If only Geffen had been there.

31.
sibs

Watching my grandsons go at it is a spectator sport unlike any other. It takes me back, first to when my kids were little, and then all the way back to my own childhood with my brother and sisters. Arc and Francis are seven and three now. On the couch, lying against and all over each other, they are mesmerized yet again by the story of *Harold and the Purple Crayon*, staring at a video they've seen scores of times but can never get enough of. In childhood, a four-year age difference is an eternity, but these two could be twins, they seem so connected. Later, at play, they're brothers-in-arms, a pirate wrecking crew, armed with sticks and broom handles as swords, and I pray for the safety of my expensive new porch screens. We go outside, and in the shed come across a toy scooter from last year that, to them, quickly becomes something worth fighting over. I'm shocked by the ferociousness of the ensuing struggle for possession, and if I wasn't there to separate them, these combatants just might kill each other. As a distraction I instigate a game of netless badminton. They whack away at soft-pitched shuttlecocks, kind of a kid Keystone Kop version of Antonioni's mock tennis match at the end of *Blow-Up*. After dinner and the good-night stories and songs, they are at peace again, pals and bedfellows, and lying there they morph into an entity that's plural. They are "the boys."

The boys.

I realize just how out of practice I am as I barely manage to help their mother, Martha, out a bit with the lifting, comforting, scraping, refereeing, and wiping. I know I must make sacrifices, and so I surrender to squirming, slippery, naked Francis, who, right now, would rather I *not* watch Judy Woodruff on *NewsHour* but instead focus on tickling him. After dinner, Arc and I slip off to the local ice-cream shop, where I turn my grandson on to my favorite flavor, mint chocolate chip. Initially he's generous and cautiously lets me have a lick or two of his cone, until I fill him with alarm by pretending I'm about take a huge bite and gobble the whole thing up, cone and all. When he laughs at my joke, I realize I haven't had this much fun in a long time.

A while back, there was a memorial service on Shelter Island for my brother Andy's wife, Alice, so my sister Teddy flew up from Florida, and Sloan made the commute from Brewster, New York. My siblings and I are all in show business, in one way or another. Sloan is a singer, songwriter, and voice teacher, Teddy is a personal manager, and Andy is a professional Santa Claus. We four* are still close, and when we reunite it's a powerful and, at times, unsettling experience. Our parents long gone, we have been orphans for years. Our kids have all grown up, with the exception of Teddy's only son, Jack, who tragically died in 2005 at the age of eighteen. We have experienced and survived divorce, the death of a spouse or a child, bankruptcy, addiction, cancer, and joint replacement. We've all been through the mill, and it shows. The sibling pecking order has pretty much stayed the same, and resentments, guilt, and regrets have remained in place for entire lifetimes. But we hug and kiss one another when we meet, and, when we are apart, and we remember, we call to check in.

My father was an only child, so he never had a sibling experience, but my mother had three sisters, her twin, Mary, living the longest, lasting into her nineties. My mom's daring move, in 1945, to marry an educated Yankee WASP and live up north separated her from her pack, and I had little contact with our southern aunts growing up. A few years ago, after my mother died, I paid a visit to my

---

* Our half sister, Anna Wainwright, who also attended the memorial, took a pass and stayed the hell out of show biz. In 2017 she got her doctorate in Italian Renaissance studies and has embarked on an academic career.

Martha and Mary in 1944.

Aunt Mary in Norfolk, Virginia. As I was turning into her driveway in my rental car, she emerged from her house to meet me. I hadn't seen her in more than twenty years, but her carriage and demeanor—her vibe, if you will—shook me. She was my mother incarnate. Her voice, laced with its south Georgia accent, was my mother's. The smell and resiliency of her body when I hugged her was my mother's. The look of her hands, right down to the cuticles on her fingers, was my mother's. Both sisters were made from the same stuff. It was as if my mother had paid me a visit from the beyond.

In the guest bedroom of my house there's a framed picture of a reunion of the Taylor family, my mother's people. On the back of the frame, *Asburn, GA November 28th 1929* is written in pencil. Although their faces look distinctly different in the picture, seven-year-old Mary and Martha are dressed identically, right down to their knee socks. They sit side by side, cross-legged on the far left of the first row. They lean slightly in toward each other as if magnetically pulled, and because they are wearing the same black jackets they appear to be attached at the shoulder. I look at my mother's serene smiling face and I see all of us—Arc and Francis, my siblings, my kids, and, most strikingly, my nephew, Teddy's dearly departed Jack.

32.

OZ

In 1982 I toured Australia for the first time, and part of the deal was plane tickets and hotels for two, so I invited my father to come along. He'd quit drinking a few years back, was in a solid relationship with Martha Fay, and was soon to be a father again at the age of fifty-seven. I hadn't quit drinking, was a new dad (second family), and was in a relationship that was beginning to unravel. My dad and I had a good time together on this two-week jaunt down under, and he wrote about it in his April 1982 *Life* column "Oh, To Be in Melbourne at Moomba": *The best part of the trip was the company I kept. We traveled well together, my son and I. We gave each other plenty of room. We talked about things we hadn't mentioned in years. Our down periods never coincided. We were happy with the same food and laughed hard at the same jokes. We didn't mind our differences. And somewhat to my surprise I enjoyed being in his limelight. I hummed his tunes, his lyrics ran through my head. The story in the Adelaide paper marking his visit there was headlined: "Dad's in Loudon's baggage." So I was. We were* not so much father and son on the trip as just two guys with a long history, out for some fun and hoping to enjoy each other's company. After my dad died, I read though his notes of the trip in little black notebooks he had written in. It confirmed what he said in the column—he really had enjoyed himself, and took real pleasure in watching me perform. There was some regret in these little black books, though. He had scribbled in one of them, "I Want a Double Lifetime." He wanted a do-over, another chance, three more wishes, the strength to lift the travel playpen in and out of the car one more time.

I want a double lifetime, I wanna start over
One lifetime's not enough, I need another
Sixty-five years on a practice run
Practice makes perfect, I'm about half done
I wanna double lifetime

I wanna double lifetime, I don't wanna snuff it
Three score and ten just ain't enough
It feels like I finally got it all figured out
Almost free from the shame and the doubt
I wanna double lifetime

A lot more time, that's what I need
I can make my move, I can do the deed
I know I'm greedy, but what do I care
For the afterlife, I don't wanna go there!

I wanna a double lifetime, man, I deserve it
I want it so bad, I even got the nerve
To get down on my bended knees

And beg and pray and say "pretty please"
Gimme a double lifetime
I wanna double lifetime, I wasted my first one

The first time around, that's always the worst one
You don't know what you're doin', and you just can't wait
So you go ahead and do it, and then it's too late
You need a double lifetime

I led a double lifetime in public and private
I wanna lead it again, I'm not gonna deny it
I'm just like you, it's true you know
Ask yourselves, are you ready to go?
No, you wanna double lifetime!

A little more time, 'cause you know I'd never
Wanna keep livin' forever and ever
I know it sounds funny if the truth be told
But 120 don't seem that old
I wanna double lifetime

I wanna double lifetime, probably not gonna get it
But if a miracle happens, you know I'm gonna let it
If I eat enough yogurt maybe I might
And the second time around I'm gonna get it right
Give me a double lifetime!

—"Double Lifetime," 2012

33.

the sum of recollection just keeps growing

1972

The word has come that an old friend died suddenly, and bits of recall about him keep breaking past the frail guard of work I set against them. As I look out the window, he pushes his glasses up over his forehead, his voice is on the other side of the phone's ring. Stared at upside down, a piece of handwriting on the desk could be his. Fragments of him play back like short bursts of mnemonic film, and I cannot look away.

Nothing in the tumble of images surprises me about him, and they show me how little I knew. It's hard to get to know a friend better. A lot of long relationships develop almost formal rhythms, and we learn to know each other's margins and bruising places. Conversations often ply between unsaid limits, and we respond to proffered cues with grooved fidelity. Exploring stops. New ground is left untouched while we glide comfortably along, turning over old stones, safe with rediscoveries.

Obviously we present clear variations of ourselves to different people. Our friend, another man recalled, had known a lot about the romantic poets and liked to talk about them. Not to me he didn't, and I had an absurd flash of wounded feelings, like a child who's been left out of a secret. But who can claim to know anyone? Indeed we are all the sum of others' recollections about us. The gathering of them goes on for a long time.

A few years ago I saw a collection of old home movies that my father had made in the mid-1930s. Since he had held the camera, he never appeared in the films, although his long afternoon shadow occasionally fell across the scenes he shot. But his presence, the way he thought about some things and how he felt were extraordinarily evident.

To make his movie during one bitter winter, he had walked out on the frozen bay near our house and shot a long piece of film looking back toward the land. What obviously interested him were the shapes the camera lingered on—great heaves of broken ice and pilings of docks wrenched into jagged angles against the sky. Watching, I was astonished at his selections. I had always thought of him as a completely direct man with no interest in abstractions of any kind. But here he was on film, working hard with the camera to find the right framing for the stark forms he saw. As it had been with my friend's love of poetry, this was a large insight into my father's being that I had missed completely.

The film showed me more than that about him. In another section he was photographing me as I skated near him. First I watched the movie with the fascination one usually feels when he looks at pictures of himself, especially pictures of a self in child's packaging. Delighted with my own gay awkwardness on ice, I suddenly had the sense that the camera was projecting a clear quality of love. The child fell, the camera lurched as its holder moved to help, then steadied when the boy rose smiling. The camera moved in for a close-up, then drew back and held as the child bent-ankled in one crude circle after another. Decades later the photographer's tenderness quite overwhelmed his subject.

Even if we're late, we can still reach out for fathers and old friends, and find good moments for ourselves in what they left behind.

Seated: Me with Lucy on my shoulders, Martha, and Dad.
Standing: Suzzy, Martha Fay, Anna, and Rufus.
Jack the dog is lying on the lawn. 1985.
Photograph by Steven H. Begleiter (begleiter.com)

34.
hospitals

A few years before my mother died, she went crazy. She'd been experiencing depression for some years, but then she suffered a series of small cerebral stokes that, we were told by a neurologist, pushed her into full-blown derangement. It was advised that she be hospitalized at New York–Presbyterian psychiatric hospital in White Plains. Built in 1894 and the second oldest freestanding psychiatric hospital in America, the place has a foreboding, Gothic feel about it. The first thing a visitor to Mom's ward experienced, after stepping out of the elevator, were the chilling shrieks and shouts coming from the patients on the other side of the securely locked door. My mother had completely withdrawn, to the point of not wanting anyone, including her own children, to see her. We were just authority figures now, coaxing and then eventually forcing her to communicate, eat, and bathe. She seemed in a rage at us, as if our wanting to help her was some kind of disobedient behavior. She was terrified of everything. Mom used to joke to us about winding up in the crazy house, what she called "the e-nee-i-nee." Then it happened to her. She didn't like us turning up, but each of our visits ended with a tearful, desperate plea for us to get her out of there and take her home. Our explanations as to why we couldn't felt like betrayals to her, and the emotions we experienced in the elevator ride back down to the lobby and on the walk out to the parking lot to freedom were guilt, sorrow, relief, and then more guilt.

After several months of jiggering with powerful antidepressant drugs, the doctors stumbled onto a combination that finally seemed to work, and Mom was discharged. She came home, diminished but calm, and no longer raging. A few years later, when we visited her at the Country House, a benign nursing home in Yorktown Heights, it was, comparatively speaking, a piece of cake.

With the exception of the maternity ward, hospitals are not known as places where happy things occur. During his three-year losing battle with colon cancer, my father had some serious surgeries at New York Hospital on East Sixty-eighth Street, and though the care provided for him was excellent, it wasn't much of a fun hang there. The visitor always feels like an intruder, a duty-bound, guilty alien from the world of the relatively healthy; the patient experiences the shame, anger, fear, and envy that goes with being infirm and temporarily banished from that world. During one of his stays at New York Hospital, Dad had a pretty lively roommate, a guy who was in for just a few days for a minor procedure, something along the lines of a hernia repair or a vasectomy. They shared a small room; the only privacy-affording barrier between them was a flimsy hanging nylon curtain. Usually you bitch about your hospital roommate—the loud, bad TV they watch day and night, the emptying of their bedpans and catheters, their disturbing moaning and groaning, the intensified snoring brought on by heavy-duty pain and sedation meds. And the other patient's stream of visitors can be a real pain in your hanging-out-for-all-the-world-to-see hospital-gowned ass. But one day Dad's roommate had quite an interesting guest. She appeared to be a nurse, although she was dressed in such a stylized fashion I immediately realized she had to be an imposter. The starched nurse's cap, precariously bobby-pinned to her hair, was way out of date, and the dress she had on, though white, was too tight and skimpy to allow for any practical movement other than a sashay. She had a toy-store stethoscope draped around her neck and was toting a portable boom box. To top it off, this not-so-young lady was wearing black fishnets and high heels. She was definitely not a real nurse. I was sitting in a chair next to my dad's bed in his half of the room, and we both got a good view of the shenanigans, vicariously experiencing our first Strip-O-Gram. It was pretty weird and ridiculous, and decidedly unsexy. The visiting "nurse" began with a spoken preamble in a Betty Boop voice:

> *This is for Joey, in bed he must lie.*
> *Our buddy Joey, one helluva guy.*
> *But a guy can get horny just lying there,*
> *So Nurse Susie will cure all Joe's tension and care.*

Then Nurse Susie pushed the play button on the boom box. David Rose's "The Stripper" blasted out, and Joey's special surprise did a series of bumps, grinds, and gyrations as she slowly wriggled out of her dress, ultimately revealing red tasseled pasties and a pair of frilly knickers with a matching garter belt. That was, mercifully, as far as it went. Susie seemed a little nervous, maybe because she hadn't expected two extra pairs of male prying eyes, and I guess Joey might have gotten more bang for his friends' bucks had my dad and I not been there. But Joey's buddies certainly knew what Joey got off on. He was grinning widely and flushed with happiness, absolutely delighted with his surprise. A few of the real nurses eavesdropped from a distance in the hallway and seemed to enjoy the show, too. I suppose that stripping and nursing are somewhat similar in that, to a degree, they both deal in a basic carnality and the alleviation of suffering.

On one of my last hospital visits to see my old man, I selfishly brought up an old bugaboo—the roman numeral issue. Just before my career began, we'd had a discussion about our name, that hefty WASP moniker—Loudon Snowden Wainwright. My father had strongly urged that I include the roman numeral III on my first album cover, so that any confusion about which Loudon was which might be avoided. He also felt that my grandmother Nanny would want her husband Loudon the first's memory to be preserved and honored. In the end, I agreed, and used my preppy and pretentious full legal name, with its roman numeral tag. Twenty years later, as Dad lay dying, hooked up to tubes, machines, and bags, I couldn't resist calling him out on something that had always bothered me. He had never professionally used his "Jr." His byline always had simply been "Loudon Wainwright." After I conveyed my grievance, he looked up at me from his bed, smiled weakly, and said, "When I'm dead you can have the name."

35.
nanny's ashes

The day before my father died in bed in his Upper West Side apartment, my sister Sloan and I arranged to have our grandmother, my dad's mother, interred in the Wainwright family plot out in East Hampton. Her cremated remains, literally her grounds, had been sitting in a Martinson's coffee can for three years on the shelf of my dad's hall closet, because he'd never gotten around to burying them, which is to say he just hadn't been able to bring himself to do it. Now that Dad was about to die, Sloan and I took it upon ourselves to put an end to this ridiculously Freudian procrastination. Like drug cartel mules, we transported the genetic contraband out to East Hampton via the Long Island Expressway and, with the help of our uncle Stuyvesant Wainwright II and a paid-off church warden, we managed to get what was left of Nanny put into the frozen hallowed ground, burying her alongside her long-gone husband, Loudon I. We mumbled a prayer, had a drink at Stuyvie's place, and then drove right back into the city. This wasn't the first time I'd filled in for my old man. A few years earlier, at my sister Teddy's wedding, I was called upon by my mother to formally introduce her, for the first time, to the attractive younger colleague for whom my father had left her. Dad, terrified, lurked somewhere at a safe distance. I still can't believe I agreed to stand in for him. This surrogacy was tough, and I resented it. You'll recall that my mother's name was Martha. My oldest daughter was named after her grandmother and my sister. And the name of my father's new love? Martha. So I said what I had to say, which was, "Mom, this is Martha Fay."

After the 1988 graveyard drop, Sloan and I got back to town and were able to report to my frail, fading father that his mother had been finally put to rest. He died later that night. The next morning I took a shower before heading back up to the apartment on West Eighty-second Street that my dad had shared with Martha Fay and Anna. I wasn't feeling terribly sad, certainly not distraught. His death was expected. In a way, what I felt was a sort of strange and powerful release—his? Mine? Ours? Then, standing there in the shower, I began to make a loud, very audible moaning sound. I suppose the downstairs neighbors might have concluded that I was having sex.

I've slumped in your chair
Tossed and turned in your bed
Lurked in your lair
I have lived in your head
Where others were closer
No one is nearer
As I glimpse you in me
In the hallway mirror

I've grabbed from the plate
And I've stabbed with a knife
On day one, my first date
I slept with your wife
My common-law stepmom
I desire and fear her
I compare you to me
In the full-length mirror

Sharing hair, forehead lines
Scowling, worrying, thinking
With a penchant for white wines
A disposal toward drinking
You had 'em, I got 'em
I move my face nearer
Broken blood vessels
In the bathroom mirror

And your doormen all know me
It's not bizarre
And it shouldn't throw me
To go move your car
But the ghost of your father
He couldn't be clearer
He's there where he haunted you:
The rearview mirror

—"Four Mirrors," 1998

36.
tracking the storm

November 1985

There was a time waiting for Gloria when I didn't know what to wish for. It was as if the dropping barometric pressure had addled me, and I couldn't decide whether I wanted the hurricane to slam right into the city, or to curve away from us and do its howling worse somewhere else. We'd laid in extra food and fresh batteries for the flashlight—even though we couldn't find the transistor radio and hadn't taped the big panes that looked east into the rain driving against our 14th-floor window—and I felt tempted (as if I had any real choice) by the challenge of the great storm.

My secret foolhardiness came to nothing. Almost before the hurricane trackers in their television studios could get the urgency out of their voices, the so-called blow of the century had passed us by and roared off to test the preparedness of neighbors to the east. Within minutes, it seemed, the sun was out, and the sidewalks outside our apartment, deserted an hour before, were thronged with strollers, chattering and smiling in a kind of giddy relief. I took a bus downtown and, looking out a window, I could see—high above the trees in Central Park—a kite some opportunist had launched in the diminishing breeze.

A few nights after the storm I got a call from the nursing home about 150 miles up the coast where my mother had spent the last four years, alert and quick in spite of her increasing infirmity. There had been many bad spells in her long illness. But the nurse's kind, careful voice was itself a special message, and I decided to drive up the next morning.

The route I traveled lay along the path of the hurricane, and I could see signs of damage from the highway—many trees uprooted, others raw and broken at the tops as if they'd been sheared off by artillery fire. As I drove a weird cacophony of thoughts battered me. Was my mother going to die this time? Would I be, at last, an orphan at the age of 60? Why had I never looked into any of her funeral arrangements? Could she be buried with my father? Why had I cried when I sang to my three-year-old daughter the night before? For her eventual fatherlessness? Should I have brought along the tape of my son's new album of songs and tried to play it for his adoring grandmother? Would television where I was going carry the Mets-Cards series?

When I got to the town where the nursing home was, I took a little side trip, perhaps to delay seeing my mother, to the nearby village where she'd lived and where in 1900 my great-grandfather had built a stone house that looked out to the sea. The hurricane had hit there, too, not with the impact of the terrible storm of 1938, when many were swept away, but still leaving shocking, raw rips in the ground where trees had been pulled up by their roots. Leaves on the trees left standing had been burned a dull brown by the clouds of salt spray the storm had blown ashore. The sounds of power saws tore the air, and here and there monarch butterflies wafted over the roads on their scarcely interrupted migration south.

Even in the semidarkness of her little room, I could see that things were awful with my mother. Waxy-pale, cheeks deeply sunken, plastic oxygen harness tugging at her nostrils, she seemed beyond frailty lying there propped high on pillows while a nurse held her hand. She knew me when I spoke, and we talked a little before she drifted back to sleep. She loved family stories, telling and hearing them, but she was almost out of their reach that day.

The next day or so passed like that with her moving in and out of consciousness. We talked, between gasps and silences, in jagged pieces—about her grandchildren, great-grandchildren, and pennant races. Down the hall a senile old man howled. "Oh, shut up!" she whispered fiercely. The slightest movement or sound woke her, and now and then she stopped breathing for 10, possibly 15 seconds, and her eyes were dark with fear when the big lids blew back. She asked for water often, and while she slept, I kept looking around the room. We'd just celebrated her 82nd birthday 10 days earlier (now she'd matched her mother, who'd died at 82), and there were many cards mixed in with dozens of snapshots of various babies taped to the wooden doors. On one wall was a big 1985 Boston Red Sox schedule with the headline "Catch Fenway Fever," and on another, above a dresser choked with dried flowers and a big TV set, was a small framed picture of me at the age of seven or eight in a white linen suit. On the wall right next to her bed, in between sedate needlepoint portraits of marching horsemen, were two large and amazingly black-and-white photographs of my mother taken at least 50 years ago. In one she is sitting on the running board of an old car (I think it was a green and black Hudson). She is wearing shorts and a halter top, as she is in the other picture, where she is clowning with my father and a good friend, and she looks glowing and simply marvelous in both. The juxtaposition of the exhausted old woman and the shadow pictures of her joyful past was suddenly too much. As I'd wished for the hurricane to hit, I wished now she could die.

I put aside the old reluctance and called the office of a local funeral director. The building itself was long and low, like a bowling alley, and when I finally found the proper entrance and was led to an office, I had glimpses of empty, darkened rooms with chairs and displays of artificial flowers. The director was out for the moment, I was told. Another man, soft-voiced and slightly rumpled, interviewed me. We got off to an odd start. "It's for yourself?" he inquired courteously. Demurring and explaining, I suddenly recalled that when I grew my beard, my mother had said it made her look old. I knew I wanted to tell her this new, silly story and that, somehow, I wouldn't.

She seemed better the following morning, her color less pale, and the nurses who watched over her so carefully were cheered up by her requests for food. "How do you feel today, Eleanor?" one asked. "I wouldn't give you 10 cents for it," she replied tartly. "Well, you look fine." "Everybody tells me I look fine," she came back. The nurse grinned at me. "We can tell she's better when she gets mean."

As the day wore on, she ate ice cream and put her on glasses so she could identify people as they came into the room. The electric power had failed again that morning, and we talked some about the great hurricane of '38. Her mother almost got caught in it, she told me. How, I asked, remembering. Well, she'd been playing bridge at a friend's and when she started to drive home, the wind and rain forced her off the road and she had to take refuge at a neigh-

Nanny on the Hudson
running board.

bor's. Then just as the blow was at its worse, my mother said, some men struggled up to my grandmother's house and pushed the piano against the front door to keep out the storm. Looking pleased at the story's outcome and tired by telling it, my mother closed her eyes.

Deceived by the turn in her weather, I went back home then, with promises to return in a few days. And that was the last story my brave, honest, funny, beautiful mother told me.

37.

the home stretch

If the day off doesn't get you
Then the bad reviewer does.
At least you've been a has-been
And not just a never was.
And you know it's not a mountain,
But no molehill is this big.
And you promise to quit drinking
As you light another cig.

—"The Home Stretch," 1986

Some years ago I ran into the legendary folksinger Dave Van Ronk in the aisles of the Integral Yoga health food store in New York City. He ruefully noted that if word got out we were seen in such a place, our reputations as hell-raisers would plummet. The brown rice and green tea managed to hold off the hands of time for a while, but hard-living Dave died in 2002, at the age of sixty-five. I'm seventy now, and every week in the obituary pages I see that another song-writer, bass player, guitarist, or lead singer of some band or other from my era has shuffled off. It's My Generation's turn to kick now.

I've been writing songs about getting older ever since I was in my twenties. The first line of the first song on my first record is "In Dela-ware when I was younger." A few years later I wrote "New Paint," declaring, "If I was sixteen again I'd give my eyetooth / I'm tired and I'm hungry and I'm looking for my youth." Then, in 1976, my song "Hollywood Hopeful" contained the line "In a matter of months I'll be thirty years old and the panic I feel can hardly be told."

And ten years ago there was "60":

All our days are numbered, none more than the big SIX-O
Sixty is the whisper that says, "You got to go."
Sixty's gonna shake you. It will be your wake-up call.
Sixty is the stumble that goes before the fall.

—"60," 2006

Some choose not to stick around for the stumble, opting out of ripe old age by giving full rein to their self-destructive tendencies. One of my musical heroes was the singer-songwriter Tim Hardin, who died of a heroin overdose in 1980. Hardin started using junk at eighteen, when he was a marine posted in the Far East. He and I had one crazy night together in London in the early seventies, and it has stayed in my memory, serving as a kind of cautionary tale. We met at the Speakeasy, a notorious music business after-hours club in Oxford Circus. Tim was very friendly, seemingly happy to hang out with an up-and-comer like me. After several drinks at the Speak, we went to

Ronnie Scott's in Soho to catch the jazz drummer Elvin Jones's last set. At first Tim seemed fine, but after a while something seemed to shift and he became maudlin, rambling, and increasingly incoherent. He spent what seemed like an inordinately long amount of time in the men's toilet. I was thrilled to be drinking with the composer of "Misty Roses," "If I Were a Carpenter," and my favorite, "Black Sheep Boy," but after a few hours in Hardin's raging and discombobulated presence, I couldn't wait to get away. By two a.m., we were back at the Speakeasy, parked in front of the club in a black cab. Tim said he must have left his wallet back at Ronnie's. Then he began to angrily accuse the taxi driver of stealing not only his wallet but also his passport. When he started trying to pry up the passenger seats in the back to look for his documents, I knew it was time for me to cut bait. Somehow, I managed to calm Hardin down enough to get him out of the cab. Then I slipped him a ten-pound note and said I would see him the next time, realizing that there probably wouldn't be one. I experienced some guilt about abandoning him on the street at three a.m., but only a twinge. I told the cabbie to take me to my hotel, and left the Black Sheep Boy to his own devices. Eight years later he was dead at the age of thirty-nine.

> *Once again, you're in the home stretch,*
> *But you're not sure where you live.*
> *You recall a small apartment*
> *and a government you give*
> *Large amounts of money to*
> *So you're allowed to stay*
> *And rest until you're well enough*
> *To leave again and play.*

When you're in the company of people out to kill themselves, you generally know it, and you're rarely shocked when they pull it off. On a few occasions I spent time with the singer-songwriter Phil Ochs. It was toward the end of his life and career and he was drinking "with a vengeance," a phrase the Random House dictionary defines as "to an unreasonable, surprising, or excessive degree." There must have been a number of causes and complex reasons for his alcoholism, but I have a theory about Phil. After Bob Dylan made his radical and bold artistic move to plug in and go electric at the 1965 Newport Folk Festival, his singer-songwriter contemporaries, including Ochs, once his principal rival, were left behind. Dylan, reinvented, roared ahead, and Phil and the others never managed to catch up. This dogged Ochs for the rest of his days. In 2016, I watched Stephen Curry and the Golden State Warriors on TV win Game 7 of the NBA Western Conference Finals. On that night, Curry outclassed every other player on the court, flashing his cocky grin after draining each three-pointer, happily gnawing on his protruding mouth guard. He reminded me of the arrogant young Bob Dylan, someone who was just better than everybody else and knew it. For some corroboration, I went to YouTube and rewatched Bob's cutting session with Donovan in the D. A. Pennebaker documentary *Don't Look Back*. There's a scene in the film when Donovan plays his pleasant but rather innocuous "To Sing for You" for Dylan and a handful of people in a hotel room. When he finishes, they all clap, and Bob says, "Hey, that's a good song, man." Then Dylan removes his shades, takes the guitar from Donovan, and sings "It's All Over Now, Baby Blue." Not only was it all over, but it wasn't even close. Pennebaker pans the camera over to the young Leitch, who we see nervously dragging on a cigarette, trying to stay cool. But it's clear that he knows he's been, as Muhammad Ali used to put it, "whupped." Donovan survived being blown out by Bob Dylan that night, and he's gone on to have a long and relatively successful career. Not so Phil Ochs, and I think the psychological fallout of being bested by Bob was a major factor in his early demise. In 1976, he hanged himself at the age of thirty-five.

Then there's the sad tale of my friend David Blue, a Dylanesque singer-songwriter from that era, who dabbled in self-destruction for many years, but then reformed and finally got clean and sober. In 1982, he dropped dead while jogging around Washington Square Park. You just never know.*

---

* In 1972, I was performing at Max's Kansas City and Dylan and Doug Sahm showed up backstage. Bob singled out one song of mine in particular for praise, stating, "Hey, man, that's a good song." He was referring to "Dead Skunk." Fortunately, he didn't ask to borrow my guitar.

38.
day player blues

The smallest role I ever had in a big movie was FBI Agent #2 in *Mission: Impossible*, which was released in 1996 and starred Tom Cruise. His producing partner at that time was Paula Wagner, a friend of mine from college, and she called me out of the blue and asked if I wanted a day's acting work on the blockbuster. Paula warned me it wasn't much of a part: "You probably don't want to do it. There might be a line or two of dialogue. But maybe not." However, remembering Stanislavski's famous remark, "There are no small parts, only small actors," I thanked her and said, "Sure." They were filming the movie at Pinewood Studios in North London, which was handy, because it was just an hour's car ride from St. John's Wood, where I was living in those days.

In advance of the job, I was sent a script and I thumbed my way through it until I found the scene the three FBI agents were in. One of them did have a line, which for some strange reason I did not go to the trouble of familiarizing myself with. I guess I assumed it would be given to one of the other two day players. Not only are there small actors, there are really stupid ones.

On the appointed day, I was picked up in a very nice car and driven up to Pinewood, where a production assistant took me in to meet the director, the formidable, grumpy, chain-smoking Brian De Palma. As I nervously approached to shake his hand, I tripped and stumbled forward slightly. Recovering, I made a lame joke about how good I was at pratfalls, a bit of jesting that failed to elicit any response whatsoever from the legendary auteur. He asked me a few random questions along the lines of "What have you been doing?" and "How do you like London?" Then, having been sufficiently vetted, I was excused, apparently passing FBI agent muster. The PA took me off to hair and makeup, and after that I was escorted to the "honey wagon," a long tractor-trailer affair that has several small staircases attached, leading up to little compartments. These cells each have a mirror, a tiny closet, and a short narrow couch to sit or lie down on (in a fetal position, if you're over five foot ten). They serve as dressing rooms/ holding pens for insignificant actors. The name of your character ("bartender," "sexy woman," "FBI agent #2") is usually written on masking tape and stuck to the door of your cubicle. When I looked up the term "honey wagon" on Wikipedia, the first definition given was "A wagon or truck for collecting and carrying excrement or manure." Still, you wouldn't trade it for a sack of gold.

A day player is an actor hired on a temporary daily basis with no long-term contract. It's a tough gig because you're on the location once, and once only. You are among scores of other people you've met for the first time who are secure in their jobs, and who have been there for weeks, if not months. They all expect you to nail it. A day player is a tiny, disposable cog in the very large, complicated, and expensive wheel that is a major motion picture.

Outside the "honey" I met my similarly dressed fellow FBI agents, a man and a woman, both, like me, American expats living in London. The three of us settled in to do the thing all actors must do, be they great or small, known or unknown, movie star or lowly day player. We waited. Eventually there was a knock at my cubicle door. They were ready for us on set for a rehearsal.

The set of a big movie like *Mission: Impossible* is its own world. Scurrying around is a small army, composed of electricians, carpenters, the lighting crew, the camera crew, the sound crew, actors, production assistants, continuity, makeup, hair, and costume folks, and, last and most certainly least, extras. Everyone is waiting for the almighty director to arrive, accompanied by the translator and conveyer of his wishes, the first assistant director. On many of the movies I've been in, there's a lot of talking and general hubbub on the set, and there are always several underling ADs shouting out for quiet. On a Brian De Palma movie, or, for that matter, a Tim Burton or a Martin Scorsese picture, when the director appears on the set, it gets quiet fast.

Mr. De Palma arrived, and the first AD called for a rehearsal. De Palma decided that I would be the FBI agent who spoke in the scene. Gulp. Wish I'd spent a bit more time with the script. But it was just a rehearsal, so it was cool for me to use my "sides," a little printed-out pamphlet of the day's dialogue that actors refer to when they don't quite know their lines.

"Rehearsing," the first AD called out.

Then, "Action!"

The rehearsal began.

Other Actor: "Blah, blah, blah . . ."

FBI Agent #2: "Those plans must have been Phelps's. They must have belonged to him."

Other Actor: "Blah, blah, blah."

"Cut!"

I nailed it. Brian seemed satisfied, anyway. He was whisked away to his palatial three banger,* and we FBI agents were shuttled back to the honey wagon, where we waited for the few hours it took to get the shot set up and lit. I was pretty revved up, having been given the one FBI agent line. This was a big-ass movie, and I was going to be in it!

Finally the time arrived to shoot the scene and we were taken back to the set. There was now a palpable sense of tense concentration in the air. Cameras would be rolling and some real money was about to be spent. "Last looks" were called by the first AD, and the makeup, hair, and wardrobe people briefly powdered and primped us FBI agents as if we were stars. One of the reasons people want to be actors is that they want to be fussed over. "Last looks" is a bit like the grooming among primates you see in nature programs, except that it's completely one-sided as opposed to mutual.

It was time for the first take.

"Sound . . . Speed . . . Marker . . . Set . . . Action!"

Other Actor: "Blah, blah, blah . . ."

FBI Agent #2: "Those plans must have been Phelpseses'. They must have belonged to him."

There was a discernible pause. Then De Palma called out *"Cut!"* We were instructed to do it again.

"Sound . . . Speed . . . Marker . . . Set . . . Action!"

Other Actor: "Blah, blah, blah . . ."

---

* A three banger is a spacious and luxurious trailer with three separate doors inhabited by the stars, director, and/or producers of a major motion picture.

FBI Agent #2: "Those plans must have been Phelpseses'. They must have belonged to him."

Again Brian yelled, *"Cut!"* and he said to the first AD, "Something's not right."

At this point, all two-hundred-plus people on the set were getting nervous, and some of them probably knew precisely what was "not right," but nobody had the guts to say what it was. It was the day player's nightmare. I was fucking up. I gave De Palma a quick line reading: "Those plans must have been Phelpseses'. They must have belonged to him." "Okay," he said curtly. "We'll try it one more time." One of my fellow FBI agents sidled up to me and hissed under her breath, "'Phelps's,' not 'Phelpseses'. You're adding a syllable." But I was so rattled at that point I couldn't take in what she was trying to tell me.

"Sound . . . Speed . . . Marker . . . Set . . . Action!"

Other Actor: "Blah, blah, blah . . ."

FBI Agent #2: "Those plans must have been Phelpseses'. They must have belonged to him."

"Cut!"

And cut he did. My line. He cut my one line. Basically, I was fired in front of two hundred people.

"Sound . . . Speed . . . Marker . . . Set . . . Action!"

Other Actor: "Blah, blah, blah . . ."

FBI agents stand there in silence.

End of scene.

They "checked the gate," confirming that there weren't any technical problems, and then moved on to a "new deal," the next scene in the day's schedule. Along with the two other former FBI agents, I was returned to the wagon or truck for collecting and carrying excrement or manure.

That night, back at the flat in St. John's Wood, still depressed and somewhat in shock, I recounted the sad tale of my *Mission: Impossible* humiliation to my girlfriend, Tracey. I still had no understanding of what the problem had been. She did her best to cheer me up, but I was pretty much inconsolable.

The sting of it all started to fade in a day or two, and I just chalked up the incident as inexplicable. Then, a week later, I was taking a shower, mulling things over, general and particular. As the warm water cascaded over me, I found myself reconstructing the fateful scene at Pinewood. I ran my line in my head and then muttered it out loud.

FBI Agent #2: "Those plans must have been Phelpseses'. They must have belonged to him."

Something *didn't* sound right.

"Phelpseses'?"

"Phelps's?"

"Phelpseses'?"

"Phelps's?"

"Phelps's!" Fuuck!

"No job is too dangerous, difficult, or deadly for the Impossible Missions Force."

I'm in a trailer, here all day long.
Stuck in this trailer, singin' this song.
I'm in a movie, that's what I'm in.
But in this trailer, that's where I've been.
I'm in a trailer, inside a trailer.

I'm wearin' makeup, they dyed my hair.
I'm in an outfit I'd never wear.
It's just a movie, it's make-believe.

I'm in a trailer and I can't leave.
I'm in a trailer, stuck in a trailer.

I'm in a trailer, I can't complain.
At least I got one in case it rains.
That honey wagon is just a hole,
But this two banger keeps out the cold.
Warm in a trailer, dry in a trailer.

Got running water, a sink to shave in.
I got a TV, I'm microwavin'.
With all this waitin' you need some perks.
I got a toilet, it kinda works.
Inside a trailer, I'm in a trailer.

I'm in a trailer, outta my mind.
I'm in a trailer, I'm killin' time.
They're spendin' a fortune makin' this flick.
It's my time and their money, it's makin' me sick
Inside this trailer.

Something is coming, I gotta hunch.
It's almost 5:30, they just called lunch.
Escape this trailer, go fill up your plate.
I'm in a movie, let's gain some weight.
Stuck in a trailer.

Back in my trailer I should be glad.
Out in the real world it's really bad.
I read the paper and it's still true,

Under that old sun ain't nothin' new.
Inside this trailer, still in this trailer.

Hey, wait a minute, I hear a knock.
They've come to get me, it's such a shock.
I gotta go now, it's time to act
For a few minutes, then I'll be back.
Inside this trailer, life in a trailer.

—"TRAILER," 2005

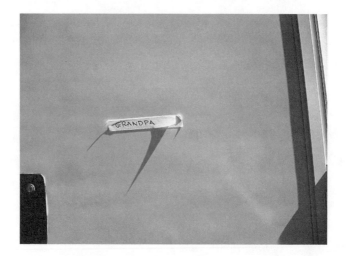

39.
paris

People in northern Europe have a pretty good grasp of English, and, throughout the 1970s, I frequently performed in Amsterdam, Belgium, Germany, and Scandinavia. I would explain certain concepts or lyrics to the audience before each song and was careful to sing slowly, enunciating the words with care. And overall, audiences in those countries appreciated my shows. They got it. However, down in France, fewer people spoke English. The French had their own folk and rock stars who sang in their native tongue—Johnny Hallyday, Françoise Hardy, Serge Gainsbourg. There was never any demand for me to play in France, until a French music journalist named Jacques Vassal wrote some very complimentary things about my first few records for *Rock & Folk* magazine. His articles created a bit of interest and somehow he managed to convince a promoter to book a Loudon Wainwright concert in Paris. Cool.

The venue was a lovely, old-fashioned theater with a capacity of a few hundred. Those who attended the show were mostly French, though there also was a sprinkling of British and American expats. The opening act was an Irishman who played the uilleann pipes, the distinctly characteristic national bagpipes of Ireland. They are also known as the "elbow pipes," because the air that's required is produced not by lung power but by a pumping bellows mechanism strapped to one of the musician's elbows. It's an ax that's been around for hundreds of years, but unless the uilleann pipes are in the hands and on the elbow of an expert, they are likely to produce an even more squawking and unpleasant dissonance than the more widely known Scottish war pipes. Unfortunately, my opening act was no expert. In addition to that, he was from Belfast, and so his declarations sounded like questions, every sentence ending in the distinctively Ulster rise in pitch. This would have been okay in English, but this guy had been living in France for years, so he chose to speak in French. It was explained to me that what came out of the piper's mouth was grammatically correct but atrociously jarring to the French ear. To make matters worse, the French-speaking Irishman was a pedant. He went on and on between each song, launching into long, boring introductions that detailed each tune's history, dating all the way back to when the blind piper Turlough O'Carolan in 17-something-or-other taught it to Joe Blow. At first, the audience was amused, but soon their amusement gave way to restlessness, and then to irritation. The guy was dying and he didn't know it, and I watched nervously from the wings as people started to leave. The room was hemorrhaging. After forty-five minutes that seemed like an eternity, the piper finally finished his set and walked off to a listless smattering of applause. Rather than warm the audience up, my opener had managed to completely turn them off. This was not a happy crowd.

As a performer, every once in a while you can have an inspired moment, when exactly the right thing to say or do comes to you for some reason. Why this happens I'm not sure. Let's call it divine intervention. I walked out onstage that night and simply said to the crowd, in English, "I'm sorry, but I don't speak French." A cheer went up and the audience members rose to their feet. It turned out to be a great show. They loved my American ass.

40.
over there,
then back

I n 1984, after nine years of living with Suzzy Roche, and due in no
small part to my aforementioned roaming tendencies, I got dumped.
The U.S. dollar and the British pound were roughly at parity then,
and I decided to buy myself a flat in London and move there. Leaving
Suzzy and our three-year-old daughter, Lucy, in New York was painful (broken family number two), but I felt I needed to get away and
try something new in a different location. At that point, being an
expatriate seemed like the way to go. My career in the UK was relatively solid, and I had a terrific, hardworking agent over there, Paul
Charles, who got me a record deal with Demon Records, the hip new
label owned by Elvis Costello and his manager, Jake Riviera. The flat
I bought was in West Hampstead—31c Inglewood Road. It was the

second place I looked at. One of the living room walls was completely papered with a large color photo of a tropical beach scene, with coconut trees at the shoreline and sailboats in the distance. It was something you might see in a travel agent's office. I suppose I found it comforting.

My first trip to London had been in 1967, a Christmas visit to my parents, who had relocated there while their house in Bedford was being rebuilt after the fire. They were living in posh Belgravia, and the exciting rumor was that Brian Jones of the Rolling Stones lived in a mews house across the street. A few years later, in the early seventies, when I was married to Kate, I rented flats in Kennington and Holland Park (five pounds a week), and I got to know the sprawling town pretty well, particularly North Central London. There were nights spent hanging out at the Tally Ho in Kentish Town, a legendary pub rock venue. I was buddies with the American expat country-rock trio Eggs Over Easy, who played there regularly, as did the Eggs-influenced English band Brinsley Schwarz, which featured Nick Lowe.

During the mid-1980s, while moping around London, feeling sorry for myself, I managed to write a lot. I was lonely, the "sad American man" by himself in a restaurant that's mentioned in my song "I Eat Out." Other songs had to do specifically with the break from Suzzy, including "Your Mother and I," "Unhappy Anniversary," and "Expatriate."

You can keep my bicycle and all of my records and tapes.
Might seem sentimental or sound like sour grapes.
Sell my clothes and furniture or give 'em to the Goodwill store.
I'm going overseas, I'm not coming back anymore.

Maybe it's a little romantic for a middle-aged man like me.
I'm gonna be an expatriate, just you wait and see.
Livin' in a garret in Paris, a houseboat in Amsterdam,
Smokin' a beard, growin' a pipe, and doin' the best I can.

—"EXPATRIATE," 1986

The mighty Richard Thompson had played on my 1982 record, *Fame and Wealth*, back in New York, and when I got over to London I enlisted him as my producer on *I'm Alright* (1985), and again as a coproducer (with Chaim Tannenbaum) on *More Love Songs* (1986). Both those albums were nominated for Grammys. In 1987, Paul Charles got me a gig as the resident American topical singer-songwriter on Jasper Carrott's BBC TV show *Carrott Confidential*. Every Saturday night I would sing a song, usually one I'd written earlier in the week, and it went out live to ten million UK viewers. "Harry's Wall," a meditation on my new visibility, was one of those songs.

Rich and Loud at McCabe's, mid 1980s.

Everywhere I go in this town, people recognize me
Probably 'cause they seen me singing these songs on TV
In the last few weeks I've found a gold mine of exposure
My career has taken off, I'm a celebrity

The guy I buy my grapefruit from, smiles at me every morning
All the tellers at my bank are at my beck and call
Harry owns the shop in town where I take my dry cleaning
I gave him my 8 x 10 to hang up on his wall

Pretty soon I'll be a name in each and every household
A lifelong dream is coming true, it's happening for me
On the street the people stare, and I can hear them whisper,
"There he goes, there's what's-his-name, we saw him on TV"

—"HARRY'S WALL," 1989

When I bought the flat on Inglewood Road, there was an old rotary-style, black Bakelite telephone on the premises, and for some reason, probably clerical error or computer screwup, I never received a phone bill from British Telecom. This went on for several years, and in those landline-only days, I had it pretty good for a while. Plenty of long-distance calls, many to the States and some to Australia and Japan, were made with impunity, seemingly free of charge. Friends and various 31c sublet tenets were discreetly invited to avail themselves of my "free phone," as long as they followed strict instructions to keep quiet about it. However, my cover was eventually blown when BT was tipped off by a vengeful girlfriend of mine after she and I parted company. Claiming to be "Mrs. Wainwright," my angry ex put in a call of complaint to the company about not getting a bill.

That's all it took. I consulted with a lawyer and, after a long wrangling negotiation, got the bill whittled down from fifteen thousand to six thousand pounds, or about twelve thousand dollars in those days. Hell hath no fury, et cetera.

I was busy and creative in London in the mid-eighties, but I was miserable and felt in exile, so I started coming back and spending more time in New York. It was good to be with Lucy, and Suzzy and I, no longer a couple now, had begun our long-lasting, close friendship. My father had been diagnosed with colon cancer in 1985, and that was another reason to return home. But I kept the flat back on Inglewood Road and spent stretches of time there.

Things got much better for me in London in the early nineties, when I fell in love with the writer and broadcaster Tracey MacLeod. We met when I was a guest on her BBC radio show. After our interview, I went with her to a hardware store on Marylebone High Street, where she bought an ironing board cover. Romantic, I know. Tracey and I were together for three years, and the list of songs written for or about her is

Tracey in Budapest.

a long one. They include "Grown Man," "Housework," "Breakfast in Bed," "I Suppose," "Out of Reach," "OGM," "So Damn Happy," and "Little Ship." A previous boyfriend of hers was former Brinsley Nick Lowe, and his list is pretty long, too.

Just before I got together with Tracey, I'd had an affair with a talented actress I'd met in New York named Ritamarie Kelly. Not long after Rita and I stopped seeing each other, I got a call from her with the news she was pregnant and that I was the father. This was a totally unexpected shock. It also seemed like a variation on a theme. I couldn't help but think of my father's affair in L.A. with Gloria in the 1950s, and the child he possibly had fathered back then.

On May 2, 1993, Alexandra Kelly was born in New York. Rita and the baby were living with her parents in an apartment across from Carnegie Hall; that's where I saw Lexie for the first time, when I was passing through New York. She was three weeks old. The next time I saw her was about a year later, bringing along twelve-year-old Lucy, who was eager to meet her baby half sister.

The only time I've seen you was about a year ago.
I was afraid to hold you, but I wanted you to know,
I touched your tiny perfect hand before I went uptown.
I didn't pick you up because I'd have to put you down.

For reasons that don't make much sense and you won't understand,
I've stayed away for your first year, it's sort of what I planned.
But I've been in your neighborhood, sometimes just blocks away.
I didn't come to visit you because I couldn't stay.

There was a baby on a plane and maybe she was two,
And she was smiling at me—I was not sure what to do.

I've kept my distance from you. A year's much more than a while,
And so I looked away from her, too ashamed to smile.

When I saw you last year, I knew that there was no mistake.
Amazing things can happen, why just look what life can make.
But life can get so hard sometimes, some feelings can't be tamed.
And people get so angry, frightened, and ashamed.

You've been a sort of secret, for a year I've told but few.
Although I'm sure that where you are so many must love you.
And I've passed by your window, but haven't dared look in.
Although I know I'd love you, too, I'm too scared to begin.

—"A YEAR," 1995

My fiftieth birthday was on September 5, 1996, and Tracey took on the daunting task of organizing a party. I'd decided I wanted a bash to mark the landmark occasion—to "go whole hog," as my mother used to say. The gathering took place in a funky old Victorian house my sister Teddy and I had rented for many summers on Shelter Island, New York. My father had died in 1988, and my mother wasn't well enough to travel to the party, but, aside from them, I had the whole crazy family tangle there—brother, sisters, good friends, and my four kids and their three moms. Kate, Rufus, and Martha came down from Montreal. Suzzy and Lucy were there. Rita and three-year-old Lexie came out from the city. Tracey was a gracious and welcoming hostess, and overall I'd have to say the celebration was a success, though there were some moments of anxiety, and at various points in the evening I had to go for some short walks (and one long-ish bike ride) to clear my head and gather my senses. The vignette that sticks in my mind the most from that night is Kate and Suzzy's mom—the magnificent Roche matriarch, Jude Roche—side by side at the piano, drunkenly singing opera arias together. I also heard a few days after the party from Rita that when Kate greeted Lexie for the first time with a gruff and scary "Hello, little girl," the three-year-old burst into tears.

My mother died unexpectedly in March of 1997. I was back in London, living with Tracey at her house in St. John's Wood, when I got the early-morning phone call from Teddy with the news. I walked to the top of nearby Primrose Hill and found myself baying at the sky. It was a visceral reaction, somewhat similar to my moaning underneath the shower in 1988 when I received the phone call about my father. His passing was, in a sense, liberating for me. My mother's death was anything but liberating. I went into a severe depression and couldn't eat, sleep, or stop crying. I was prescribed drugs and was told that their beneficial effects would take a while to kick in. But then I became manic and felt like I was coming out of my skin. When I wasn't lying on the couch chain-smoking, I was washing and re-washing windows in Tracey's house, or else riding my bike three or four times a day to the Hampstead Ponds, to jump in the water, in order to experience some momentary distraction and relief. I simply couldn't handle the ramping-up process, and after tearfully explaining that to the doctor, he took me off the antidepressants.

When you were alive I was never alone.
Somewhere in the world there was something called home.
And as long as you lived I would be all right;
There were reasons to live and incentives to fight.
Now I'm smoking again, I thought all that was through,
And I don't want to live, but what else can I do?

And I feel like I've faked all that I ever did,
And I've grown a gray beard, but I cry like a kid.

—"Homeless," 2001

I had to come home to America. Tracey and I decided to split up. She had wanted to start a family together, which for me at that point would have been psychologically impossible. I wound up living in the Mouse House, the little cottage in Katonah where my mother had last lived. As I put it in the liner notes for my 2001 album, *Last Man on Earth*: "Twice a week I took the train into the city to see my shrink. I told him I didn't think I'd be able to write songs anymore. He told me not to worry, always good advice for pitching slumps and bouts of impotence. Back up in northern Westchester I went swimming in and walking around Lake Waccabuc, waters I consider sacred and medicinal. Then I began to write again."

I also began to see Lexie with some regularity, and that also meant spending time with her mother. Rita and I became romantically involved again, and before long I was in family unit number three. It seemed sudden and strange, but was also somewhat logical, since this was a family that was already in existence. It was as if the three of us had been, in a way, waiting for one another. After my mother died, the bottom fell out of my life. Then, at the age of fifty-two, I suddenly had another shot at domestic life and being a father. I went for it.

AROUND THAT TIME, I GOT a particularly nice career boost when the producer, director, and writer Judd Apatow contacted me about an acting job in *Undeclared*, a TV show he was creating, his follow-up to *Freaks and Geeks*. I hadn't seen *Freaks and Geeks*, and had no idea who Judd was, but after watching a few episodes, I knew I wanted to be involved with his new show. Apatow had become a fan of mine as a Syosset, Long Island, teenager when he saw me on the first incarnation of *The David Letterman Show** in 1980. In *Undeclared*, I was cast as Hal Karp, the dysfunctional dad(!) of college freshman Steven Karp, played by Jay Beruchel. The show only had one season on Fox (2001–2), but it was a critical success and a fan favorite. It was also the beginning of my working with Judd on a number of projects, including acting roles in his movies *Knocked Up* and *The 40-Year-Old Virgin*, and contributing songs to *Love*, his show on Netflix. As of this writing, Judd and my old pal Christopher Guest† have been working together on the idea of filming my theater piece *Surviving Twin*.

---

* For a few weeks I was the musical sidekick on Letterman's original morning show. Then Dave moved to late night, hired Paul Shaffer, and the rest, as they say, is history.

On Cavett.

My first appearance on American national TV was in 1969 on ABC's *The Dick Cavett Show*. Cavett introduced me as Luden (as in the cough drop) Wainwright III.

Do you know that I appeared on *Saturday Night Live*, in season one, episode five? The host was Robert Klein, but do you recall (or even care) who the other musical guests were that night? That's right: fresh from their win of the 1974 Eurovision Song Contest, four very cute unknown Swedish kids called ABBA! They also apparently were the only group to ever lip-synch on SNL.

† Another LW3 TV fun fact: Chris and I first met back in 1973, when I went to see him in the National Lampoon stage revue *Lemmings* at the Village Gate in New York. Also in the cast were John Belushi, Chevy Chase, and Alice Playten. Guest and I also were both friendly with Michael McKean, whom I had gone to college with. When Chris and Michael teamed up with Harry Shearer, Tom Leopold, Martin Mull, and others to be in the Rob Reiner 1979 ABC comedy special *The TV Show*, they created a sketch about an English heavy metal band called Spinal Tap. Check it out on YouTube. I'm in a wig playing keyboards with Tap.

Me and Jay Baruchel in *Undeclared*, 2001.

After *Undeclared*, Rita, Lexie, and I moved out to L.A., and I bought a house in Woodland Hills in the San Fernando Valley, where we lived for almost eight years. I owned and sailed a Catalina 25, which I kept moored up in Ventura. We had a beautiful garden in the back of our house, with fruit trees, roses, vegetables, and plenty of roaming room for our dog, Harry. A bit more acting work came my way, with some episodic TV, and good parts in Tim Burton's movie *Big Fish* and Cameron Crowe's *Elizabethtown*. It was also during this period that I worked with the producer Joe Henry and his fabulous crew of musicians on two albums. Rita and I got married in 2005.

In 2008, my friend Dick Connette, who was back in New York, pitched an idea to me about making a record based on the recordings of Charlie Poole (1892–1931). Poole was a wild singer and "banjo-playing son of a bitch" whose recordings I'd first heard in the early 1970s. I'd been knocked out by Poole's work the way just about anyone in their right mind would be, but there were also parallels between the two of us. I grew up a northerner but, like Charlie, I was born in North Carolina. My mother was born and raised way down

Photograph by Paula Court.

in the rural South, and if you wanted to be genteel about it, you might say she was a "country girl." A not-so-nice appellation would be "white trash," which is what Charlie was. I think I have a genetically tinged sense of where Poole was coming from. The themes and subject matter of his music also happen to be some of my favorites when it comes to writing my own songs—mother, booze, nonsensicality, and death, to name a few. Dick Connette and I worked on *High Wide & Handsome: The Charlie Poole Project* for about two years, and our efforts were rewarded in 2010 when the double CD won a Grammy.

In 2009, Rita, Lexie, Harry, and I moved back to the East Coast. But there the marriage began to fray, and then it faltered. In 2014, Rita and I separated. We had raised our daughter, Lexie, through her adolescence and teenage period, and that was certainly something important. In the case of my other three kids, I'd been pretty much missing in action for those crucial years.

> *The slap of the paper, the hiss of the sprinkler, the beep of the coffee*
> *machine*
> *The drone in the distance that says there's a freeway*
> *The gardeners will soon make the scene, cause it's Thursday*
> *Soon they'll arrive on the scene*

Me, Rita, and the kids, including Harry from
The Village of the Damned (my obedient son).

I pick up the paper, I'm spritzed by the sprinkler, inside I take
*   in my caffeine*
Then I hear the dog door, I know he's gone out there
To mark and to mess up the scene, they're illegal
Soon they'll arrive on the scene

Our leader's an actor who speaks with an accent
Who's able to procure our love
But life is a movie out here in the Valley
What else were we all thinking of?

The clack of the skateboard resounds in the Valley, next door the
*   kid's starting a band*
Their morning rehearsal is making me crazy
The volume is way out of hand, it's not music
To my ears it's way out of hand

The slap of the paper, the hiss of the sprinkler, the beep of the coffee
*   machine*
The drone in the distance that says there's a freeway
The gardeners will soon make the scene, cause it's Thursday
Soon they'll arrive on the scene, they're illegal
To mow, blow, then go from the scene

—"Valley Morning," 2007

41.
rite of passage

wrote this in 2009:

My sixteen-year-old daughter, Lexie, is taking her road test soon, and if she passes she will be legally licensed to operate two tons of moving chrome, glass, and steel day and night, pretty much anywhere in the western world. She got her learner's permit a while back, and since then, both her mother and I have logged quite a few hours in the shotgun seat with our darling young one behind the wheel. That's a tough gig, because kids hate being told what to do by their idiotic parents, so, in addition to being scared out of our minds, we were often insulted by our teen. A meek parental suggestion to stay in the middle of the road in order to avoid an oncoming school bus was often met with an emphatic and terse *"I know!"* followed by a withering "God, you just make me nervous." It's at this point parents think maybe they should have sprung for the five-hundred-dollar driver's education course at the high school, or even gone for the eighty-dollars-per-hour private instructor. But the voice in my head said, "Hey, you can do this," as I instantly recalled my long-gone father showing, telling, and kind of teaching me how to drive. Cue calendar pages flipping back to 1962, with me and my dad side by side in the front seat of a green Rambler station wagon on an abandoned dirt road in Bedford. Forget about automatic or even four on the floor, because back then it was three on the column, baby. I can still hear the grinding of gears as I tried to go from first to second, not to mention even scarier reverse. I recall that maneuver being described by my dad as pulling the stick in, and then up, as if you were trying to punch yourself on the chin. I'd say that clutch operation is all but a lost art in the early twenty-first century. Way back in ancient days, it seemed like hours were spent just getting that Rambler to lurch forward. How many times did I stall out? It had to be hundreds, if not a thousand. My father was not a particularly patient man, and anything resembling an emphatic *"I know!"* on my part would have been pushing it. As for "God, you just make me nervous," that was inconceivable, though Dad himself was certainly capable of taking the Lord's name in vain when the red lights on the Rambler's dashboard came back on, yet again.

Like Lexie, I was late getting my driver's license. I flunked my first road test at seventeen, which was particularly humiliating because my one-year-younger sister, Teddy, passed hers on the very same day. More than forty years later, I can still feel the shame of that double failure—being bested not only by a girl but by my own kid sister. I can't recall what went wrong during my road test; perhaps I failed to employ the weird and now virtually vestigial ninety-degree right-turn hand signal. A friend of mine recently revealed to me that at the very beginning of his road test, way back when, he honked at a blind man in a crosswalk. Game over.

Lexie recently attended a five-hour pre-licensing course required by Motor Vehicles, and her mother and I were relieved to learn that, in addition to instruction on blood alcohol levels, there were plenty of "this is what can happen to you" cautionary car wreck videos shown. Apparently these films were "gross-out" horrific and certainly made an impression on Lex, because when she got home later that night she went online to search YouTube for more of the same.

I suppose teaching your kid to drive is one of the last life lessons you can impart as a parent. You start out showing them how to tie their shoelaces, and before you know it, they're knocking off your side-view mirror while attempting to parallel park. Then you lend them your car and pay the increased insurance premium so they can drive away, out of your life and, hopefully, into their own. This is a rite of passage, and is as it should be— a part of the natural order of things.

Lexie in 2000.

As her road test approaches, Lex still has to fulfill her fifty hours of supervised practice driving, and it's possible we may chicken out and spring for a few private lessons. That's what my father did. Yes, Dad eventually threw in the towel and paid for me to go to Fred's Driving School in Katonah. Coincidentally, there was an outfit in town called Fred's Auto Body.

42.
montreal

'm back in Montreal, here to do Rufus and Martha's Christmas show. It's December 4, 2015, and a few days ago some crazed married couple shot, killed, and wounded a lot of people in San Bernardino, California, which is about thirty miles away from where my youngest kid, Lexie, goes to college. What a world. We do the show in a few days, and I'm tempted to perform "I'll Be Killing You This Christmas," but probably won't. Still, allow me to quote myself. The last verse goes:

> I'll be killing you this Christmas,
> And the NRA, they lobby, so it's so.
> I love our great nation, the real world is my PlayStation.
> I'll blow you away beneath the mistletoe.
>
> —"I'LL BE KILLING YOU THIS CHRISTMAS," 2014

But people don't want to hear that agitprop stuff, especially right after another shooting, so I'll probably stick to "I Saw Mommy Kissing Santa Claus."

I've been coming to Montreal for close to forty-five years now. After my marriage to Kate broke up in 1976, she and the kids moved up here, back to her hometown. Then I became the visiting, repentant dad. Usually when I came up from New York it was to look after Rufus and Martha when Kate and her sister Anna were out touring. I always thought these visits would make a good movie. Dad shows up in a town where they literally don't speak his language, and for a few weird days takes a stab at being a loving, authoritative but fair father. It never works out, of course, because even though they are little kids, they still know the man is a fraudulent interloper, someone their mother once loved but now despises. There would be shots in my movie of the dad standing on the Metro platform, isolated and alone (kids in school?). Also a scene depicting my attempt to cook spaghetti that goes disastrously and comically wrong, à la the French toast scene in *Kramer vs. Kramer*. Of course, some hugging and kissing and laughing, too. Then after a few days, the mother returns, and it becomes obvious which parent the children really love and know and need. The trip to see the kids was just a strange dream that in the end doesn't amount to much. So the father takes a cab to the airport and flies home to New York and his other family. The authorities let him back into the country. On the immigration form there is a question about the reason for the visit. In pen he prints the word "Expiation."

But now I'm back in Montreal, and it's 2015. I spend the afternoon with my six-year-old grandson Arc. I pick him up at school, where he introduces me to his young, ridiculously cute teacher, Audrey. He explains to her in his broken French that I am his *grand-père*, and I smile at her and shake her dainty little hand, feeling about six myself. Then he and I take the 80 bus downtown to my hotel. Anytime there is a lull in the conversation, he asks me somewhat nervously, "What are you doing?" I answer that I am "waiting" and "thinking," and then I give the most honest answer of all, which is, of course, "Nothing." We go for a swim in the hotel pool and take a dip in the Jacuzzi. The sauna scares him, I think because it is so dark and enclosed. Then, back up in the room, we order room service. He has a burger and a Pepsi; I go for the pasta with shrimp and a big-ass glass of Mondavi white wine. Forty years ago, I did all of this with Rufus, Arc's uncle, and all my feelings now are the same as they were then: somewhat excited, thinking it's going pretty well, that I'm not doing a bad job. I'm delighted by my grandson's spontaneity, and truly enjoy sitting him up on my lap, helping him get his shoes on, and even wiping his ass ("I need help," he calls out from the bathroom). I effusively congratulate him on his rather impressive shit. But after a while, the old boredom kicks in. After four hours of being *Grand-père*, I'm exhausted and falling asleep. At last, it's time to take Arc home to his parents. He's yawning now, too, and that makes me happy. I spring for a cab, do the drop, and then, heading back to the 80 bus, who should I run into on the corner of Querbes and Fairmount but his uncle Rufus! He's on his way to Martha's for a Christmas show meeting. My son is forty-two and looks handsome and tall, but also tired and jet-lagged. We do the double-cheek kiss thing and I say I'll see him tomorrow. In a sense I already spent time with him today. Once I'm on the bus, someone offers me a seat, and, senior that I am, I take it. What a world.

Your mother and I are living apart
I know that seems stupid but we weren't very smart
You'll stay with her, I'll visit you
At Christmas, on weekends, in the summertime, too

Your mother and I are not getting along
Somehow, somewhere, something went wrong
Everything changes, time takes its toll
Your folks fell in love, love's a very deep hole

Your mother and I will do all we can do
To work this thing out and take care of you
Families get broken, I know it's a shame
It's nobody's fault, and you're not to blame

Your mother and I are both feeling bad
But things will get better, they won't stay this sad
And I hope when you grow up, one day you'll see
Your parents are people, that's all we can be

Your mother and I.

—"YOUR MOTHER AND I," 1986

43.
surviving twin

I t started in Maine in 2009. I was up in Vacationland to do a show, and since there were no hotels near the gig that met my primary on-the-road requirement that windows must open at least a few inches,*

---

* The reason for the open-window requirement dates back more than thirty years ago when I was cast in my first major motion picture, *The Slugger's Wife*. This baseball/rock and roll wannabe comedy came out in 1985 and was a disastrous flop, both with the critics and at the box office. The stars were Michael O'Keefe and Rebecca De Mornay, the script was written by Neil Simon, and Hal Ashby directed. I had the small but (I'd like to think) pivotal part of Gary, the guitar player in Debby's (De Mornay) rock band. I spent ten weeks in Atlanta working on this flick, and it was rough going. The straight-ahead comic sensibility of Simon never really meshed with the shoot-from-the-hip style and somewhat drug-addled imagination of Ashby. Ray Stark was the producer, and his lizard-like countenance and scary vibe added extra tension to the proceedings. It was my first acting job in a big movie and I was pretty scared and, as a result, not very good. There was, however, some real drama during the making of *The Slugger's Wife*. One afternoon a tornado swept through our Peachtree Street location, and Rebecca De Mornay's trailer was knocked over with her inside of it. Luckily, all she sustained was a bad facial bruise,

I was housed in someone's cabin. Not really a cabin per se, since there were modern amenities, among them cable TV, laundry facilities, and an automatic dishwasher. But the place had a cabinlike feel to it, with a trace of Cracker Barrel Old Country Store ambience. Deer antlers and a pair of antique wooden cross-country skis were mounted on the interior walls. There were black-and-white photos in carved wooden frames—a picture of a Sunday school class from the 1920s and one of men with handlebar mustaches in a logging camp from the 1800s. In the middle of the room was a swaying upholstered easy chair, and on the floor next to it a wooden magazine rack containing copies of old *Life* magazines. At some point I sat down and pulled out an issue from 1971 with Tricia Nixon on the cover, knowing it was possible that one of my dad's "The View from Here" columns might be in the front section of the magazine. Sure enough, there was one, and not just any column of his but one of his best; for my money, the very best. It was "Another Sort of Love Story," a twelve-hundred-word essay about having to put our family dog John Henry to sleep. I started to read it and was laughing immediately. By the time I got to the payoff at the end of the piece, I was sobbing, the perpetual

---

but they had to shoot around her for several days. The most fun part of the experience for me was hanging out with Martin Ritt, who regaled us during the many hours of downtime with his colorful stories of Hollywood and the days of the blacklist. Ritt was an acclaimed director (*Hud*, *Norma Rae*) and originally was hired in that capacity for *The Slugger's Wife*, but then he suffered a mild heart attack before the movie began and was replaced by Ashby. Marty was then cast as an actor, a less stressful job, I suppose. He played the baseball team manager. Anyway, back to the windows. I lived those ten weeks in the downtown Atlanta Hilton Hotel, where none of the windows opened, and being hermetically sealed for that amount of time made me very anxious. The claustrophobia was intense, and it's lingered with me in the ensuing thirty years. Whenever I check in to any hotel anywhere, my first question at the front desk is "Do the windows open?" If they don't, I seek accommodation elsewhere.

Gordian knot in my gut having been loosened and relaxed for the first time in God knows how long. Of course, I knew both the writer and the dog, and had loved them, although expressing that love to the former had always been a pretty tall order for me, practically an impossibility.

The experience in Maine affected me, so much so that I decided to find and read all of my dad's columns. When they first appeared in the magazine throughout the 1960s and '70s, I often ignored them, because having a famous father had mostly been a drag. I was the son of the famous *Life* magazine writer Loudon Wainwright. Wasn't that great? Wasn't I proud? Those two questions always led to a third one, which I invariably asked myself: How the hell was I going to top that?

Finding all "The View from Here" columns was not easy. Some, but not many, are available on the Internet, and I located a few in the microfilm files at the New York Public Library on Forty-second Street. Then I hit pay dirt. I did a show at the main library in Louisville, Kentucky, in 2010, and had gotten friendly with Craig Buthod, the administrator there. His library had every issue of *Life*, going all the way back to the first one published in 1937, with its iconic Margaret Bourke-White cover photo of the Fort Peck Dam in Montana. All the *Life*s were chronologically arranged and bound in big dusty hardcover books, just like the ones I'd pored over in the early 1960s at the St. Andrew's library. In those days, however, I wasn't looking for my dad's columns. I was just curious and horny, on the lookout for titillation that could lead to some kind of release and satisfaction back in the dorm after lights out. There was some sexy stuff in *Life* if you were willing to look for it, like shots of skimpily clad female Eastern European javelin throwers and shot-putters, with their exciting and previously unseen taboo tufts of underarm hair. There was a photo-essay about breastfeeding and another rather provocative one in the early 1940s about how to undress in front of your husband. How to turn on teenage boys trapped in boarding school is more like it. But I digress. Craig and his hardworking staff in Louisville found the columns I needed, and scanned and then e-mailed them to me.

"The View from Here" column appeared throughout the 1960s, '70s, and '80s, when *Life* was ubiquitous, on every coffee table in America, way back when there were coffee tables. My father wrote about politics and current events, the big stories of his day, but my favorite columns of his are the personal ones: the ones about having to put the dog down, the fire that destroyed our house, buying himself a Savile Row–tailored suit in London, and visiting his mother for the last time in a nursing home. His political stuff didn't really grab me as much when I read it, simply because it was of its own time, and that time had passed. I did, however, enjoy Dad's forays into criticism. Occasionally, he would write about a movie (loved *Dr. Strangelove*; hated *E.T.*), and he took a pretty nasty swipe at Linda Ronstadt's 1983 rerecording of old standards, *What's New*. He also relished reporting on the cultural movements of that time and its cast of icons and clowns, be they baseball's Billy Martin, the hippies, Richard Nixon, or the Maharishi. Dad interviewed Martin Luther King Jr. and was with the press corps traveling with Robert Kennedy when the senator was gunned down at the Ambassador Hotel in L.A. He wrote the profiles of the original Project Mercury astronauts and counted John Glenn and Scott Carpenter among his good friends. I remember as a kid watching in awe the trim, athletic Carpenter doing backflips off the diving board at the Bedford Golf and Tennis Club pool. Initially my father, a former marine, was a grudging supporter of the Vietnam War, but that changed as the conflict worsened and dragged on. In 1969, he and his close friend and colleague at *Life*, Phil Kunhardt, came up with the daring idea of publishing the photos, names, and hometowns of a single week's war dead in the magazine. *Life* had always been pretty middle of the road, so this was a radical and provocative move, and it prompted angry letters and cancellations ("You have succeeded in turning the knives in the backs of grieving parents"), but also high praise ("Your story . . . was the most eloquent and meaningful statement on the wastefulness and stupidity of war that I have ever read").

Martha Fay, the woman who lived with my father the last twelve years of his life and is the mother of my half sister, Anna, lent me a collection of letters that Dad wrote to his mother when he was in the Marine Corps from 1942 to 1945. Some were typed, but most were handwritten in pencil and pen, and a few were blackened and singed from the 1966 family fire. The letters were a trove of information for me and an important source and starting point for *Surviving Twin*, the eighty-minute theatrical show I developed, in which I combine and connect some of my songs with my father's writing. Dad was just seventeen when he wrote the first of these letters, but already his abilities as a writer were apparent. He never saw combat in World War II, but his observations, fears, and complaints about life as a young recruit are funny, moving, and revealing.

1943

In San Diego now, Mom. It's a dull, sailor crammed town. Can't get a drop to drink because I'm not 21 and they won't serve me. I'm going to write to the new governor Earl Warren and tell him I don't like the liquor laws in his lousy state and that if he doesn't have them fixed immediately so that all men in uniform can imbibe, I'll depart. If Errol Flynn being accused of the seduction

and statutory rape of 2 minor girls is an example of the
purity of glorious California then why can't I have a
beer? To be truthful I long for a little younger, female
companionship. Although you realize, Mom, there's
nothing I'd rather do than see you! –love Louds

I've been performing *Surviving Twin* for several years now, and this posthumous collaboration I've been having with my father has become a rich and rewarding experience. Sharing his work with my audience makes me very happy. My old man and I are getting along better than ever now.

Last week I attended a family affair,
And a few remarked upon my recent growth of facial hair.
"You look just like your father did with that beard," someone said.
I answered back, "I am him," even though my old man's dead.
I didn't want to be him, well, at first I did,
When I loved and looked up to him as a little kid.

He sent me to his old school, I was a numeral with his name.
And he gave me this gold signet ring and he wore one just the same.
And I guess that I believed him and probably it was true
When he told me I was just like him—that's what some fathers do.
But a father's always older, and my dad was rather tall.
Who says size doesn't matter? He was big and I was small.

I needed to be big enough to be someone someday.
And I learned I had to beat him, that was the only way.
I learned I had to fight him, my own flesh, blood, bone, and kin.
But I felt I was just like him. Can a man's son be his twin?

First, we fought for my mother. That afforded little joy.
When he left she was heartbroken. I was still their little boy.

But I started to get bigger and to win the ugly game,
When I made a little money and I got a bit of fame,
And I saw how this could wound him—this could do the trick.
And if I made it big enough I could kill him off quick.
But how can you murder someone in a way that they don't die?
I didn't want to kill him. That would be suicide.

I got frightened and I backed off, I let up and I was through.
And in the end he did himself in, usually that's what we do.
Now I'm alive and he is dead and neither of us won.
It's spoiled for the victor once the vanquishing is done.
A man becomes immortal through his daughter and his son,
But when he fears his legacy a man can come undone.
And the beard is a reminder I'm a living part of him.
Although my father's dead and gone, I'm his surviving twin.
Although the old man's dead and gone, I'm his surviving twin.

—"SURVIVING TWIN," 2001

44.
me & my *mechuten*

I suppose you could say that Leonard Cohen and I were related, inso-far as we are the grandfathers of the sweetly irrepressible Viva Katherine Wainwright Cohen. My son Rufus and Leonard's daugh-ter Lorca are Viva's parents. Chaim Tannenbaum tells me that the Yiddish for what Leonard and I are, in relation to each other, is *machatonim*. The great singer-songwriter was my *mechuten*. I met Leonard (or, as Nashville record producer Bob Johnston pronounced his name, "Len-erred") in 1968 when I was working as a waiter, cook, janitor, and dishwasher at the Paradox, New York City's first macro-biotic restaurant, in the East Village. I'd begun writing and singing my songs by then, but was still a label-less unknown. Occasionally, people of note—"knowns," you might say—would show up at the Paradox for a plate of brown rice and vegetables. One lunchtime I was manning the cash register when Robin Williamson of the Incredible

String Band came up to pay his bill, and I had to explain to the ethereal, shy Scot the value of the quarters, nickels, and dimes in his possession.

Excitement ran through the Paradox on the day Leonard Cohen dropped by. The magnetic, dapper Canadian had released his first album in 1967 and was a new star on the scene. He was also known to be a seeker of sorts, interested in Eastern philosophy and alternate disciplines, and rumored to be a dabbler in Scientology. Leonard's waitress must have mentioned that there was a talented employee on the premises, because after a little coaxing I sat down with my guitar at the long communal table in the restaurant and played my song "Four Is a Magic Number" for him. He seemed impressed, and after I finished he enthusiastically declared, "You can really write." This was a major validation for me. I had suspected and hoped that I had some ability, but I wasn't really sure.

Three decades went by before Leonard and I met again. Our kids, Rufus and Lorca, had been close friends for years, though they hadn't yet decided to become parents together. One night in 2001, there was a dinner party at Musso & Frank ("The Oldest Restaurant in Hollywood") to celebrate the release of *Poses*, Rufus's second record for DreamWorks. I was running a little late when I walked into the restaurant. In addition to Rufus and Lorca, Sally and Van Dyke Parks were there, as well as Pierre Marchand, who produced *Poses*, and Lenny Waronker, who ran the DreamWorks label. Leonard was seated at the head of the table. When he and I saw each other, we were surprised: we were wearing identical shirts—the same cut, the same fabric, the same color pinstripe. This felt more synchronistic than just coincidental, and everyone was struck by the spookiness of it. A harbinger of something, or someone, perhaps?

Viva was born on February 2, 2011, in Los Angeles, and, on the eve of her arrival, there was a gathering at the Cohen residence, a modest two-story house in Hancock Park that Lorca and Leonard shared. Lorca had already passed her due date and was hugely and uncomfortably pregnant. Rufus was there, not just expectant, but nervous as hell. My daughter Lucy and I happened to be in L.A., and the two of us were invited over. Leonard, smiling and looking positively rabbinical in his suit and tie, Star of David lapel pin, and signature felt trilby, greeted us at the front door with a sonorous "Welcome, friends." I couldn't help but wonder if my *mechuten* still had "our" shirt. In the living room, sweet white wine was poured for a celebratory toast. Then Leonard brought out some old photo albums and showed us formal black-and-white portraits of long-gone relatives: rural peasants from Poland and Lithuania, some of whom had been annihilated in pogroms in the late nineteenth and early twentieth centuries. After about forty-five minutes, our gracious host bid us good night and retreated upstairs to his part of the house.

The last time I saw my *mechuten* was in December 2012. He was a football field away in a basketball arena, onstage at a sold-out comeback concert at the Barclays Center in Brooklyn. A few days earlier he had sold out Madison Square Garden. Cohen hadn't toured for some time, but financial necessity had forced him back out on the road. Lorca got a pair of tickets for me and my friend David Nichtern for the Brooklyn show. I arrived a little early, and while I waited for Dave to get there, I watched Leonard's devoted fans pour into the huge venue. I was struck by the age range of his audience. His demographic started with teenagers and ended with people in their nineties. Once we got to our seats and the show began, it started to feel a lot like church, almost like a kind of Mass, but with a seventy-eight-year-old

Don Juan pontiff punctuating his prayers and supplications with James Brown knee drops. During the songs, the silence in the room was complete. I hadn't seen anything quite like it before. Leonard held his audience rapt for more than three hours. After the show, Dave and I went backstage and chatted with some of the musicians. A few close family members, Lorca and Leonard's older sister Esther, were allowed to meet with the star in his dressing room. I'm sure my charismatic *mechuten* must have been tired.

Dave and I got to share a limo back to Manhattan with Esther, and on the ride she happily told us about how she'd always known that her baby brother would be someone special one day. I told her the story of meeting Leonard at the Paradox forty-two years earlier, way back when he told me I could really write.

Me and Viva.

Four is a magic number
But then again so is five
There's a sinking sinner in your gutter
And he's the happiest man alive

Every time I sit you down
To tell you what is so

For safety's sake, remember please
This boy he don't know

The cross is a sacred symbol
But then again so is the fish
And the priest who makes you tremble
Prays for stars on which to wish

Every time I sit you down
To show what must be shown
For safety's sake, remember please
None of it is known

Earth is a mystery mother
But then again so is Mom
Jesus didn't go no further
Then any Harry, Dick, or Tom

Every time I sit you down
To tell you what is true
For safety's sake, remember please
I'd shut up if I knew

—"FOUR IS A MAGIC NUMBER," 1970

45.
working the room

In Anchorage recently I witnessed Rufus play for a rapt crowd of his people. He was seated at the piano, and since I was in the wings all I could really see was his back, though his head bounced from side to side and was often dramatically thrown back for effect. He had them mesmerized and was totally in control, and I flashed back thirty-something years to when he was nine, his sister Martha was six, and their half sister Lucy was just a babe in arms. I was living with Suzzy then, and she and I and the kids were at the wedding reception for my sister Sloan and her husband, George McTavey. My parents, recently separated, were also there, posing together for family pictures but otherwise staying as safely far away from each other as was possible. Actually, now that I think about it, my dad put in an appearance at the church but quickly hightailed it back to the city after the ceremony. I can certainly relate to that tendency of his to flee. At the reception, there was food and wine and a Dixieland band. I remember dancing with Pounie—the nickname for my daughter Martha—me doing the box step with her standing on the tops of my feet, along for the ride, both of us looking down. The party was in the old Historical Hall in Bedford. At one end of the hall there was an empty stage, and on it was an old, dusty, out-of-tune upright piano. At one point, Rufus clambered up onto the stage, sat down at the piano, and performed something he had recently learned from his mother, Kate, back in Montreal. It was a few bars of boogie-woogie, just a snatch, really. People were charmed and gave him a rousing ovation. For the next two hours it seemed like every ten minutes he went back to that upright and tore off those same four bars of music. It didn't take too long for the enthusiasm in the Historical Hall to wane, and finally Rufus was asked, and then ordered, to stop playing the piano. In the end he had to be physically restrained from mounting the stage. It was an object lesson in the boy's strong and innate determination and need to dazzle. And dazzling is something he continues to do.

In the late seventies, the Roches began a tradition of doing Christmas shows at the Bottom Line in New York City. Even before they were signed to a record deal with Warner Bros., in 1977, they had caroled during December all over Manhattan, at private Christmas parties, in train stations, on street corners, and underneath the arch at Washington Square Park. For these occasions, the trio expanded the group to include four or five of their singing female friends, and this larger group became known as the Caroling Carolers. At the Bottom Line shows, everyone performing was dressed as Christmassy as possible, wearing spangles, tinsel, and red, green, silver, and gold garlands from head to toe. The carols were printed out for the audience, but everyone onstage knew all the lyrics and all their singing parts. The Roches took their music seriously, and as groups go, they were well rehearsed. Their musical arrangements were always meticulously worked out and almost obsessively gone over. Maggie, Terre, and Suzzy liked to have it nailed down; as a result, their performances were, like their harmonies, very tight. The McGarrigle sisters, on the other hand, often chose to wing it. They had a much looser work ethic and were often under- or even, on occasion, unrehearsed. When Kate and Anna did a show, there always seemed to be a great deal of pre-song buildup—discussions of which key, lots of nervous onstage tuning, plenty of hair flipping, and a great deal of picking up and putting down of instruments. Critics often observed that their shows had a "living room quality." Their fans loved their naturalistic, relaxed performing approach, but its shambling, chaotic nature always made me, as an observing boyfriend/husband, nervous. To a degree, though, the duo's onstage fumbling-around was also a means of ratcheting up dramatic tension. When a Kate and Anna show finally coalesced into song, a palpable release of audience tension could be produced.

This tight versus loose McGarrigle/Roche thing was on display at one of the early 1980s Bottom Line Roche Christmas shows. Eight-year-old Pounie was visiting me for Christmas that year, and at the last minute she was made an honorary junior Caroling Caroler, dolled up in tinsel and garlands and brought out onstage, albeit completely unrehearsed. In terms of the carols themselves, she knew what any kid would know—"Jingle Bells" and the opening lines to "The First Noel" and "Silent Night." There was no time for her to learn lyrics, much less any musical parts, but, like her brother, she has always been fearless onstage. Pounie stood up in front of the sold-out Bottom Line crowd and basically lip-synched her way through the entire show (including all the tricky verses to "Good King Wenceslas"). Her lips, however, were not really in synch; she just opened and closed her mouth, batted and rolled her eyes, and waved her arms around. This combination of total commitment and over-the-top animation worked, and she sold it. The audience was delighted. After the show, she had to go home to bed, and as I walked her out of the Bottom Line, an excited middle-aged audience member detained us. "Little girl!" he exclaimed. "That was wonderful! You were marvelous!" My eight-year-old, cool as a cucumber even back then, smiled a gracious, slightly condescending thank-you in the direction of her admirer and continued her exit.

Me and Pounie, Cayamo Cruise, 2017.
Photograph by Boom Baker.

Lucy resisted getting into the family business. There were too many performers—her mom and dad, uncle and aunts, not to mention her half brother and sister. We knew she could sing and that she loved music, but whenever the guitars came out at a party, she would contrive a way to get out of the room, or would sit quietly by herself in the corner, witnessing her family members as they expressed themselves, usually with a frown on her face. One summer she went away to a music camp in Connecticut, but upon her return she continued to maintain her low profile, and there was still no indication that she had any desire or need to break into show biz. After college and graduate school, Lucy became an elementary school teacher, and we pretty much figured that was that. But then her performer genes asserted themselves, and she began writing, singing, and doing shows. Whereas Rufus and Martha go out and grab, practically attack, an audience, Lucy gently coaxes and lures them in with her songs, almost as if they, the audience, were a class of her second graders. Her singing voice is clear and unadorned. And she's funny, with great comic timing. When she sweetly, but with just a smidgeon of whimsical drollness, asks her audience, "Are there any questions so far?" we feel we are in a happy classroom with a teacher we love.

In the last few years, Wainwright, McGarrigle, and Roche family members have sung together in various groupings on different occasions, like Rufus and Martha's Christmas shows, the Wainwright Family Show on the 2017 Cayamo Cruise, and 2015's Wainwright Family Alaskan Adventure, when our audience actually traveled with us throughout the forty-ninth state. I wrote a jingle for that one:

Meet the Wainwrights—on the train, the boat, the bus.
Join the family—come on, rub elbows with us.
We're the Wainwrights, that singing family.
For five days and five nights come sample our reality,

In Alaska, that wild & crazy state.
It's a safe distance from the lower forty-eight.
We're the Wainwrights—we get looks and we get stares.
More than eagles, Eskimos, glaciers, moose, and bears.

Meet the Wainwrights—now we finally have a show.
Forget the Osbournes! Those Kardashians must go!

We're the Wainwrights—we can play and we can sing.
Our Sound of Music, kind of a screwed-up Von Trapp–type thing.

Rufus Wainwright—sure you remember him
Once was a tit man, now he checks pecs out at the gym.
He has a trainer traveling with him on the bus
'Cause he's more famous and much richer than the rest of us.

Yeah, we got Roches—from that awesome singing crew
Suzzy and Lucy—they're a daughter-mother twosome.
But they're Wainwrights—and for that we all are glad.
Once upon a happy time Suz slept with Lucy's dad.

Sloanie Wainwright has a voice that will not quit.
Bears and eagles and whales are afraid of it.
And Sarah Palin runs the other way.
Is Sarah in Alaska or has she moved to L.A.?

Martha Wainwright* and Lexie Kelly are not here.
Lex is in college. Martha just chose to steer clear.
Bein' a Wainwright can be a little much,
But Martha and the bloody motherfuckin' asshole stay in touch.

Loudon Wainwright—he's the patriarch.
He's the skunk man who can get a little dark.
He is important and would like to make it clear:
If it were not for Loudon none of you folks would be here!

---

* Pounie.

So meet the Wainwrights—on the train, the boat, the bus.
We're the Wainwrights—come on, rub elbows with us.
We're the Wainwrights—that singing family.
For five days and five nights come sample our reality.
The adventure of a lifetime with the Wainwright family!!!

—"MEET THE WAINWRIGHTS," 2015

When I turned seventy in 2016, most of the whole far-flung friends and family gang gathered out on the east end of Long Island to mark the occasion. My girl friend Susan Morrison, a magazine editor, organized the weekend of festivities and there was a bit less melodrama than at my fiftieth. Rufus is married to a tall, handsome German guy named Jörn Weisbrodt. In addition to being a successful arts impresario, Jörn is a welcoming host and a terrific cook, and the afternoon before the birthday he and Rufus threw a barbecue for us at their place in Montauk. Afterward we all watched the sunset on the beach. The next morning Susan led me on a goofy birthday scavenger hunt around my garden in Shelter Island and then cooked lunch out on the porch for everybody. Tracey MacLeod, now the happy mother of two strapping teenage boys, sent greetings from London, along with a bottle of fine wine. The centerpiece of the birthday itself was a musical celebration in Amagansett the next night at the Stephen Talkhouse, a funky room that I've been playing at for more than thirty years. There were plenty of highlights at the show, including my sister Sloan's version of my song "The Man That Couldn't Cry" and Rufus performing "Out of This World." Lucy and her mom tore it up on another of my songs, "Human Cannonball," and Suz sang a special number about me she had written for the occasion, as did Chaim Tannenbaum. It was all beginning to feel like *This Is Your Life*, and

I kept expecting Ralph Edwards to turn up. Dick Connette, Chaim, and my longtime musical cohort Li'l Davey Mansfield performed "Charlie's Last Song" from *High Wide & Handsome*. Close friends from Ireland, Renee Lawless and Peter Fallon, flew over for the occasion, and Peter graced us with a few of his beautiful poems. My friend and former manager/agent Mike Kappus and his wife, Saori, came in from San Francisco. Extra special

Susan Morrison and me on the South Ferry, 2015.

guests included my brother Andy, his son Taylor, Teddy, and my daughter Lexie. Suzzy's ninety-two-year-old mom, Jude Roche, who had also been at my fiftieth, was happily in attendance. Her date that night was Suzzy's longtime boyfriend, Stewart Lerman, who produced my CDs *Last Man on Earth* and *So Damn Happy*. After the show was over, and Susan and her daughter Helen had brought out a giant cake, which thank goodness did *not* have seventy candles on it, we were surprised to discover that former New York Met Keith Hernandez had stopped by the Talkhouse and was tending bar that night, just for the fun of it. At that point the selfies started, and the focus shifted from the septuagenarian birthday boy over to the legendary World Series champ and broadcaster.

> It's all in a family, that's no lie
> Even stays that way after we die
> Leaves, branches, twigs on a family tree
> And the forest can be hard to see

Mother and father are in charge
And the brand-new baby will loom large
Brothers, sisters, uncles, aunts
It's a family life, so take a chance

It's a work in progress, can't you see?
And the why, wherefore, is a mystery
When the family fights they know next door
No one wins in a family war

Then there's that thing it's all made of
Dare we sing that the thing is love?
Love heals heartache and familial pain
And what family is not insane?

Just give them all a hug and a kiss
At the wake, the wedding, birthday, bris
At the function let dysfunction rule
No shallow end in the family pool

We gather for the holiday
And pray for a quick, safe getaway
No one's so close, nothing's so real
And the smallest thing is the biggest deal

That so-and-so did such and such
How can you love someone so much?
Forgive, forget, and finally see
The forest from the family tree

It's all in a family, that's no lie
Even stays that way after we die
You forgive, forget, and finally see
When you get to hold the new baby

—"All in a Family," 2012

46.
my biggest fan

My biggest fan's a four-hundred-pound man.
Who knows how many stone hang on to his bones?
And you ask, "How come?" but, hey look,
His mother was a professional cook.
When he was one his father took off.
It was a trauma that he never shook off.
He was dealt that hand. My biggest fan.

Recently somebody was telling me about seeing a singer-songwriter contemporary of mine do a bad performance at a club. Hearing such a thing would usually lift my spirits, because, like most performers, I have a jealous, frightened, competitive, and insecure nature. If someone else fails or falters I can be perfectly happy to hear all about it, and, in certain cases, I've been absolutely delighted. For some strange but primal reason, when someone else is trashed, I feel safer. I guess that's because, deep down, when I'm not thinking of myself as the greatest singer-songwriter that ever lived, I consider myself to be a talentless fraud. When the guy (he was a fan I'd met at the

CD table) was bitching about how lousy this other singer-songwriter had been, my response was surprising. I found myself defending the other performer. I said something like "Well, he probably had an off night," or "He might have been tired." I must be getting soft, because my usual reaction would be to quietly gloat. It was especially weird because I'd done shows with performer X and he'd always had a superior and condescending attitude toward me. There's a pecking order in the barnyard of life and, I suppose, there has to be. But in order to do the job, any job, you have to believe in yourself. I read something the novelist Martin Amis once said and it's stayed with me: "You haven't got a chance of being the best unless you think you're the best." I think what he's saying is, you have to employ the power of autosuggestion. For strictly practical reasons you have to lie to yourself. You have to think, "I'm better than Saul Bellow," or "I'm better than Dylan." You know it's probably bullshit, but you have to trick yourself into believing it, otherwise you wouldn't bother sitting down in front of a blank piece of paper or picking up a guitar.

> *After the show, fans say "Thanks" and "Hello."*
> *They proffer something to sign or deliver a glib line.*
> *And you know there's never any escape*
> *From the fan who wants to give you his tape.*
> *But when all of those hounds are all done,*
> *In the dressing room there remains but one,*
> *And it's my main man. My biggest fan.*

As far as defending that other performer, it's not really that I'm getting soft. I just know now how hard it is to be any good night after night. Audiences don't really appreciate this, and I guess in order to preserve the magic of show business, they shouldn't have to. Performers, just like prostitutes and presidents, let people down. We've all been disappointed by our heroes. Thirty years ago I saw Ray Charles at the Royal Festival Hall in London. I hate to speak ill of a dead legend, but he stank. He didn't give a shit. I don't think he was high or drunk, he just didn't care. He played for about forty-five minutes, did one perfunctory encore, and left the building. The amazing thing was that the sold-out audience let him get away with it. They gave him a standing ovation! I felt ripped off, so I stayed seated. After all, in 1961 I had taught senior prefects at St. Andrew's to shake their little WASP booties to the throbbing strains of "What'd I Say," for God's sake. Today, however, I know better and have a more forgiving attitude. In addition to being tired or having an off night, that poor motherfucker had to show up and be Ray Charles.

Some fans harass and stalk. The big guy likes to talk.
He knows every song, what's been good and gone wrong.
He knows the story of my whole cheesy life:
The name of each kid, ex-girlfriend, and wife,
Every label that I've ever been on.
He's obsessed but he doesn't fawn.
No, he understands. He's my biggest fan.

There are "Loud Heads" out there. It's true, they're dying out, but stragglers keep showing up. You initially meet them at the CD table or maybe out in the parking lot after the show. An opening Loud Head gambit might be "Your songs changed my life," or "I just have to thank you for your work." They mean it and it's taken some of them a lot of courage to blurt it out. Of course it's nice to be on the receiving end of such a compliment. You're flattered and delighted. Suddenly you've been transformed from the jerk hauling his guitar and a three-quarter-full box of CDs back to the car into some sort of Albert Schweitzer. These fans keep showing up at the gigs and you love them for that, too, so one night you agree to let them buy you a drink. What the hell, it's either that or go back to the hotel and stare at Bill Maher on TV. And then after a wonderful wine-infused hour of adulation, you stupidly wind up giving them your e-mail address. The next time you show up in their town you've left them some comps. What the hell, you don't pay for comps.

Most fans are average guys and gals,
Anxious to be your bosom pals
For a night or just an hour,
For a bite, some kind of shower.
They got a plan, you understand?

Some Loud Heads stay on board for years, and seeing them again and again is a bit like looking in the mirror. You watch them thicken and gray as time passes, aging before your very eyes. And you are a witness to the calamities that befall these people. There was a group of Loud Heads from the UK who traveled great distances to see all my shows when I toured there in the eighties and early nineties. It was a small posse of three guys and their wives. The leader of the pack was a bookie, and his best buddy was a frustrated wannabe drummer. I think the third man might have been the bookie's brother. Initially, not only was I flattered by this group, I was taken with them, especially the bookie. He had the rakish, charming, and persuasive qualities that I imagine go with being a gambler. These people brought me presents and drinks for years, and in return I provided them with occasional comps and an hour or so of my presence after shows. But eventually things soured. They knew my story from the songs, and they had filled me in on their histories, but after a while we ran out of gas. Maybe they thought that hanging out with me might somehow change their lives, which like most people's were humdrum and uneventful. They began to bore me, and I began to disappoint them. The drummer's wife got sick and the bookie's wife finally left him. The bookie turned up at one gig with his teenage daughter as his date. The girl was the spitting image of her beautiful mother. I had provided the kid's father with a life soundtrack, and she seemed thrilled to meet me. But he seemed bitter. I hadn't been solicitous enough to him over the years, hadn't bought or stayed for enough rounds. Then, one time, just the drummer and his wife turned up, almost out of a sense of duty.

My fan is so large, he's a one-man entourage!
There's so much more there to him than Tom, Dick, Harry, or Jim,
And if you wanna know just how big a fan he is, he comes to
*   every gig.*
Sometime I sell out. Hey, man, that's no sin.
Somehow my fan always manages to squeeze in.
And he's happy to stand, my biggest fan.

Life, as it will, had beaten the couple down, or so it seemed to me that night. It was nice enough to see them, but there was no joy in the occasion. And that was the last I saw of those UK Loud Heads. It was as if they just stopped going to church. Or they'd simply tired of my music. My pessimism might have been engaging when they were in their twenties, but now, twenty-five years on, it had lost its charm. Our love affair had ended. They realized that Albert Schweitzer was human, or even worse—at the bottom of it—a kind of bum.

Occasionally, a new Loudster shows up, usually just one lone obsessive—young and strong and full of adoration. Maybe his dad or even grandfather was a fan. But my policy these days is nobody gets my e-mail address and I never drink with the patrons. After the gig, I just trudge back to the car, put the CDs in the trunk, and let the GPS lady on my phone tell me the way back to the hotel. Bill Maher is waiting up for me.

> *But the biggest surprise, aside from his size,*
> *Is just how hip he is when it comes to show biz.*
> *There's a triumvirate, a kinda top three.*
> *Yeah, there's Bob, then there's Neil, then there's me.*
> *Naturally, Bob's number one, the runner-up, that's Mr. Young.*
> *I'm number three in command, but he's still my biggest fan.*
> *I'm his third man, but he's still my biggest fan.*

—"My Biggest Fan," 2005

47.

graduation

'm going to Lexie's college graduation. She's my kid and I have to be there. Gotta do it. Just like I had to take her to the Universal Studio Tour, years ago, when we moved to L.A. My friend Danny told me then, "You gotta do it, man," and he was right. I don't like amusement parks, but, by God, I did it. Another rite of passage. But don't get me wrong. It's not that I don't want to be at the graduation. It's just that it will be the first time in over a year and a half that my daughter's mother, Rita, and I have seen each other, and it's not going to be easy. I picture us exchanging tense little nods, since it's a little too early for the perfunctory peck-on-the-cheek stage. I'm sure we'll eventually get to a better place, but you can't push these things. Years ago, at my son Rufus's boarding school graduation, I stood there with him and his mother, Kate, while somebody took our picture. In the snapshot, he's in the middle, and he's happy that his parents are there, flanking him. His mother is grinning. She didn't really have much of a smile, come to think of it. It was always more of a grin. I'm wearing a tie and a sports jacket, with sunglasses and a faintly ironic look on my face. You can see that I want to get the hell out of there. But our son is happy and expansive, acting as a bridge between his parents, but also as a buffer, keeping us apart, the way a boxing referee by nature will insert himself between two weary prizefighters leaning on each other in the late rounds. What the snapshot shows, though, is that we were all in it together. And we got through it. You get through it somehow.

What worries me the most is that Rita and I might wind up after the graduation having to have a meal together in a restaurant. So much of it seems to take place in restaurants—the first date, the courting, the planning, the celebrations, the first fight, the umpteenth fight, the discussions about splitting, the patching it up, the deciding to split; all the way to the bitter, awful, gruesome end. We started out being a mom and a dad, in it together, there for the school plays, the field days, and the birthdays. We sat in the folding chairs in the auditoriums,

Graduation with Rufus and Kate, 1991.

excitedly beaming as we witnessed our kid's dazzling performances, especially her portrayal of one of the spoons in *Beauty and the Beast*. We stood on the sidelines of the soccer field, shouting fearful encouragement when the ball somehow got to our kid, infectiously terrified she'd screw up. And we nervously hovered at her early birthday parties, so anxious she was having the time of her life, praying there wouldn't be tears, and always ready to provide auxiliary puffs in the blowing out of the candles, as if that very young life of hers depended on their extinguishment. Now it's many years later, and we're needed there primarily as witnesses, tokens of an earlier time. We are the reasons and reminders of her creation and existence. Offer thanks or blame, if you will, but if it weren't for us, she wouldn't be here.

All this reminds me of when I graduated from boarding school in 1965. My parents drove down from Westchester for my commencement in Middletown, Delaware. They were in a bad marriage and had been for many years, but their plan was simply to stay put there. That's what people did then, and, even though they separated in 1976 and my father started a new family, my parents stayed married until my dad's death in 1988. Being divorced in America, like being an alcoholic, was not such a matter of fact back then as it is today. There was a real stigma attached to it, and much more than just a whiff of failure. And like a lot of things in life, it was much harder on the women. You were damaged goods if you were a divorcée. A divorced man, on the other hand, got to start all over again—a seasoned veteran, a survivor, an escapee, back in the game to take another shot.

At my graduation, more than fifty years ago, I gave the valedictory speech. My grades weren't particularly good, but I was the best speaker and funniest performer in my class, so I got the gig. When I woke up that morning, I thought, "This is the last day I'll ever have to be at this place." And that stayed with me all day, even during the ceremony. I don't remember much about my speech or how it was received. I was also given the drama prize that day, a collection of Shakespeare's plays that, a few years later, like so many of the artifacts of my youth, would be consumed in the family fire. At commencement, on the day of beginning, I just wanted it to be over. I wanted to get my clothes and my shoes, my records and record player, my fan and all of my other crap out of the dorm and into the car. The faculty members I thanked and said good-bye to on that day, even the ones I liked, suddenly appeared to be what I had always suspected they had been, small and insignificant men whose jobs had been to hold a few hundred boys in their thrall for four years. But on graduation day their power evaporated, like a spell does in a fairy tale, and my slavery was suddenly ended. Before we left, I politely thanked some of them, and I suppose I meant it. They had done their jobs, shepherding me through the experience somehow, and I was grateful for that. But my plan was to never return to the school, and for more than a half century I've pretty much stuck to it.

Now it's a few weeks after Lexie's graduation, and I'm happy to say that, despite my fears, it went quite well. At the ceremony, her mother and I sat side by side in the quad, huddled under umbrellas, wearing rain ponchos. We shared our disapproval of the cell phone chatter going on around us. I got pissed off when one of the graduating student speakers went on a tirade, a sort of lecture about how much certain lives matter, her implication being that certain other lives don't. Behind her sat the college faculty, decked out in their somewhat goofy robed finery and floppy hats, attentive but also looking embarrassed about what they were hearing. I moved ten rows forward, to be in position and at the ready with my phone to take a picture when my kid's name was called and she trooped up there to get her diploma. Then it was over, and the sun came out and there were hugs and more pictures and tears. Sure, I got choked up. Rita, Lexie, and I and a few of Lex's friends went out and had a perfectly enjoyable lunch together. Then I dropped Mom and daughter back at the dorm. Rita and I hugged, and one of us said to the other, "We did it." Maybe we both said it.

Bein' a dad isn't so bad, except that you gotta feed 'em
You gotta shoe 'em and clothe 'em, and try not to loathe 'em, bug 'em
*   and hug 'em, and heed 'em*
Bein' a dad can sure make you mad, man, it can sure drive you crazy
It's as hard as it looks, you gotta read 'em dumb books, and you end up
*   despising Walt Disney*
Bein' a dad starts to get radical when they turn into teenagers
You gotta tighten the screws, enforce the curfews, confiscate
*   weapons and pagers (remember pagers?)*
But a daughter and son can be sort of fun, just as long as they don't
*   defy you*
They'll treat you like a king, they'll believe anything. They're easy to
*   frighten and lie to*
Bein' a dad can make you feel glad when you get paperweights and
*   aftershave lotions*
Yeah, it feels pretty great when they graduate, that's when you're
*   choked with emotions*
But bein' a dad takes more than a tad of good luck and divine
*   intervention*
You need airtight alibis, foolproof disguises, desperation's the father of
*   invention*
So sometimes you take off for a few rounds of golf, and you stay away
*   for half of their lifetimes*
The result of it all is you're captured and hauled off before a tribunal
*   for dad crimes*

Bein' a dad can make you feel sad, like you're the insignificant other
Yeah, right from the start, they break your heart, in the end every kid
  wants his mother
Bein' a dad

—"Bein' a Dad," 1997

48.

unplanned
obsolescence

I've written songs that mention pagers, long-playing records, and telephone answering machines. One, "Overseas Call," goes a bit further.

> *The fish in the ocean will gather around*
> *That telephone cable they will fathom the sound*
> *Of a lost human voice finally found*
> *Gonna make me an overseas call*
>
> —"OVERSEAS CALL," 1986

I wasn't sure there was such a thing as a transatlantic cable anymore, so I looked it up on Wikipedia:

TAT-1 (Transatlantic No. 1) was the first transatlantic telephone cable system. It was laid between Gallanach Bay, near Oban, Scotland and Clarenville, Newfoundland between 1955 and 1956 by the cable ship *Monarch*. It was inaugurated on September 25, 1956, initially carrying 36 telephone channels. In the first 24 hours of public service there were 588 London–U.S. calls and 119 from London to Canada . . . TAT-1 was finally retired in 1978. Later coaxial cables, installed through the 1970s, used transistors and had higher bandwidth.

All cables presently in service use fiber-optic technology. Many cables terminate in Newfoundland and Ireland, which lie on the great circle route (the shortest route) from London, UK to New York City, USA.

It's nice that my song is not completely obsolete.

I've been writing topical songs for almost my entire career. Initially they were assignments, like the songs I wrote for the TV show *M*A*S*H*. That's when I realized I could write to order and on deadline. In 1976, on my album *T Shirt*, I began in earnest to tackle current events—people and things that amused or pissed me off. In addition to "Bicentennial" and "Talking Big Apple '75," I wrote "California Prison Blues" for that record, and it's when I got my first lesson in the shifting sands of topical songwriting. There are four people in the song—Squeaky (Lynette) Fromme, Charles Manson, Patricia Hearst, and Eldridge Cleaver—and they were all incarcerated in California at that time. Hearst's legal situation was constantly in flux, even after I wrote and initially recorded the song. The lyrics for the Hearst verse, like the others, had to be submitted and printed for the liner notes, before the album was mixed and mastered. On the sleeve they still read:

Patricia was kidnapped there's not a lot of doubt
And Tania's granddaddy was a man with clout
Yeah, but now Patty's in prison and she might not get out

But, due to late-breaking news stories about Hearst's improving legal situation, I wound up rewriting and rerecording the verse. What you hear on the record is different from the printed lyrics:

Patty's in prison, yeah, but I think she might get out
Patty's in prison she just might get out
Patty's gotta daddy and Daddy's got a lotta clout

My first and foremost influence in musical social commentary was not Phil Ochs or Pete Seeger but rather the great Tom Lehrer, whose records I heard in the early sixties. Some have accused him of being condescending or even mean-spirited, but I love how he made fun of everything and everybody—the church ("The Vatican Rag"), the right ("We Will All Go Together When We Go"), and the left ("The Folk Song Army"). Lehrer was willing and able to send up everything—Hollywood, rock and roll, romance, the Boy Scouts, drug dealing, and Christmas. He reveled in being silly, and, if he chose, macabre, as evidenced in his wonderful line from "Poisoning Pigeons in the Park": "My pulse will be quickenin' / With each drop of strychnine." On his early live recordings, you hear the audience roar with laughter, not only at the songs but also at his droll, biting patter. In 2012, I managed to get in touch with eighty-nine-year-old Tom via e-mail, and I humbly implored, which is to say begged, him to play piano on a song of mine called "My Meds." He politely declined, but said that he liked my song, mostly because it mentioned Mercurochrome. I was disappointed that Lehrer passed on my invitation, but I was also thrilled to have had the correspondence with one of my heroes.

Over the years I've continued to come up with various musical harangues, broadsides, laments, parodies, and political potshots. My targets are usually broad ones—the Internet, Jesse Helms, the O. J. Simpson trial, and that bad girl of Olympic figure skating, Tonya Harding. But "Tonya's Twirls" is a good example of how you can start out by poking fun at someone in a song, and then swerve from the particular to the general, and get into something a bit bigger.

You knew she was in trouble when you saw her bodyguard
When you saw those two together, you knew it wasn't hard
To see that she was different, not just one of the girls
With their gliding and their sliding and their pirouettes
    and twirls

Then it turned out that she smoked and drank and posed practically
    nude
And she didn't smile all of the time, she got angry and was crude
No, she wasn't Goody Two-skates like all the other girls
With their grinning and their spinning and their winning little twirls

And her childhood was unhappy and her mom was really weird
And her husband liked to hit her, but it was poverty she feared
She grew up in the trailer park, not like most other girls
With their gliding and their sliding and their whirling little twirls

Yes, they all look like princesses, little Barbies to the core
But she was your parents' worst nightmare, the slut who moved
    next door

From the wrong side of the tracks, she liked the boys more than
    the girls
With their gliding and their sliding and their girlish dainty twirls

And it seemed like she was lying about what she didn't know
And then she started crying in the media sideshow
In practice she kept falling down more than the other girls
With their gliding and their sliding and their picture-perfect twirls

And they almost towed her truck away and the whole thing was
    a drag
Forget about Campbell's Soup or Reebok, Wheaties or the flag
There'll be books, she'll make some money, it's what they're after,
    all these girls
With their selling, kiss-and-telling, and their twisted little twirls

So play the national anthem, stand up proud and tall
Oh, we hope that ours don't stumble and that theirs slip and fall
And remember Olga Korbut. What happens to these girls?
With their triple flips and axels and their somersaults and twirls

Ice used to be a nice thing when you laced up figure skates
Now it's a thing to win a medal on for the United States
But once there were no lutzes, axels, pirouettes, and twirls
Just giddy, slipping, sliding, laughing, happy little girls

                      —"TONYA'S TWIRLS," 1994

My most recent topical song was about Donald Trump, and it was called "I Had a Dream." When I wrote it, in the spring of 2016, the whole thing was a joke—the song, him, and the idea that he could possibly be elected president. When I performed the tune, throughout that summer, most people loved it, and why wouldn't they? I was preaching to the choir. There were a few unhappy campers, people who walked out after hearing the song and/or asked for their money back, but I took a slightly perverse pleasure in ruffling their feathers, and was unconcerned. It was just a joke, right? Right.

I don't imagine I'll be singing the song for a while, due to unplanned obsolescence kicking in. "I Had a Dream" was somewhat prescient, though. I name-checked Jeff Sessions and Ben Carson as Trump cabinet picks. Cold comfort.

> *Dreams come true and there's prophesy*
> *And sometimes a nightmare is a reality*

> —"I Had a Dream," 2016

49.
memorial service

These days I've been thinking a lot about my up-and-coming, unfortunately inevitable memorial service. You know—turnout, location, catering, the vibe . . . that sort of thing. Some decisions—drawing up a living will, let's say, or picking a headstone, for instance—really should be done in advance, and one's memorial service is certainly a once-in-a-lifetime occasion, so why leave it to others to make the important choices? You always hear people say, "Oh, he would have hated that," or "I'll bet she's turning over in her grave right now," and that's not good, so I've decided to jot down some of my thoughts on the matter while I'm still here. These are not so much last wishes as just a few helpful preemptive guidelines.

I know they're all pretty busy these days, but I sure hope my kids can come. It's one thing to constantly forget my birthday or disregard umpteen text messages, but it would be a bit weird, kind of ridiculously passive-aggressive, for them to just opt out of my memorial service. Yes, I know it's all about remembering, but can't there also be a little forgive and forget at this point? Or how's about some plain old "He's dead, so just get over it"? Whatever. In addition to my progeny attending, it would be nice if their mothers showed up, too, since those women were the principal beneficiaries of my largesse and, I suppose, the greatest victims of my occasional indiscretions. I like the idea of my exes sitting side by side in, say, the second or third row, holding hands and gently leaning against one another for support, if and when they are overcome with emotion. Further back, but liberally sprinkled throughout the room, would be all my former girlfriends. Ideally they should be unobtrusively incognito, initially remaining on the periphery of the proceedings, evoking whispers of "Who could that terribly attractive, sad woman be?" or "Is that who I think it is?" But after the speeches, videos, and songs, when friends and family are standing around oohing and aahing at the snapshots and photos on display of my childhood, youth, and vigorous middle age, I imagine my old flames, perhaps emboldened by a glass of wine or two, might approach each other to introduce themselves. This very well may result in hugs, spontaneous expressions of sorrowful solidarity and shared loss. I love the thought of that kind of a tableau and I sincerely hope my exes and all the kids are friendly and forgiving toward the sorrowful, repentant home wreckers. But of course you never know.

Unfortunately, due to fire regulations and venue capacity, my fans and the general public won't be able to attend the memorial itself, but I expect there will be a throng of mourners gathered in respect and sorrow outside the building. These, after all, were the people whose lives I touched the most.

Naturally, I'm very concerned about what people will say about my work, how it affected and inspired them in particular and what it might mean to the world at large. I trust that all the speakers at the service, including any secretly gloating, contemporary rivals of mine in attendance, will be thoughtful, fair, and considerate when preparing their remarks. Presumably there will be a plethora of funny and/or moving anecdotes offered, which is nice, but sometimes people can get a little overly effusive and maudlin at the podium, and that can be a turnoff. Short and sweet is always the way to go.

In addition to songs, poems, and stories, some lovely unobtrusive music played softly during the service might be nice; that sad movement from Mahler's Fifth Symphony, for instance, or the Samuel Barber adagio they used at the end of *The Elephant Man* movie.

As for the weather, a light drizzle would be appropriate, something that will gently complement the sweet melancholy that my memorial undoubtedly will produce, an appropriately low-barometric atmosphere for my bereft friends, family, exes, loved ones, and admirers as they leave the service and head homeward to resume their futile, humdrum, and now much emptier existences après me.

Oh, when I die, and it won't be long
You're gonna be sorry that you treated me wrong
You're gonna be sorry that you treated me bad
Yes, and if there's an afterlife I'll gloat and I'll be glad

Oh, it might be a plane crash, or some sort of OD
Hey, there's gonna be a photograph with my obituary
You're gonna see it and you'll cry a lot, you're gonna wanna wear
    black
I'll be dead, but you can bet your life I'm gonna get you back

I'm tired of being left up on your shelf
I might not wait around, I might kill myself
Not only would you miss me, but you'd feel guilty, too
Oh, I'd be dead, but it would be too late, the joke would be on you!

Ha, ha, ha, ha
Ho, ho, ho, ho
Chuckle, chuckle, chuckle, chuckle
Snicker, snicker, snicker, snicker
Guffaw, guffaw, guffaw, guffaw
Yuk, yuk, yuk, yuk
Chortle, chortle, chortle, chortle

So you better take warning and start treating me good
Start doin' the things that I think you should
And you better not pout and you better not cry
Hey, the grim reaper is comin' to town, and I just might die

—"Unrequited to the Nth Degree," 1975

50.
the 75-90

Out on the road, out on the road,
You're Willy Loman and you're Tom Joad,
Vladimir and Estragon,
Kerouac and Genghis Khan.
Out on the road, out on the road,
That's where your wild oats were sowed.
You start out a prince and you end up a toad,
Livin' out on the road.

—"Road Ode," 1993

Getting there is not half the fun; it's almost none of it, really. Getting there can be hell.

The travel is what we performers are paid for. It's the hard, brutal, boring part of the job. Due to financial realities and in conjunction with lone wolf tendencies, some of us go it alone: no backup band, no tour manager, no one to carry the guitar. Just a piece of paper that tells you when the flight leaves, where the hotel is, what time the sound check is, what the merchandise split is, when the show starts, and how much money to pick up at the end of the night.

It's true that if you are in a town you've been to before, there might be a friend to call or a favorite restaurant to visit. If you know of a real pool at a good Y, maybe there will be time for a swim. But these are activities best suited for a day off. If it's a show day, the most important thing is whether or not there will be a chance for a nap.

Quarter to three, it's time to nap
He always says, "No nap, I'm crap"
His motto is "No nap, I'm crap"

—"Missing You," 2001

Yes, getting there is mostly a drag and almost none of the fun. The fun is the seriously important part, the seventy-five to ninety minutes onstage performing in front of your people—those strange, gullible, wonderful folks who have gone to the trouble and expense to come out to see you and hear you play your songs. Perhaps they had nothing better to do, but I think not. Most of them want to be there, probably because they saw you on an earlier occasion—last year, maybe, or perhaps forty years ago—and they had a good time. They came away with something. They got their money's worth. They never forgot it. It made them forget something else. They saw your show when they were young, when they were in college, when they were in love, when they had kids, after they got divorced, when they were really drunk, when you were really drunk, before they had surgery, and after their mother died. You were funny or you made them cry or maybe both.

We shall best understand the genesis of the yield of humorous pleasure if we consider the process in the listener before whom someone else produces humor. He sees this other person in a situation, which leads the listener to expect that the other will produce signs of an affect—that he will get angry, complain, express pain, be frightened or horrified or perhaps even in despair; and the onlooker or listener is prepared to follow his lead and call up the same emotional impulses in himself. But this emotional expectancy is disappointed; the other person expresses no affect, but makes a jest. The expenditure on feeling that is economized turns into humorous pleasure in the listener.

—*Sigmund Freud, Art and Literature*

What you did for the 75–90 stayed with them afterward, for forty years, or as long as it took for them to walk back to the parking lot. It affected them. You provided a service. You entertained the troops. You disappointed their emotional expectancy. You economized their expenditure on feeling. You made a jest. You touched a nerve.

When you're on the stage, you can feel your audience. They take on a distinct personality. There is an element of the unknown, because you're in a room that's cloaked in darkness with a large, changeable, amorphous human entity. It sounds scary, and it is. And even if the room is packed with fans, they might be wondering if you're still any good.

When you were younger you were so much better.
When you were younger you were really hot.

Now you're much older and you're colder than ever.
Why won't you hang it up? Why don't you stop?

—"How Old Are You," 1985

It's an exciting and dangerous situation. When I first started sing-ing for money fifty years ago, I squirmed and twitched, stamped my foot and stuck out my tongue. A lot of that had to do with wanting to be noticed, but I was also unconsciously employing the extreme phys-icality to tamp down the terror of being onstage. My gyrations have lessened through the years, although recently I overheard someone within earshot describe me as "spastic with a nervous tic." Even now when I play a new song for the first time for a friend or a loved one in a kitchen or a living room, I tightly close my eyes. I'm afraid to see they might not like it.

In the meanwhile you've stopped writing songs, there's nothing left
    to say
You'd like to get your old job back and mow lawns again one day
But keep lifting up your left leg and sticking out your tongue
There's nothing else that you can do, and you're too old to die young

—"The Home Stretch," 1986

On occasion, within an audience there can be a straying faction, a person or people who have come late, or who don't really care about being there, or who have had too much to drink. Then some wran-gling has to take place, order must be established, you have to take charge.

You deal with hecklers, drunks, talkers, and texters carefully, in the ways you would handle unruly children. You first ask them to behave, and if they don't, you gently warn them. If that fails, you shame or embarrass them. After that, you call for backup and assistance. If you lose your temper and come down too hard on an offender, there is a risk you will also lose the rest of your audience, since you will suddenly appear disagreeable, all too human, like anyone else, no longer above it all, which is where the audience wants you to be. Not long ago I had a female audience member sitting directly in front of me at a show, at a table in the first row, who would not stop taking pictures with a very large, loudly clicking camera. I bent down after a song and gently asked her to desist, quietly explaining that what she was doing was distracting me. When she continued, I switched into a higher gear and poked fun at her—okay, I embarrassed her—in front of the rest of the audience. I probably said something along the lines of "Look, folks, the paparazzi are out tonight." It worked, and she stopped taking pictures, but she was not happy. She had been humiliated. She sat there during the next song pouting. So after that song, I apologized in the nicest possible way, employing just the barest minimum of irony, but my apology only increased her humiliation and she left her table, rolling off in her wheelchair, which until that moment had not been visible in the darkened venue. You have to be careful. You never know what's out there. Still, the show has to be protected. They pay you, but it's still your show. You own it.

The heckler heckles and he gibes and he japes.
Listen to him, you're gonna make mistakes.
He really hopes that your leg breaks.
He's a heckler and he's out to get you.
Some say he's drunk, some say he's stoned.

He wants you deposed and dethroned.
A crank caller would have telephoned.
His aim is out to get you.

—"The Heckler," 1978

Even though it's a performance, only a show, merely a bit of make-believe, you are offering up the best part of yourself—the smartest, boldest, strongest, funniest, saddest, meanest, most fucked-up, most joyful, and most truthful part of yourself. You are sticking your neck out, and you are dropping your pants.

Every goofing-off session in grammar school, every tiny part you had in a school play, every minute watching others perform onstage, on TV, or in the movies has led you to this. It's what you always wanted to do, what you were born to do. You were, someone once said, a natural performer, and that is why you feel at home onstage.

It's no wonder you have next to nothing left to give when you're finished, when the show is over, when the tour has ended and you have to go home to your actual home, back to the real but in many ways inferior world. This is reentry, back to where you attempt, in a half-assed way, to be a decent person, husband, boyfriend, or father, but where so often you fall short. Yes, you're self-centered, but you also don't have much left to give. You're played out. The real world requires a performance, too, but you already gave at the office. Because of your inability to cut it in the real world, you feel worthless and inconsequential, the very same feelings that drove you into show business in the first place.

When it's time to come back to reality
And you're road sick and you're half crazy

Well, you fit right in quite naturally
Home from out on the road
Back to see family and friends
And to face the music and to make amends
But comin' up for air you can get the bends
In from out on the road.

—"Road Ode," 1993

So after a break, you take some more gigs, and when you walk into that room at the Holiday Inn or the Marriott or the Courtyard, you sometimes feel you're really back where you belong again. It's all the same room, really. Art on the walls you barely notice, much less bother to look at. These days the phone by the bed is as likely as not mute and dial-tone-less, remnants of ye olde analog days. The big black monolithic flat-screen TV faces the bed, as if to say to whoever enters, "When you lie down you *must* watch me." The pillows, sheets, and comforters on the bed are supplicant, happily awaiting their inevitable thrashing and rearrangement, quietly eager to be shaped into something poetic and meaningful, like the mountain of mashed potatoes in *Close Encounters of the Third Kind*. The windows open a few inches, just enough to let in some air and the three a.m. police sirens. Then there's the ice bucket or, if you must, the plastic trash container, to be used later during the night as your very own personal chamber pot. There's a twinge of guilt about the maids, so in the morning you will give the pee jug an extra rinse and consider leaving a sawbuck behind. The shampoos and conditioners seem vaguely familiar, but your mind is capable of convincing you they are sui generis. Slide open the closet door and there is a plastic laundry bag hanging there, waiting to receive your dirty clothes and/or wet bathing suit. Nine hours later you return to the room from the gig and you're much too jazzed to sleep. You're in the charisma business, and you've just put out for three hundred or three thousand people. And now you're alone. In the old days you got into the nasty and destructive habit of picking up women after shows, bringing a sort of love hostage back to the hotel room, a raunchy token of esteem, someone to serve as a proxy for the adulation you experienced during the gig. It might be a waitress who worked at the venue or an attractive female audience member, every once in a while even the opening act.

He was checkin' her out at the sound check.
She was soundin' and lookin' real good.
Kind of a cross between Edith Piaf
And Little Red Riding Hood.
She was young enough to be his daughter
And old enough to have been around,
Good enough to blow him off of that stage
And good enough to bring a house down.
He said, "You must be my opening act,"
And she said, "I've heard a lot about you."
They made small talk about her direct box
And all his record company blues.

—"APHRODISIAC," 1989

After a few decades of this furtive, regretful behavior that makes everyone unhappy—maybe you most of all—you begin to report back to the hotel with no one in tow but yourself. That's fine, because all the magic, payoff, reward, real love, and fun has already happened. It happened with you and your audience. It took place during the show itself, the 75–90.

> *For twenty-odd years I have strummed on guitars,*
> *Five thousand lost flat picks, four fingertip scars.*
> *I must have broken a million G strings,*
> *Picking and strumming and playing these things,*
> *Banging and tuning and playing these things.*
>
> *And it's been twenty years that I've written songs,*
> *Over a hundred and still going strong,*
> *About drinking and hockey and flying above,*
> *Again and again about unhappy love.*
> *Over and over, unhappy love.*
>
> *And it's music for money, but I do it for fun.*
> *Oh, I know how to do it, it's easily done.*
> *To stand on a stage doesn't make me afraid.*
> *I'm comfortable up there, it's gotten me laid.*
> *And it always amazes me when I get paid.*
>
> *So here I am doing all that I can do.*
> *I'm playing, you're paying, I'm grateful to you.*
> *Indoors and outdoors, at home and abroad,*
> *I sing these songs and you people applaud.*
> *You haven't changed much, you still applaud.*

—"CAREER MOVES," 1985

acknowledgments

Peter Gethers, my editor at Blue Rider, started this ball rolling. He and I first met some years ago after he tracked me down and overpaid me to perform at his fiftieth birthday party. He was a fan. When Peter saw my theater piece *Surviving Twin* in 2014, he made the bold assertion that I had some kind of a book "in me." That felt a bit like an unwanted medical diagnosis, and at first I resisted the idea of joining the burgeoning ranks of singer-songwriters who write their memoirs. My forays into prose writing had mostly been confined to coming up with liner notes for albums, and the idea of writing an actual book scared the shit out of me, just as it had my old man. But Peter nudged, my initial fears were sufficiently allayed, and with the help of my agent, Liz Darhansoff, an understanding was reached with Blue Rider and a plan was put into action. The indefatigable and discerning Brant Rumble has also been of invaluable assistance throughout the entire process.

At the outset there were good friends who assured me that writing a book just might be possible. My thanks to Suzzy Roche, Dick Connette, Chaim Tannenbaum, Mike Kappus, and Peter Fallon for their encouragement and support.

When family members got wind of the project, their overall response was somewhat muted, the expression on a few faces one of bemusement, bordering on concern. Perhaps they were thinking "Here he goes again." I've tried to write carefully about the people I love, but I acknowledge that some might feel exposed, underappreciated, or misrepresented. It's my book, but maybe I got parts of it wrong, so my apologies to any and all unhappy campers.

On an every-day-and-night basis, my girlfriend Susan Morrison has helped me with *Liner Notes*. Not only did I avail myself of her considerable chops as an editor, but I also lapped up her unflagging encouragement, and benefitted from her astute, on-the-money suggestions, as well as a few gentle warnings. In the margin of one my earliest drafts, in response to a pathetic stab at some self-confessional risqué humor, Susan kindly discouraged me by writing in pencil, "Save yourself!" My love and thanks go to her for that excellent advice, and for plenty more.